JOHN JANTSCH

The Self-Reliant Entrepreneur

366 DAILY MEDITATIONS
TO FEED YOUR SOUL
AND GROW YOUR BUSINESS

Published by John Wiley & Sons, Inc., Hoboken, New Jersey.
Published simultaneously in Canada.

For general information on our other products and services or for technical support, please contact our Customer Care Department within the United States at (800) 762-2974, outside the United States at (317) 572-3993 or fax (317) 572-4002.

Wiley publishes in a variety of print and electronic formats and by print-on-demand. Some material included with standard print versions of this book may not be included in e-books or in print-on-demand. If this book refers to media such as a CD or DVD that is not included in the version you purchased, you may download this material at http://booksupport.wiley.com. For more information about Wiley products, visit www.wiley.com.

Library of Congress Cataloging-in-Publication Data

Names: Jantsch, John, author.
Title: The self-reliant entrepreneur : 366 daily meditations to feed your soul and grow your business / John Jantsch.
Description: First Edition. | Hoboken : Wiley, 2019.
Identifiers: LCCN 2019037261 (print) | LCCN 2019037262 (ebook) | ISBN 9781119579779 (hardback) | ISBN 9781119579755 (adobe pdf) | ISBN 9781119579762 (epub)
Subjects: LCSH: Entrepreneurship. | Self-reliance. | Creative ability in business. | Success in business.
Classification: LCC HF5415 .J36 2019 (print) | LCC HF5415 (ebook) | DDC 658.4/21—dc23
LC record available at https://lccn.loc.gov/2019037261
LC ebook record available at https://lccn.loc.gov/2019037262

Cover Design: Wiley
Cover Image: © svtdesign/Shutterstock

Printed in the United States of America

V318067 082919

To Carol, who makes every day the best day of the year.

To the makers, founders, owners, start-ups, side hustlers, intrapreneurs, and entrepreneurs everywhere who courageously choose to insist on themselves.

Acknowledgments

My girls, Jenna, Sara, Ellen, and Mary, for your contribution to every word in this book and for occasionally acting like you think I'm funny.

My friend and literary agent Stephen Hanselman, without whom this book would not have happened.

Amanda Rhode, whose research and care for our literary collaborators was invaluable.

Jay Baer, who should recognize his suggestions sprinkled throughout.

Todd Henry, for pushing me to lighten up a bit.

Carrie Wilkerson, for constantly admiring my work without question.

BJ Ward and Karin Kraska, for being true readers.

The team at Wiley, for recognizing immediately that this book needed to be written. Elizabeth Welch, your copyediting was such a gift.

Team Duct Tape, Sara, Jenna, Tricia, Carly, Michelle, and Rachelle, for creating the space for me to give this project so much time.

Crow's Coffee in Kansas City, Missouri, and Salto Coffee Works in Nederland, Colorado, for letting me hang out for long writing sessions infused with coffee and eventually beer.

The hundreds of authors cited in this work, both dead and living—your inspiration and audacity will always find a home with me.

Introduction

In this book I invite you to take inspiration from a renegade minister, a handyman turned political activist and naturalist, and an innovative educator and early feminist voice, though they may seem at first an odd collection of mentors to guide today's entrepreneur.

Each of these sources of inspiration produced their primary body of literary work in the mid-1800s, during a time that many cite as America's first period of a truly spirited counterculture.

I'm speaking of the period often referred to as American transcendentalism, a brief time that experienced its heyday just prior to the American Civil War and left a lasting impact on American literature, religion, philosophy, art, political activism, social thought, and as I propose in this work, a goldmine for today's enlightened entrepreneur.

It doesn't matter what you call this point of view or even what you call yourself. You can possess the spirit of self-reliance and independence no matter your profession or job title. Being an entrepreneur is as much about who you choose to be as what you choose to do for a living.

In addition to blossoming independent thinking, this was a period of unparalleled awakening in American literature, when perennial classics such as *The Scarlet Letter, Leaves of Grass, Moby Dick, Little Women, Uncle Tom's Cabin, Self-Reliance, Walden,* and *Civil Disobedience,* along with a great deal of the catalog of Emily Dickinson, Mark Twain, and Edgar Allan Poe, sprang forth.

This was a period when America's literary voice finally broke free of the influence of other cultures. There's a reason your teachers asked you to (made you) read most of these works. I invite you to revisit the golden nuggets of these classics in the context of your entrepreneurial journey. Don't worry; there will no pop quizzes.

Not to overcomplicate the history lesson here, but some of the writers sourced in this book would be seen more as coming from a period also referred to as American romanticism. Romanticism and transcendentalism have many commonalities and some differences. Both placed great emphasis on the individual as well as inspiration from nature.

The time period identified as each's heyday overlaps; however, romanticism did not concern itself at all with God or religion, whereas spirituality was a founding aspect of the transcendentalist philosophy. Transcendentalism flourished perhaps as a natural outgrowth of American romanticism.

Even though some of the authors of the works listed here didn't consider themselves transcendentalists, in all of these voices you can hear the emergence of a self-reliant, self-searching, and at times self-torturing protagonist—a common motif driving this new form of American literature. In the end, it doesn't matter what you call it; the lessons for entrepreneurial thinking abound.

There is an undeniable element of a counterculture, or even internal disobedience, in most entrepreneurs. So, I suspect that, if you have not already done so, you will find kindred spirits in these pages.

The simple idea that runs through the works I've curated for this book is that all individuals possess self-knowledge that transcends what they might see and hear from others around them.

You must trust yourself to be the ultimate authority on what is right. And this is the ultimate definition of self-reliance.

Many of the transcendentalist writers made a case for what, at the time, were seen as radical ideas:

- that holding and sticking to your own beliefs is more important than following the well-worn track of others;
- that producing value rather than acquiring possessions is a far more useful contribution to the world;
- that the essence of success is gained through individual experience and self-examination more than by following prescribed doctrine;
- that observing nature provides the most perfect example for how to live;
- that inner peace is a goal worth diligent pursuit;
- that present moment awareness is the secret to lasting joy; and
- that the essence of life is to explore how all things are connected.

Transcendentalism was initially a religious undertaking—albeit more of a movement to question the given religious doctrine, particularly Calvinism. The movement, however, quickly became a force in many areas of life beyond religion and found its most notable spokesperson in Ralph Waldo Emerson.

Although this book does not intend to tackle the subject of religion, the connection between the entrepreneurial journey and the human spiritual journey has many parallels found in the underpinnings of transcendentalist philosophy and writing.

Emerson's philosophy of self-reliance, as with many of the transcendentalist works, clearly borrowed heavily from ancient Eastern sacred texts such as *The Upanishads*, *The Tao-te Ching*, *Bhagavad-gītā*, and *The Vedas*. These works spoke of a god not as a separate being or Trinity but as a force of energy within every individual waiting to be awakened.

If that doesn't sound like inspiration for the entrepreneurial spirit, I don't know what does.

Change is perhaps the only constant in the world of the entrepreneur. Transformation, as a constant influence, is at the heart of the transcendentalist philosophy, and the persistent search for a process of transformation serves the entrepreneur well.

Emerson's self-reliance finds a catalyst in self-awareness and calls the entrepreneur to create a space for inner and outer observation in an attempt to join mind, body, and spirit in the achievement of individual transformation and the transformation of the entrepreneurial enterprise.

A common theme contained in many of the works of the period is that of individualism—that the source of truth was contained within rather than from the inspiration of others. These ideas burn brightly still today as hundreds of thousands pilgrimage to Walden Pond and the Thoreau Institute's Walden Woods Project each year as a tribute to these teachings.

So, yes, in this sense, this book reveals a vital spiritual component to this awakening of the self-reliant entrepreneur. The spirit of the entrepreneur is understood as much as a force of energy as an institution.

Once you find your unique self-reliant point-of-view and voice, your one voice of truth, you can find freedom in every decision you make. This is true for anyone and not just entrepreneurs. What's healthy for the self-reliant entrepreneur is equally useful for anyone wishing to gain a measure of self-reliance.

Self-reliant entrepreneurs do not consider themselves constrained by their circumstances; rather they ignore the call of common wisdom on the way to shining a light on what only they can make manifest.

This is not an appeal for recklessness. It is a form of thought that is perhaps less an act of self-confidence than it is one of self-trust. And the difference is ultimately practical.

How This Book Is Organized

Much like the annual passing of calendar seasons, there are four distinct phases or seasons that most entrepreneurs experience as they move from start-up to traction to growth and profit and back to what many confess feels like instability all over again. These "seasons" are part of how entrepreneurs move from one phase of business to the next.

Of course, this observation is one of hindsight because, unlike the turning and tumbling leaves that signal fall, the seasons of the entrepreneur are much more difficult to detect—but look for them, both inside and out, and you will see them.

This metaphor offers the perfect way to organize the readings and reflections into seasons while further focusing on thematic elements that make up the core tenets of self-reliant thinking.

In *The Self-Reliant Entrepreneur,* the seasons of the entrepreneur are named Planning, Discovering, Evolving, and Growing. In furthering the season metaphor, these easily line up with the attributes we most associate with summer, fall, winter, and spring:

Planning		
January – Trust	February – Creativity	March – Freedom
Discovering		
April – Love	May – Commitment	June – Security
Evolving		
July – Failure	August – Resilience	September – Congruence
Growing		
October – Change	November – Impact	December—Grace

How to Use This Book

The format of this book allows you to reflect upon tailored, timeless guidance each day without investing too much time. You may wish to study deeply every day in order to center your thoughts for that day or dive in from time to time as your schedule allows or as you need to wrestle with a particular challenge. There are countless ways to use and to gift this work.

Each day you will start with a reading from a transcendentalist-era author, followed by my reflection and application for today's entrepreneur. Each passage concludes with what I call a "Challenge Question" in an effort to nudge you to apply the day's lesson to your current situation or goal. Use the brief space found at the bottom of each page to record your initial thoughts to the question. You may find that you return to your answers over and over again.

A word of advice here—don't be surprised if you find answers to these questions coming from somewhere deep inside. Don't ignore that voice. We are often quick to dismiss our own insights in favor of advice from others—listen to yourself; it's probably your soul speaking up.

Pick this book up every day or every once in a while and use the wisdom of the transcendentalists (some feisty entrepreneurs and revolutionaries) to keep you showing up, keep you inspired, and most important, to keep you boldly self-reliant.

Also, it doesn't matter where you start or when you start. If you found this book in July, jump in there and you catch the first six months next year. This book will remain fresh to you year after year as each reading will mean something new when you revisit after 12 months of growth on your self-reliant path.

There is an element of irony in teaching the idea of self-reliance. See, the "self" part of the equation is on you. The lessons that follow will never truly impact your life until you embark on the intense self-exploration required to embody the themes. Only you can make the concepts contained here practical, personal, and ultimately relevant.

For that reason, you'll find numerous references in this book to the practice of meditation, journaling, and solitude as tools to help you experience the internal cultivation of these notions so that you might ultimately express them in your everyday external reality.

Author's Note

A number of the meditations used in this book have been lightly edited from their original form in an attempt to modernize pronouns and address words no longer in common use that may serve to confuse the meaning of the quote. Every effort has been made to retain the original meaning of the passage.

January

Ralph Waldo Emerson (1803–1882)

Every revolution was first a thought in one man's mind and when the same thought occurs in another man, it is the key to that era.
—*Ralph Waldo Emerson*

Source: Wikimedia

Ralph Waldo Emerson is considered the father of the transcendentalist movement. He was born in the bustling seaport of Boston, Massachusetts, in 1802. His father, a Unitarian minister and learned man, instilled in him an interest in literature from a young age.

Emerson enrolled in Harvard at age 14, where he developed a keen interest in Asian culture, religion, and literature. He continued his study at Harvard Divinity School to become a minister, like his father, and took a post at a Boston church in 1829.

However, when his wife passed away from tuberculosis in 1831, he questioned his faith and decided to move away from the Church. After quitting his job, he left the United States to travel throughout Europe, where he met such literary giants as William Wordsworth, Samuel Taylor Coleridge, and Thomas Carlyle.

Upon his return to the States, he became a public lecturer—a career he would hold for the next 50 years of his life. This is also when he became involved with transcendentalism.

He published *Nature*, a seminal text of the movement, in 1836, and together with Margaret Fuller founded *The Dial*, the journal that became the primary vehicle for transcendentalist writers to publish their works, in 1840.

He published two collections of writings, *Essays* in 1841, and *Essays: Second Series* in 1844, that helped cement his place as a literary celebrity in America. In his later years, his writing focused more on poetry and contained strong influences from Eastern religions.

He continued to write extensively until 1880, and he died in Concord, Massachusetts, in 1882.

January 1

The Force of Nature

Why should we be in such desperate haste to succeed, and in such desperate enterprises? If a person does not keep pace with their companions, perhaps it is because they hear a different drummer. Let them step to the music which they hear, however measured or far away. It is not important that you should mature as soon as an apple tree or an oak. Shall you turn your spring into summer?

Henry David Thoreau—Walden (1854)

Nature has no desire to succeed—one season inevitably folds into the next, a year marked by changes in weather, ecology, and daylight—no matter how much force we might exert to contain it.

If we attempted to mimic nature, one thing is for sure, we would release the need to control any aspect of our lives. We would give in to what naturally needs to happen.

This is a fundamental element of self-reliance. And ironically by releasing the need to control we eventually find that we gain access to greater control.

Think about the last time you forced or tried to force something to happen. How did that feel? How did it turn out? If you succeeded, did the result last?

Now think about the last time something came into your life by way of what felt like luck. Isn't it possible that your lack of control actually created what you characterized as luck? Your letting go created your fate.

Today, and as you journey through this book, consider the many things on your path that worked out well for you even though you didn't or couldn't control them—listen closely for this tone, for it is your beat—the beat of your "different drummer."

Challenge Question

Can you describe a time you benefited from luck? What does luck feel like?

_____

_____

Planning: Trust

January 2

Wear Your Truth

I may be deemed superstitious, and even egotistical, in regarding this event as a special interposition of divine Providence in my favor. But I should be false to the earliest sentiments of my soul, if I suppressed the opinion. I prefer to be true to myself, even at the hazard of incurring the ridicule of others, rather than to be false, and incur my own abhorrence. From my earliest recollection, I date the entertainment of a deep conviction that slavery would not always be able to hold me within its foul embrace.
Frederick Douglass—Narrative of the Life of Frederick Douglass *(1845)*

So much about the quest for self-reliance is counterintuitive. The way toward the light often looks like the darkest choice. The true measure of our strength comes clothed in our ability to be weak.

But to speak and assume your truth in an effort to follow your passion as those around you seek to drag you into their fear and doubt also requires extraordinary wisdom.

You must first recognize how foolish following the path of others is so that you may embrace the posture of self-reliance.

Douglass stated he knew he would be freed from slavery long before it happened and that he welcomed the ridicule of others for speaking his truth in his version of "to thine own self be true."

Today, be mindful of what you think, do, and say and consciously note how often your thoughts and actions betray your essential truth and how often you stand firmly clothed in your truth.

Challenge Question

What is something you are sure of, even if it does not yet exist?

_____

_____

January 3

You Are Blendingly Distinct

Who in the rainbow can draw the line where the violet tint ends and the orange tint begins? Distinctly we see the difference of the colors, but where exactly does the one first blendingly enter into the other?
Herman Melville—Billy Budd, Sailor *(1924)*

Blendingly is a word every entrepreneur should embrace as it perfectly defines the contradiction inherent as you struggle for progress, all the while holding your breath in fear of failure—where does one end and one begin?

We often fail to see or trust our greatness because our feelings of unworthiness tell us we have accomplished far too little at this point. Read in context, Melville's character is explaining insanity, and there's certainly a little madness to be embraced in being an entrepreneur.

It shows up a little like striving to make it while pushing aside a persistent feeling that we are a fraud.

Here's are some questions to ponder. What do your feelings of unworthiness want from you? Why do they scream the loudest right when you are on the edge of something particularly significant?

Today, let go of the need to achieve. Get comfortable with being somebody and nobody at the very same time, and perhaps you'll finally catch a glimpse of your greatness once and for all.

Challenge Question

Can you describe a belief that might be holding you back? Where did that belief come from?

_____

_____

January 4

Who Are You to Be Great?

A foolish consistency is the hobgoblin of little minds, adored by little states-men and philosophers and divines. With consistency a great soul has sim-ply nothing to do. He may as well concern himself with his shadow on the wall. Speak what you think now in hard words, and to-morrow speak what to-morrow thinks in hard words again, though it contradict every-thing you said today.—"Ah, so you shall be sure to be misunderstood."—Is it so bad, then, to be misunderstood? Pythagoras was misunderstood, and Socrates, and Jesus, and Luther, and Copernicus, and Galileo, and New-ton, and every pure and wise spirit that ever took flesh. To be great is to be misunderstood.

Ralph Waldo Emerson—Self-Reliance *(1841)*

What, then, is it to be understood? Is it to have what you are doing, say-ing, thinking, and feeling fit into someone else's consistent view of the world?

Emerson felt that to be great was to be different, but he also knew that different was a more difficult way to go. An impressive lot—Socrates, Jesus, Luther, Copernicus, Galileo, and Newton—were all labeled different and per-secuted long before their ideas would be branded genius.

Different for the sake of difference may not make you great, but if your ideas today are not causing some to question your sanity just a bit, you may not be trying hard enough.

Different is often misunderstood, and those willing to change the world may eventually face the label of different, or weird, or crazy, or, the age-old favorite, a dreamer.

Dreaming big and being willing to be different is the hallmark of a self-reliant entrepreneur.

It's game time again—how will your dream be misunderstood today?

Challenge Question

How are your dreams misunderstood? Describe a time.

_____

_____

January 5

You Are Enough Right Now

All around us lies what we neither understand nor use. Our capacities, our instincts for this our present sphere are but half developed. Let us confine ourselves to that till the lesson be learned; let us be completely natural; before we trouble ourselves with the supernatural. I never see any of these things but I long to get away and lie under a green tree and let the wind blow on me. There is marvel and charm enough in that for me.

Margaret Fuller—Summer on the Lakes *(1844)*

The call to compete, stay relevant, follow the social media draped existence of others, robs us of our focus.

And, of course, the chase for more belies the fact that we already possess so much. Find less to do, think about, and observe, and it is likely you'll discover that your idea, your innovation, your silly little thing that nobody gets is quite perfect.

Strip the essence of your business down to no more than two or three priorities each month, each quarter perhaps, and go to work brilliantly on those ideas.

New ideas and new ways to make money are tantalizing, but the real fortune is in fully realizing the essential nature of your unique point of view, and that is expressed by doing less rather than more.

You are *enough* does not mean that you are *everything* right now. It says you had this idea of yours because you needed to shine a light on something, and even though you may need lots of help and you may make lots of mistakes, you trust that, right now, at this moment, you've got what it takes.

Step back, take in the wind, learn, smile, and stay focused on what's right in front of you. Everything is perfect, everything is perfect, everything is perfect—right now.

Challenge Question

What is one thing you feel is holding you back? Why are you letting it?

_____

_____

January 6

Peaceful in Your Intent

I exist as I am, that is enough, If no other in the world be aware I sit content,
And if each and all be aware I sit content. One world is aware and by far
the largest to me, and that is myself. And whether I come to my own today
or in ten thousand or ten million years, I can cheerfully take it now, or with
equal cheerfulness I can wait.

Walt *Whitman*—Song of Myself *(1855)*

The world is going to happen today—with or without your permission.

We have little control over what happens through the day, what is said, what we deem success or failure, and certainly how others react to whatever it is that we do.

The one thing we control universally is our intent. Intent powers, often unconsciously, our everyday actions and reactions and, if we choose to direct it so, powers the overarching vision for our entrepreneurial journey.

What is the ultimate intent for your journey? Not so much precisely where you are going but how you will impact others because you are going.

To realize intent of this nature, you must simultaneously hold this vision and let it go. You must be content with your progress. The thing is no matter what you do it is likely you'll get to where you want to go someday, but intent will get you there faster.

As a self-reliant entrepreneur, you are able to be one with your business and simultaneously able to stand apart from your business, letting things happen without trying to control the outcome.

Today, be at peace while holding your intent steadfastly.

Challenge Question

How do you plan to positively impact others today?

_____

_____

January 7

Consistency Brings Trust

They must be the poor creature that does not often repeat themselves. Imagine the author of the excellent piece of advice, "Know thyself," never alluding to that sentiment again during the course of a protracted existence! Why, the truths a person carries about are their tools; and do you think a carpenter is bound to use the same plane but once to smooth a knotty board with, or to hang up their hammer after it has driven its first nail?
  Oliver Wendell Holmes, Sr.—The Autocrat of the Breakfast-Table *(1858)*

The key to success is to do things others aren't willing to do and to do them over and over again.

That may not sound like advice for one intent on becoming a headline-making overnight success, but it is terribly sound advice for one intent on making a long-term impact on some corner of the universe.

Your unfailing word is how you let people know you mean it. Your reliable deed is how you lead others. Your constant practice is how you master your journey.

It is likely you will grow tired of expressing your truth long before even a trifle of those who most need it will ever experience it.

Today, tell your story, express your truth, enlist others in that story, and never stop sharing some version of it.

Consistency—showing up again and again and doing what you promised you would do from the start—is the hallmark of one to whom trust is extended.

Challenge Question

Can you describe one positive habit that has served you through consistent practice? How did you turn it into a habit?

_____

_____

January 8

Respect Your Dream

Far away there in the sunshine are my highest aspirations. I may not reach them, but I can look up and see their beauty, believe in them, and try to follow where they lead.
Louisa May Alcott—From the scrapbook of Elbert Hubbard (1915)

What is it that you most love about what you do or aspire to do?

Who else finds peace, joy, and happiness when you do it? Respecting this notion is how you unearth the joy that will always be with you.

Live in constant appreciation of your highest aspirations and you will attract what you need.

Challenge Question

What element of what you do brings you the greatest joy?

_____

_____

January 9

A Life Imagined

If one advances confidently in the direction of one's dreams, and endeavors to live the life which they have imagined, they will meet with a success unexpected in common hours. They will put some things behind, will pass an invisible boundary; new, universal, and more liberal laws will begin to establish themselves around and within them; or the old laws be expanded, and interpreted in their favor in a more liberal sense, and they will live with the license of a higher order of beings.

Henry David Thoreau—Walden *(1854)*

You are 100 percent unique (just like everyone else!)—there is no other human being exactly like you. That fact of science alone should be enough to allow us to choose whatever path we like rather than follow in the steps of others or choose a life determined by those who would judge right and wrong for us.

Are you living your life based on past prescriptions, or are you asking, "What do I want, what am I afraid of, what must I change?"

Or are you comparing yourself to others?

To live more fully, you must stop reinforcing judgments on yourself made by others and you must stop imposing your judgment. These are the mental exercises that compound daily to rob us of our essential, 100 percent unique nature.

Here's the thing: there's nothing to win. There's only your essential nature, and when you discover the awesome power of that, when you start to feel that in your heart, you'll discover the key to this entire game.

All day today, take note of things that are unique and essential to you and only you.

Challenge Question

Can you describe something about yourself that is completely unique?

_____

_____

January 10

Cast Your Bread

Mother's motto was "Hope, and keep busy," and one of her sayings, "Cast your bread upon the waters, and after many days it will come back buttered."

Louisa May Alcott—Her Life, Letters, and Journals *(1914)*

The message contained in today's reading is a playful version of a notion as old as all of civilization. It appears in the book of Ecclesiastes 11:1–6 (v. 1—*Cast thy bread upon the waters: for thou shalt find it after many days*) and could be seen as a literal characterization of the practice of the ancient Egyptian farmers who would cast seeds on top of the spring floodwaters of the Nile so that when the water receded the now-germinated seeds would settle into the rich soil and produce a fruitful harvest.

In *Her Life, Letters, and Journals*, Alcott recounts a winter when a neighbor lacked firewood, so her parents gave half of their dwindling pile to the neighbor in need without any real idea of how they would provide enough heat for their own home.

Shortly after a woodcutter passing by feared the drifting snow and asked if he could drop off his load there; he told them that because they were doing him a favor, they needn't hurry about paying for it.

The universe has an amazing scorekeeping system, and those who trust that what they need will show up at the appropriate moment can stay focused on acting in a mindset of prosperity.

An essential element of self-reliance is the belief that all things are connected and that what is good for others is good for you and is good for all. Keeping the continuous cycle of giving and receiving flowing—investing and reaping—is how abundance appears at precisely the moment nature intended.

Challenge Question

When was the last time you shared something unconditionally?

_____

_____

January 11

Light Within

*A person should learn to detect and watch that gleam of light which flashes
across their mind from within, more than the luster of the firmament of
bards and sages. Yet they dismiss without notice this thought because it is
theirs. In every work of genius, we recognize our own rejected thoughts; they
come back to us with a certain alienated majesty.*

Ralph Waldo Emerson—Self-Reliance *(1841)*

Self-doubt fuels much of the resistance felt at some point by nearly every
entrepreneur. A complete absence of self-doubt might suggest a lack of
passion—if you aren't at least a little afraid to do something, you might not
be thinking big enough.

But ignoring your genius precisely because it is yours triggers a pattern
much worse than the paralysis of doubt alone. When our ideas are rejected off
hand or left to linger unrealized, we begin to welcome forms of incongruence
or want of integrity.

Trust the gleam of light that flashes across your mind from within or
forever risk living a lie—it's just a choice.

Emerson's passage concludes with this thought in summary: "and we
shall be forced with shame to take our own opinion from another."

Today dig deep and access how this idea might be creating friction in
your journey.

Challenge Question

Can you name one big thing (idea) you know you should be doing?

_____

_____

January 12

Your Own Crazy

Had the routine of our life at this place been known to the world, we should have been regarded as madmen—; although, perhaps, as madmen of a harmless nature.

Edgar Allan Poe—The Murders in the Rue Morgue *(1841)*

Entrepreneurs possess their own special brand of crazy—and that's just fine!

Truly self-reliant entrepreneurs bear more resemblance to artists than the traditional businessperson. To make something out of nothing requires equal parts hallucination and determination.

It's no coincidence, then, that terms like "lean" and "canvas" abound in start-up literature. Artists, like entrepreneurs, struggle for many reasons, but often it is because they determine to stay true to their vision when it would seem so much easier to just get a job and collect pay.

Today, wear your badge of madness proudly (although do no harm).

Challenge Question

What's one time when you did not stay true to your vision (word) for fear of looking foolish?

_____

_____

January 13

Life Evolving

To be wise is but to know how little can be known. The true searcher after truth and knowledge is always like a child; although gaining strength from year to year, they still learn to labor and to wait. The field of labor is ever expanding before them, reminding them that they have yet more to learn; teaching them that they are nothing more than a child in knowledge, and inviting them onward with a thousand varied charms.

William Wells Brown—Three Years in Europe; or, Places I Have Seen and People I Have Met *(1852)*

Any entrepreneurs caught believing they have mastered their craft are just about to get their butt kicked.

The lifelong practice of gathering knowledge begins with the desire to learn but blossoms with the admission that you know so little. This isn't a flaw in your education; it's an acknowledgment that you can never run out of things to absorb.

Committing to a life of practice and growth requires curiosity above all else. Curiosity is the entrepreneur's perpetual learning device and personal growth engine.

Some have more of it quite naturally, but it can be learned and embraced.

True curiosity is not simply the gathering of information—it's the questioning of information gathered.

Why not? How does this work? Why do we do it this way? What if we . . .

Excitement breeds curiosity, and few things stimulate excitement like adventure.

Today, plan an adventure, something you've never done, maybe even something you're a little afraid to do, and ask yourself as you're doing it not just what you learned, but how alive it made you feel.

Challenge Question

When is the last time you ventured into something completely unknown to you?

_____

_____

January 14

Take the Plunge

You can't sit on the bank and think about it. You have to plunge. That's the way I've always done and it's the right way for people like you and me. There's nothing so dangerous as sitting still. You've only got one life, one youth, and you can let it slip through your fingers if you want to; nothing easier. Most people do that.

Willa Cather—The Bohemian Girl *(1912)*

Few things are easier than not acting on a heartfelt desire. And the tricky thing is there are so many ways to escape into the busyness that you can actually start to feel excited about doing nothing special.

All the while you begin to shrink.

And it's understandable, because you're not smart enough yet, you don't have enough experience yet, you haven't made the right connections yet.

That's what you might tell yourself as a way to keep sitting still, all the while life is slipping through your fingers. Nothing easier.

Don't think, take the plunge, you'll have plenty of time to be afraid another day, just not today.

Challenge Question

What's one bold action you could take today that would propel you toward your dreams?

_____

_____

Author's Note: Today's reflection is provided by my daughter, Ellen Jantsch.

January 15

Have a Dream

Reformers who are always compromising, have not yet grasped the idea that truth is the only safe ground to stand upon. The object of an individual life is not to carry one fragmentary measure in human progress, but to utter the highest truth clearly seen in all directions, and thus to round out and perfect a well balanced character.

Elizabeth Cady Stanton—The Woman's Bible *(1895)*

It's so easy to fall into the trap of feeling like this thing you are doing is too hard. It *is* hard! Building your own business isn't easy, it never was, it isn't now, and it won't ever be.

One of your biggest advantages is your willingness to keep pushing ahead even when it feels like you aren't making progress.

To do something on your own can invite criticism or worse, comparison, and those self-inflicted voices become noisy distractions, but *"truth is the only safe ground to stand upon."*

Do you remember any days when you worked for someone else and maybe you didn't give it your best work? In hindsight, didn't that feel worse than putting up with the hard work you're doing on your own?

Your work has your name on it and belongs to you. You're contributing on your own terms, expressing yourself the way you want, and that is a tiny and important revolution!

Challenge Question

What's the hardest part of your work these days? How could you reframe it?

_____

_____

January 16

The Inside Edge

So, in those winters of the soul, / By bitter blasts and drear / O'erswept from Memory's frozen pole, / Will sunny days appear. / Reviving Hope and Faith, they show / The soul its living powers, / And how beneath the winter's snow / Lie germs of summer flowers!
John Greenleaf Whittier—"A Dream of Summer," The Works of John Greenleaf Whittier, Vol. II (1857)

The practice of improving anything begins with improving yourself.

The ideas of inner work and interconnectedness are central to a great deal of the transcendentalist writings.

Many scholars interpreted Emerson's use of the term "self-reliance" not to define what we might call today "rugged individualism," but to define a sense of reliance on our own internal source of spirituality that could be tended and cultivated as a lifelong pursuit.

In that interpretation, then, what you do for yourself will be reflected in how you view the world around you.

The kindness, honesty, humility, and grace you show yourself will be shown to others. And, conversely, the rage, blame, mistrust, and suffering you bear will become how others experience you.

This may seem like a lot of weight to carry around, but perhaps the solution is simple—release it.

Challenge Question

What great act of self-care can you carry out today?

_____

_____

January 17

Make Good Choices

If a person has a genuine, sincere, hearty wish to get rid of their liberty, if they are really bent upon becoming a slave, nothing can stop them. And the temptation is to some natures a very great one. Liberty is often a heavy burden on a person. It involves that necessity for perpetual choice which is the kind of labor people have always dreaded. In common life we shirk it by forming habits, which take the place of self-determination.
Oliver Wendell Holmes, Sr.—Elsie Venner: A Romance of Destiny *(1861)*

Owning a business, being an entrepreneur, is either the most freeing perspective available or it's not at all. But the good news is you get to choose.

If you don't feel free at all right now, consider what well-worn justifications you might be using to keep yourself in chains. If only x wasn't a problem, I would finally do y.

It doesn't mean there aren't substantial constraints to your ability to do what you were destined to do—it simply demonstrates that resistance is a strong force.

Deciding to overcome resistance is your most momentous choice. Often it's a choice that involves fear, drama, and courage, and it's also often one many won't make unless pushed, because the habit of justification is too ferocious.

The secret to making the choice that is right for you is to stop living in either the future or the past and to embrace fear as something you can accept in today's version of freedom.

Challenge Question

What are you willing to give up in order to be free?

_____

_____

Planning: Trust

January 18

Time to Do Less

Our life is frittered away by detail. An honest person has hardly need to count more than their ten fingers, or in extreme cases they may add their ten toes, and lump the rest. Simplicity, simplicity, simplicity! I say, let your affairs be as two or three, and not a hundred or a thousand; instead of a million count half a dozen, and keep your accounts on your thumb nail.

Henry David Thoreau—Walden (1854)

Today's culture promotes, almost cheers, doing and having more.

Another foundational element endorsed by transcendentalists was production over consumption—that you should add more value to the world by thoughtfully producing things rather than mindlessly consuming them.

Although most entrepreneurs have no issue with the mindset of adding value, the siren's call of the next new thing or new model is hard to ignore. Facebook will gladly exhibit what you're lacking.

Self-reliance, however, requires something less—fewer ideas, fewer objectives, and few distractions. And something more—additional space, additional focus, and additional discipline.

The space, focus, and discipline to gain control over the highest payoff activities in your business and your life.

Self-reliant entrepreneurs find, create, and cherish the space to explore.

It doesn't matter how many gadget-filled moments you use today, you must find the time to do less.

Challenge Question

What would it take to carve out one hour every day just to think?

_____

_____

January 19

Unlimited Power

We can fix our eyes on perfection, and make almost everything speed towards it. This is, indeed, a noble prerogative of our nature. Possessing this, it matters little what or where we are now, for we can conquer a better lot, and even be happier for starting from the lowest point. Of all the discoveries which men need to make, the most important, at the present moment, is that of the self-forming power treasured up in themselves. They little suspect its extent, as little as the savage apprehends the energy which the mind is created to exert on the material world. It transcends in importance all our power over outward nature.

William Ellery Channing—Self-Culture *(1838)*

A belief in the connection among all living things was at the core of transcendentalism. This belief might seem in conflict when juxtaposed with the guiding principle that individuals are at their best when they are self-reliant.

However, Channing's reading might also suggest that it is the careful blending of these two ideas that unlocks a "self-forming" power we are free to tap at any chosen moment no matter where we find ourselves today.

When we begin to see everything as an extension of ourselves, we can let go of comparisons and accomplishments and fix our eyes on the perfection currently dammed up by our ego's need to compete rather than allow.

Test this out by turning to social media and reading a few dozen posts. What's your gut reaction when you do this—is it joy or is something less noble? Of course, it's the latter because we are trained to judge the thoughts of others as something separate from us—and they are not.

What if instead you saw everything as a path to the realization of your goals—sending thoughts of peace, joy, and happiness toward things you might have previously deemed bad or wrong.

From this point of view, you have access to unlimited power.

Challenge Question

When was the last time you judged something or someone as wrong? How did it make you feel?

January 20

Truthful Adherence

What I mean by the Muse is that unimpeded clearness of the intuitive pow-
ers, which a perfectly truthful adherence to every admonition of the higher
instincts would bring to a finely organized human being. It may appear as
prophecy or as poesy . . . and should these faculties have free play, I believe
they will open new, deeper and purer sources of joyous inspiration than
have as yet refreshed the earth.

Margaret Fuller—Woman in the Nineteenth Century *(1845)*

When you think about how you want to live your life, do you ever get a sense of deep insecurity about a particular aspect of it? Do you worry about what others might think?

It's funny how much stock we put in what others think, yet we immediately dismiss the clarity of our own intuitive powers to determine how we should live.

You must trust your inner beingness, "your Muse," because little else actually matters.

Today, ignore the echo of outside forces (even those living only in your head) and live and breathe in complete harmony with who you are.

Challenge Question

What aspect of your life are you living influenced by the expectations of others?

_____

_____

January 21

The Wonder of Things

And I will show that there is no imperfection in the present, and/ can be none in the future, / And I will show that whatever happens to anybody it may be turn'd to / beautiful results, / And I will show that nothing can happen more beautiful than death, / And I will thread a thread through my poems that time and events are compact, / And that all the things of the universe are perfect miracles, each as profound as any.

Walt Whitman—Leaves of Grass (1855)

In his popular book *Stumbling on Happiness*, author Daniel Gilbert states, "Wonderful things are especially wonderful the first time they happen, but their wonderfulness wanes with repetition."

When we begin or plan our entrepreneurial journey, we are full of wonder. So, how are you feeling about it today?

Miracles, wonderful things, beautiful results, happen around us every day if we let them.

Challenge Question

What miracle will you witness today?

_____

_____

January 22

Leap Unapologetically

If you lend me your ears, I shall doubtless take your hearts too. That I may not lead you into any wrong, let me warn you of this. Never violate the sacredness of your individual self-respect. Be true to your own mind and conscience, your heart and your soul.

Theodore Parker—The Collected Works of Theodore Parker *(1865)*

Figuring out what it means to be true to your own mind is merely the halfway point. The real work involves holding it and finding a way to make it so.

However, if the conditions that feed your heart and soul don't exist, perhaps you'll need to make them.

Some people will tell you that you can't do that—take delight in that and leap unapologetically into the hard work at hand.

Yes, it's hard work. But wouldn't you rather work hard doing something that brings you hope? Wouldn't you be more okay with failing at something that nourished your soul?

In a *Poet's Advice to Students*, e e cummings wrote, "To be nobody-but-yourself—in a world which is doing its best, night and day, to make you everybody else—means to fight the hardest battle which any human being can fight; and never stop fighting."

Challenge Question

What's one thing you will never violate, never stop fighting for, in your search of the perfect entrepreneurial journey?

_____

_____

January 23

No Regrets

*In our nature, however, there is a provision, alike marvelous and merciful,
that the sufferer should never know the intensity of what they endure by its
present torture, but chiefly by the pang that rankles after it.*
Nathaniel Hawthorne—The Scarlet Letter *(1850)*

John Lennon wrote the song "Beautiful Boy (Darling Boy)" for his son Sean that contained the now quotable lyric, "Life is what happens to you while you're busy making other plans."

It's so darn easy to get caught worrying about tomorrow when the really great stuff is happening today, right here, right at this moment, right in front of you.

This is one of the hardest things you'll have to master as an entrepreneur and human, but you've got this. Take a giant breath and then do it two more times—feel better already?

Being mindful seems like such worn-out advice—everyone gives it and nobody takes it, but it is the secret to living a life with no regrets.

Worrying about the future is just a habit, and so is reveling in the moment. Set up daily, maybe hourly, rituals that force you to snap back to the moment at hand and build them into your day.

Today, do something that requires no thought at all, say, wash a dish. But instead of rummaging over the schedule ahead while you do it, participate fully. Feel the curve in the dish, sense the water and soap as it runs over your hands, let everything else go. Weird, isn't it? Like breathing, we do it unconsciously and so we miss the experience of it entirely.

What else has become unconscious? What else will cause the pang that rankles primarily after you've missed the moment?

Challenge Question

What can you fully experience today with your entire being?

_____

_____

January 24

Endlessly Changing

Human minds are more full of mysteries than any written book and more changeable than the cloud shapes in the air.
Louisa May Alcott—The Abbot's Ghost *(1867)*

As a self-reliant entrepreneur, you get to change your mind—good thing, too, because changing other people's mind is a big part of your job. Your ability to convince others that you can do the work, that you're not too young, or too new or just too different than their current solution may make or break your venture.

Be in constant discovery mode, not just because something isn't working, but because you can always make it better.

Being open to change means giving up your need to be right and listening deeply to another's point of view. You don't have to take someone's advice or change to meet someone's opinion, but listening is the catalyst for your change and growth.

Listening is how you discover amazing new ways to think about a problem. Listening is how you let others know you care. Listening is how you let others help you. Listening unlocks some of the mysteries of the human mind.

Challenge Question

Who can you actively recruit to listen to today?

_____

_____

January 25

Exceptions to Every Rule

History jeers at the attempts of physiologists to bind great original laws by the forms which flow from them. They make a rule; they say from observation what can and cannot be. In vain! Nature provides exceptions to every rule. She sends women to battle, and sets Hercules spinning; she enables women to bear immense burdens, cold, and frost; she enables the man, who feels maternal love, to nourish his infant like a mother.
Margaret Fuller—Woman in the Nineteenth Century *(1845)*

In his essay "Education," Ralph Waldo Emerson stated that Nature loves analogies, but not repetitions. Most innovation is created by breaking the rules rather than repeating the past.

In the simplest sense, entrepreneurs are often rule breakers, but not in the criminal sense. They are often the first to see the unjust, or at least unnecessary, in even the simplest of rules—and from there they innovate.

But innovation does not come from copying; it comes from collecting analogies in the context you find yourself and rearranging how we do it here.

Innovation benefits from analogies, but not from repetitions.

Challenge Question

How can you be the exception to the rule today?

_____

_____

Planning: Trust

January 26

How High We Are

*We never know how high we are / Till we are called to rise; / And then, if
we are true to plan, / Our statures touch the skies—
The Heroism we recite / Would be a daily thing,/ Did not ourselves the
Cubits warp / For fear to be a King—
        Emily Dickinson—"We never know how high we are"—Letters (1894)*

Today's reading is certainly a call to reflect on the subconscious limiting
beliefs that might be holding you back from accomplishing what you were
meant for, or at least capable of. "For fear to be a King" seems like an odd
notion to apply to an entrepreneur until you start to examine the sometimes
habitual behavior that runs contrary to the stated objectives of success.

You might think to yourself, "I'll write that book when I have more
time." No, you won't. For some reason, you will never find the time to
write that book. Not until you rid yourself of what's holding you back. Of
course, the key to ridding yourself of limiting beliefs and behavior is to
identify them.

This is tough, lay-on-the-couch-and-talk-about-your-feelings kind of
work, but if you look honestly at the parts of your life that aren't working
as you had hoped, you might start to see clues and remnants of deep-seated
beliefs that work to create friction in your life rather than traction. (Feel free
to blame it on your parents if you like, but then you've got to own how it
shows up now.)

Challenge Question

What areas of your life are weakened by subconscious beliefs about things
like power, money, fame, relationships, commitment, responsibility, time?

_____

_____

January 27

Gratefully Uncomfortable

The power which resides in us is new in nature, and none but we know what that is which we can do, nor do we know until we have tried. Not for nothing one face, one character, one fact, makes much impression on us, and another none. It is not without pre-established harmony, this sculpture in the memory. The eye was placed where one ray should fall, that it might testify of that particular ray.

Ralph Waldo Emerson—Self-Reliance *(1841)*

Comfort may indeed to be one of the greatest adversaries of the entrepreneur.

The moment we begin to feel we deserve something, get used to things being a certain way, or expect to be treated as though we are more important than another, is the moment we start to fade.

Entitlement creates stagnation and constrains the flow of nature in our lives.

You might actually play with this idea and find occasions to make yourself uncomfortable. It's not so much about being uncomfortable as it is about being comfortable with how it makes you feel.

You can do something very simple, like take a new way home, or something slightly more complex, like present a new idea to a room full of people you don't know.

Look for instances that make you irritated and observe why you're feeling this way. Travel is a great everyday irritant for some and presents a great opportunity for witnessing and accepting inconvenience in a gracious manner.

We take so much for granted when we strive to achieve that we forget just how great we have it.

You're always in charge of the moments you choose to think, feel, and act about something, and true self-reliance means accepting almost everything as neither good nor bad.

Challenge Question

When is the last time you gratefully accepted being uncomfortable?

_____

_____

January 28

Relative Harmony

Musicians say there are three primal notes, without which music cannot be; and there are three primal colors, without a due proportion of which painting wants harmony. Pictures by the old masters show a knowledge of this; or rather an intuition, that transcends knowledge.

Lydia Maria Child—"What Is Beauty?" (1843)

Today's reading screams two things—entrepreneurs don't really make anything new—there is nothing new—only new ways to interpret, blend, juxtapose. And that we all have the same set of tools from which to craft our big idea.

So, in the words of Austin Kleon, author of *Steal Like an Artist*, here's your job:

Draw the art you want to see, start the business you want to run, play the music you want to hear, write the books you want to read, build the products you want to use—do the work you want to see done.

Discover the three primal notes that vibrate for you and practice blending them in new ways until you've got a hit.

That's the only commitment you have to make. So make it already.

Challenge Question

What could you blend to make something new?

_____

_____

January 29

Your Granitie Truth

To speak impartially, the best that I know are not serene, a world in them-selves. For the most part, they dwell in forms, and flatter and study effect only more finely than the rest. We select granite for the underpinning of our houses and barns; we build fences of stone; but we do not ourselves rest on an underpinning of granitie truth, the lowest primitive rock. Our sills are rotten. What stuff is the person made of who is not coexistent in our thought with the purest and subtilest truth?

> *Henry David Thoreau*—Life Without Principle *(1854)*

Do we demand enough of ourselves—of others?

Ironically, the best way to demand more from others is to trust them to be self-reliant. To recognize only they know what best serves their true nature.

And the best way to embrace our granitie truth is to admit there are many things we don't know, many positions about which we may discover we are wrong.

This is the only honest point of view and allows us to stay open to the perspective of others. It also allows us to change our mind. Both are important tools for the self-reliant entrepreneur.

Today, find a piece of raw granite and hold it in your hand.

You're using a fraction of the limitless power you possess—go get the rest; this is your ticket.

Challenge Question

Who will you trust to be self-reliant today?

_____

_____

Planning: Trust

January 30

True Desire

Nothing is far and nothing is near, if one desires. The world is little, people are little, human life is little. There is only one big thing—desire. And before it, when it is big, all is little. It brought Columbus across the sea in a little boat.

Willa Cather—Song of the Lark *(1915)*

Desire, powerful as it might be, is simply one motivation in a potential sea of stuff motivating us to do what we do.

A sense of duty is a motivation, fear, tradition, obsession, joy, anxiety, shame, pleasure, sadness—all motivations masked as shallow drivers.

Connect to your true motivation, your true desire to inch forward toward something that looks like impact, tamp down all those false motivations masked as want, and you'll begin to make all that lies before you small in the wake of true desire.

Challenge Question

What is the one thing you truly desire to accomplish?

_____

_____

January 31

Doing Sacred Work

We but half express ourselves, and are ashamed of that divine idea which each of us represents. It may be safely trusted as proportionate and of good issues, so it be faithfully imparted, but God will not have his work made manifest by cowards. It needs a divine person to exhibit anything divine.
Ralph Waldo Emerson—Self-Reliance (1854)

Wow, *coward* is a strong, perhaps overly dramatic word here, but maybe, just maybe, it applies.

When we hold back and half-express ourselves, it is often driven by something like cowardice or even shame.

You got dealt a hand that wasn't that great. You repeatedly got told you weren't going to amount to much. You didn't realize this was going to be *so much work.*

Suck it up—you're doing divine work.

It's not your fault that you feel afraid and that you sometimes feel and act like a coward—but it is your fault if you stay that way.

Challenge Question

Who will be better off 10 years from now because you decided to do what you do?

_____

_____

February

Margaret Fuller (1810–1850)

Only the dreamer shall understand realities, though in truth his dreaming must be not out of proportion to his waking.

—*Margaret Fuller*

Source: Wikimedia

Margaret Fuller was a woman of many firsts: the first woman granted access to the library at Harvard, the first full-time female book review editor in US journalism, and the first female foreign correspondent for a major US newspaper.

Born in Cambridgeport, Massachusetts, in 1810, she was the first child in her family. While she was an intellectual star from a young age, her trajectory shifted when her father died in 1835. Instead of launching her literary career, she began teaching to earn money to support her younger siblings.

However, her aspirations did not fade. She remained active in Boston's intellectual circle, becoming coeditor of *The Dial*, a transcendentalist magazine, and hosting her Conversations series—gatherings for women to discuss gender roles, women's rights, suffrage, and abolition.

Her essay "Woman in the Nineteenth Century" became a central feminist piece and launched her newspaper career, which eventually took her abroad during the Italian Revolution as the first female foreign correspondent for a major US newspaper.

It was in Italy that she met Marchese Giovanni Angelo d'Ossoli, a revolutionary with whom she would fall in love, have a child, and get married.

When the revolution failed, Fuller and her family decided to return to America. Sadly, their ship sank 400 yards off the coast of New York, and Fuller, her husband, and her child all drowned.

February 1

The Adventure of Journey

It is not metres but the metre-making argument that makes a poem—a
thought so passionate and alive, that, like the spirit of a plant or an animal,
it has an architecture of its own and adorns nature with a new thing,
Ralph Waldo Emerson—"The Poet," Essays, Second Series *(1844)*

When you start a business or embark on an entrepreneurial journey of some form, you begin to realize just how much your life changes—or do you?

It is so easy to get caught in the allure of the daily chase or the stress of the to-do list that you may not have even taken note of how much things are changing—or worse, you're fighting with change.

Resistance to change is what keeps us only happy enough, justifying our fears and failures, and ultimately, playing so much smaller than we intended at the start.

Your entrepreneurial call has a shape all its own, and until you let go, recognize it, and *become it* you'll always feel stuck. You know that feeling—like you're kind of in an indistinguishable funk.

Recognizing and intentionally participating in the creation of your own change is what will make your adventure feel like the birth of something quite alive.

So, how do you recognize that call?

Say this out loud:

My life is an adventure; my business is an adventure.

What did you feel just now?

Through this lens, pass everything that happens today and know that you can run on this path if you choose to. You can shout your intentions and make a bold case for your idea and dream, and by doing so realize that today is the day to take up the call to make the dent that only you can make.

Challenge Question

What is something you know you must change to realize your most adventurous life?

_____

_____

Planning: Creativity

February 2

Create Clods

What is done interests me more than what is thought and supposed. Every fact is impure, but every fact contains in it the juices of life. Every fact is a clod, from which may grow an amaranth or a palm.
Margaret Fuller—Summer on the Lakes *(1844)*

One way to interpret this meditation from Fuller is the "nose to the grindstone"—what is done is all that matters—point of view.

Or you might prescribe to the idea that science has shown the power of thought to manifest.

But surely both thought and action come into play when you are working on your masterpiece.

When you truly believe in your clod of a thought, you will be inspired to take action. It is only when fear makes your thought impure that you tend to act accordingly

In *Bird by Bird*, a book on the craft of writing by Anne Lamott, there's a chapter titled "Shitty First Drafts." The idea is to stop editing your brilliant idea before you even get it down on paper or you just might never quit thinking and start doing.

Stop thinking so much and just create already.

Challenge Question

What is the one thing you need to create most?

_____

_____

February 3

The Life in Yourself

When good is near you, when you have life in yourself, it is not by any known or accustomed way; you shall not discern the footprints of any other; you shall not see the face of man; you shall not hear any name; the way, the thought, the good, shall be wholly strange and new.

Ralph Waldo Emerson—*"Spiritual Laws,"* Essays—First Series *(1841)*

Intuition is a concept that some embrace more fully than others, but as an entrepreneur, you will find that this is a trait that will serve you well.

Some people seem to be born with it; some learn through life's greatest teacher—failure. There's no telling how you got it.

Don't complicate it.

You know what is you, so you will also know what is right and true for you. Some might call that intuition; some might define it more simply as "You'll know it when you see it."

The key is that you must have faith in the way.

Today, go out of your way to put yourself in situations and surroundings that are new and strange and trust the life in yourself to provide light.

Challenge Question

When did you last feel something was true in your gut and follow that feeling?

_____

_____

February 4

What Is Wild?

Our village life would stagnate if it were not for the unexplored forests and meadows which surround it. We need the tonic of wildness … At the same time that we are earnest to explore and learn all things, we require that all things be mysterious and unexplorable, that land and sea be indefinitely wild, unsurveyed and unfathomed by us because [it is] unfathomable. We can never have enough of nature.

Henry David Thoreau—Walden *(1854)*

Today's overt exclamation is to get yourself outside—get very, very far outside and into the wild.

For some, modern life actually makes this more of a chore than for others, but the importance mentally, physically, and spiritually cannot be understated.

Scientific study after study makes this advice infinitely practical for those who desire things like improved short-term memory, mental energy, concentration, creativity, and stress relief.

Even as we consume more and more of the land and sea, we shall never fully grasp the whole of the natural world. So why not make it our perpetual classroom?

As you attempt to expand your entrepreneurial vision, you can tap the unfathomed expansiveness of nature to open up new ways of thinking and doing.

Today . . . let's see—I know! Go take a hike!

Challenge Question

Where will you go hike or get outside in some fashion today?

_____

_____

February 5

Own Your Art

It is a beautiful truth that all contain something of the artist in them. And perhaps it is the case that the greatest artists live and die, the world and themselves alike ignorant what they possess. I think of few heroic actions, which cannot be traced to the artistical impulse. One who does great deeds, does them from an innate sensitiveness to moral beauty. Such persons are not merely artists, they are also artistic material.

Walt Whitman—*"Talk to an Art-Union"*—Prose Works *(1892)*

In a speech at the Unesco International Conference of Artists in Venice in 1952, world-renowned sculpture Henry Moore expressed a similar thought: *"I feel that I can best express myself, that I can best give outward form to certain inward feelings or ambitions by the manipulation of solid materials—wood, stone or metal."*

That's how it is with many entrepreneurs; they express who they are by molding their vision to become something experienced by others in outward form.

Today you'll manipulate both yourself and how people experience your business—you'll become both artist and the subject of your art, and that will be the most heroic thing you can do today.

Own it.

Challenge Question

What is your favorite sculpture? (Don't have one? Then find one that inspires you! Henry Moore's work is a good place to look.)

_____

_____

February 6

Expanding Capacity

Every now and then a person's mind is stretched by a new idea or sensation,
and never shrinks back to its former dimensions. After looking at the Alps,
I felt that my mind had been stretched beyond the limits of its elasticity, and
fitted so loosely on my old ideas of space that I had to spread these to fit it.
Oliver Wendell Holmes, Sr.—The Autocrat of the Breakfast-Table *(1858)*

You are in the business of creating something new, perhaps something revolutionary.

But how does one develop what is not without a sense of what is?

Unless you intentionally feed and expand your mind, you'll be limited to borrowing from a very small pool of ideas and many of your efforts will be destined to become uninspired copies of something already appreciated the world over. (It's okay; you have terabytes of untapped storage.)

Consuming a diverse regimen of art, books, cultures, foods, and music is the secret to greater focus and greater confidence in your thinking. A key to developing breakthrough ideas is to discover how to make the complex simple. Ironically, when you have access to a greater store of seemingly random ideas you'll more readily recognize the patterns required to do just that.

Read books on architecture, calculus, wolves—anything not related to what you already do for a living—and pay attention to how your mind comes to life when you comb not simply for information but for parallel ideas.

Try a food you're pretty sure you're going to dislike, travel to a place that makes you feel a little unsafe, go see a play that presents a point of view with which you don't currently agree. If you ultimately reject each after your trial, then ask yourself why.

Intentionally stretch your mind beyond the limits of its elasticity and you will build capacity for innovative thinking.

Challenge Question

Where could you go today to experience something very new and different?

_____

_____

February 7

Suddenly Grateful

There was a time when all these things would have passed me by, like the flitting figures of a theatre, sufficient for the amusement of an hour. But now, I have lost the power of looking merely on the surface. Everything seems to me to come from the Infinite, to be filled with the Infinite, to be tending toward the Infinite. Do I see crowds of people hastening to extinguish a fire? I see not merely uncouth garbs, and fantastic, flickering lights, of lurid hue, like a trampling troop of gnomes—but straightway my mind is filled with thoughts about mutual helpfulness, human sympathy, the common bond of fellowship, and the mysteriously deep foundations on which society rests; or rather, on which it now reels and totters.

Lydia Maria Child—Letters from New York *(1843)*

All of society indeed rests on a mysteriously deep foundation, but few debate the level at which our thoughts dictate how we choose to see the world.

Do we fill our minds with grateful images of the "common bond of fellowship" available in each moment? Or do we fret about the meeting tomorrow with that pain-in-the-neck client?

See everything today through the lens of gratitude and you might be surprised how even the mundane, the arduous, gets more delightful.

It may feel absurd to proclaim "I am so thankful! I get to go tell my client I'm not going to meet the deadline for the project!" But let's face it—you have a client, you have a project, you're probably going to sleep in a warm bed tonight and choose what you get to eat for your next meal.

Today, notice any time you begin to tense up about something you have to do and see if you can turn it around into something wonderful you get to do.

Challenge Question

What are you suddenly grateful for today?

_____

_____

Planning: Creativity

February 8

As We Are

Say what some poets will, Nature is not so much her own ever-sweet inter-preter, as the mere supplier of that cunning alphabet, whereby selecting and combining as they please, each person reads their own peculiar lesson according to their own peculiar mind and mood.

Herman Melville—Pierre: or, The Ambiguities *(1852)*

In his best-selling book, *The 7 Habits of Highly Effective People*, author Stephen Covey included this thought: "Each of us tends to think we see things as they are, that we are objective. But this is not the case. We see the world, not as it is, but as we are—or, as we are conditioned to see it."

The use of this exact phrase—"We see the world, not as it is, but as we are"—is found in countless sermons and self-help literature, including some translations of the Talmud, a collection of writings on Jewish law and tradition, compiled and edited between the third and sixth centuries. Suffice it to say, it's not an entirely new concept.

Concepts, ideas, platitudes are wonderful—understanding of the ideas, however, is what makes us self-reliant.

All innovation and creativity depend on this very idea. The notion that we get to choose and arrange our own "cunning alphabet" is a powerful concept for certain. So what will you do with it?

Challenge Question

What's one word you could invent for your life today?

_____

_____

February 9

The Life in Yourself

Genius burned so fiercely that for four weeks I wrote all day and planned nearly all night, being quite possessed by my work. I was perfectly happy, and seemed to have no wants. Finished the book, or a rough draught of it, and put it away to settle. Daresay nothing will ever come of it; but it had to be done, and I'm the richer for a new experience.

Louisa May Alcott—Her Life, Letters, and Journals *(1889)*

How many days go by where you wonder what you actually got done? And then, think about those days where you consider how much you've accomplished—and it's only noon.

What's the difference? Focus.

When you have a priority so important that no distraction calls loud enough to extinguish your fiercely burning genius, you're unstoppable.

Success is rarely a matter of how much you must work, but how on fire you are about the work you must do. It takes space and air to fan the right flames—give yourself both.

Challenge Question

What's something you've been putting off that you should work on?

_____

_____

February 10

Reawakening the Bond

Undoubtedly we have no questions to ask which are unanswerable. We must trust the perfection of the creation so far, as to believe that whatever curiosity the order of things has awakened in our minds, the order of things can satisfy.

Ralph Waldo Emerson—Nature *(1836)*

A harmony exists between the world of nature and human beings no matter how distant this bond has become.

When we as humans depended on nature to provide food and shelter, we possessed senses that allowed us to smell danger and see tiny changes in our environment as signs of impending abundance. This reliance allowed us to believe in the absolute existence of nature.

Trusting and depending on the current signs mattered more than a reliance on the past, and that too is a power we must stimulate in our day-to-day entrepreneurial lives.

We still possess the ability to correspond with nature and make order of our journey by recognizing the link between our individual spirit and the entire universe.

One of the most consistent themes in self-reliant literature is the inter-connectedness of all beings, or atoms for that matter. That the joining of mind and body, spirit and universe is fully represented in nature.

By reawakening the bond with the natural world, we can further develop a level of self-trust that eventually allows us to let go of any fears that hold us back.

Today, as you create perfection you can rest assured that the world is as it should be and your dream, now awakened, is as it should be.

This is how the universe helps you create your own unique world of self-reliance.

Challenge Question

What can you do today to recognize a part of yourself in every other human being?

_____

_____

February 11

Simply Perfect

In character, in manner, in style, in all things, the supreme excellence is simplicity.

Henry Wadsworth Longfellow—Favorite Poems

Longfellow is one of America's most popular poets. His long-form poems, such as "Paul Revere's Ride," "The Wreck of the Hesperus," and "The Song of Hiawatha," were at one point required memorization exercises in many schools.

And yet in his own work of favorite poems, it is a note about yearning for simplicity that sums up his creative genius.

Simplicity, it turns out, is much harder than the opposite.

Simplicity or even brevity of thought and word forces us to distill something to its core, without excess to make our point. But being precise is sometimes the greatest work we endeavor.

Simplicity, however, may be best summed up as an aspiration. To embrace simplicity as a creative force, we might find it useful to see it in all things—choices, strategies, conversations, possessions, as well as our entrepreneurial vision. Through this lens it becomes our teacher.

Simplicity is about being less busy and more focused on what matters. Simplicity as a point of view helps us focus on the essentials that lead to the success we so desire.

In the words of Greg McKeown, author of *Essentialism: The Disciplined Pursuit of Less*:

> The pursuit of success can be a catalyst for failure. Put another way, success can distract us from focusing on the essential things that produce success in the first place.

Challenge Question

What is one thing you could simplify or eliminate completely right now?

_____

_____

February 12

Dreamers of the Day

They who dream by day are cognizant of many things which escape those who dream only by night. In their gray visions they obtain glimpses of eternity, and thrill, in waking, to find that they have been upon the verge of the great secret.

Edgar Allan Poe—Eleonora (1842)

"Daydreaming" has gotten a bad rap. It's a term often applied to people who dare to think differently, but it's a skill required by entrepreneurs.

It's the skill required to stop, plan, think, and in a cognizant state, allow the creative process to unfold.

T. E. Lawrence, perhaps better known as Lawrence of Arabia, once said that "the dreamers of the day are dangerous men, for they may act their dreams with open eyes, to make it possible."

Go ahead and daydream today.

Challenge Question

What dream occurs to you most during the day?

_____

_____

February 13

First Make a Mess

In creating, the only hard thing's to begin; / A grass-blade's no easier to make than an oak, / If you've once found the way, you've achieved the grand stroke; in the worst of his poems are mines of rich matter, / but thrown in a heap with a crush and a clatter; / Now it is not one thing or another alone, / Makes a poem, but rather the general tone.

James Russell Lowell—"A Fable for Critics" (1848)

Creativity is a messy thing.

Often it is the distillation of our heap of ideas that leads to a stunning creative breakthrough.

Lowell's poem was a popular criticism of the writing of many of the era's most notable authors, including, in this stanza, Emerson.

Your ideas will have critics. Your raw creative leanings will go unfinished. Your best, most financially promising ideas will likely spring from your ability to assemble new ideas from old concepts.

Todd Henry, the author of *Die Empty: Unleash Your Best Work Every Day*, calls this work *meshing*. It is all of the "work between the work" that makes you more effective when you are working. It consists of things like following your curiosity, studying, developing your skills, and asking deeper questions about why you are doing your work.

This is how you find your genius contribution, but only if you're at first willing to make a crush and clatter.

Challenge Question

What part of your vision contains the richest matter?

_____

_____

February 14

Artful Growth

What was any art but an effort to make a sheath, a mould in which to imprison for a moment the shining, elusive element which is life itself,—life hurrying past us and running away, too strong to stop, too sweet to lose?
Willa Cather—Song of the Lark *(1915)*

Many art forms are just that—static frames holding the unending flow of life momentarily in remission.

Want to test this? Find an image of Frida Kahlo's *Self-Portrait as a Tehuana*. She painted this in 1940 after she and her artist husband Diego Rivera divorced. It is a metaphor created to house a sentiment that was quite literal.

The entrepreneur's art, however, is a living work in a constant state of evolution—or not. You see, if not, if static or, worse, stagnant, it is dying. There is no momentary state of remission—living or dying is all there is.

The entrepreneur's form of art is change.

Get used to it, relish it, embrace it, be thankful for it. This is growth. Make it happen.

Challenge Question

What can you change today?

_____

_____

February 15

Thin Decision Making

When good is near you, when you have life in yourself, it is not by any known or accustomed way; you shall not discern the footprints of any other; you shall not see the face of humankind; you shall not hear any name; the way, the thought, the good, shall be wholly strange and new.
Ralph Waldo Emerson—Self-Reliance (1841)

Our unconscious mind is more powerful than we may acknowledge. This thing often referred to as gut instinct may indeed be our mind giving voice to what Emerson dubbed our "latent conviction"—our inner ability to know what is best for us.

Psychologists use the term "thin-slicing" to describe a person's ability to find patterns in events based only on "thin slices," or narrow windows, of experience.

More recently, the term "adaptive unconscious" has been used to describe an effortless mental process that influences our judgment and decision making.

Malcolm Gladwell brought both terms into popular use in *Blink: The Power of Thinking Without Thinking.*

The way, the thought, the good is wholly strange and new—and it's only in you.

Trust it.

Challenge Question

When was the last time you had a strong gut feeling about something?

_____

_____

Planning: Creativity

February 16

Active Procrastination

The creative action is not voluntary at all, but automatic; we can only put the mind into the proper attitude, and wait for the wind, that blows where it is bound, to breathe over it. Thus the true state of creative genius is allied to reverie, or dreaming. If mind and body were both healthy and had food enough and fair play, I doubt whether any men would be more temperate than the imaginative classes.
Oliver Wendell Holmes, Sr.—The Autocrat of the Breakfast-Table *(1858)*

Today's reading may be just what you were looking for—a reason to embrace procrastination.

And let it be.

What feels like procrastination is one of two things—fear or intuition. Discover which it is and act accordingly.

If it's fear or dread of what's ahead, then punch it in the face. If it's intuition telling you to hang, breath, gather some space and the answer will arrive, then step back and do something playful instead.

Active procrastination may allow you to make a better decision with less stress and train your mind to let go of momentary drama and pressure.

Asking yourself why you should do today what you could put off until tomorrow may seem like the lazy person's Ben Franklin, but sometimes that's just what's called for.

Challenge Question

What can you do today that feels like play?

_____

_____

February 17

Authorin g Something Beautiful

The whole plan laid itself smoothly out before me, and I slept no more that night, but worked on it as busily as if mind and body had nothing to do with one another. Up early, and began to write it all over again. The fit was on strong, and for a fortnight I hardly ate, slept, or stirred, but wrote, wrote, like a thinking machine in full operation. When it was all rewritten without copying, I found it much improved, though I'd taken out ten chapters, and sacrificed many of my favorite things; but being resolved to make it simple, strong, and short, I let everything else go, and hoped the book would be better for it.

Louisa May Alcott—Her Life, Letters, and Journals *(1889)*

Norman Maclean's novella *A River Runs Through It* includes a passage that captures today's reading well:

One of life's quiet excitements is to stand somewhat apart from yourself and watch yourself softly becoming the author of something beautiful even if it is only a floating ash.

That is perhaps the truest description of the magic trick you must perform in order to become self-reliant: to stand somewhat apart from yourself and let go in hopes that whatever it is you are engaged in would be better for it.

In the movie adaptation there is a scene where the narrator, describes how his father taught him that the art of writing lay in simplicity. The son would present an essay and the father would approve and instruct his son to make it half as long.

Challenge Question

What can you remove from your journey right now in order to make it better?

_____

_____

Planning: Creativity

February 18

Speak What Tomorrow Thinks

With consistency a great soul has simply nothing to do. You may as well concern yourself with your shadow on the wall. Speak what you think now in hard words and tomorrow speak what tomorrow thinks in hard words again, though it contradict everything you said today.

Ralph Waldo Emerson—Self-Reliance (1841)

Self-reliance anchors a great deal of its potency in self-trust. Today's reading is a kick in the self-trust pants.

Although consistency is often heralded as a pillar of stability, self-reliance calls you to trust in your ideas enough to know when they are wrong. It requires the courage to change course even if you fear the disapproval of those who today approve.

Every innovation or remarkable breakthrough occurs because someone changed their mind and decided to approach something from a new point of view. All growth requires this form of change.

It does not mean that you must abandon your current beliefs, but it does mean you must trust yourself enough to contradict your previous perceptions when it becomes clear that you must "speak what tomorrow thinks."

Early on in *Self-Reliance*, Emerson writes, "The other terror that scares us from self-trust is our consistency; a reverence for our past act or word, because the eyes of others have no other data for computing our orbit than our past acts, and we are loath to disappoint them."

It is through the disregard for what others might think that you can gain the independence of thought that breeds true self-reliance.

Challenge Question

Is there someone in your life who causes you to doubt yourself? Why do they possess this hold?

_____

_____

February 19

Thinking Makes It So

No one doubts—certainly not I—that the mind exercises a powerful influence over the body. From the beginning of time, the sorcerer, the interpreter of dreams, the fortune-teller, the charlatan, the quack, the wild medicine-man, the educated physician, the mesmerist, and the hypnotist have made use of the client's imagination to help them in their work. They have all recognized the potency and availability of that force.

Mark Twain—Christian Science *(1907)*

Think about the last time you worried about a future event. How did your thoughts about this contemplated situation make you feel physically?

The point is our mind incessantly judges every common and uncommon thing as right or wrong, and this takes a toll on how we show up physically.

If this is true, and numerous studies say it is, then it's not much of a leap to wonder what would happen if we took control over how our mind exercised influence over our body.

Here's the deal: most judgment is borne out of ignorance. When we judge someone or something as bad, it's often because we don't know the whole story and we simply fill in the blanks from our own bias and assumptions.

This is equally true when we judge something as a good result. We're often guilty of taking far more credit for making it happen than is warranted.

Today, take one hour and pledge to practice nonjudgment, no matter what happens. And just observe—don't judge yourself for judging or you'll kind of miss the point.

Challenge Question

What is one thing you've deemed bad or good that you might reconsider?

_____

_____

February 20

Child of the Mist

There is something servile in the habit of seeking after a law which we may obey. We may study the laws of matter at and for our convenience, but a successful life knows no law. It is an unfortunate discovery certainly, that of a law which binds us where we did not know before that we were bound. Live free, child of the mist,—and with respect to knowledge we are all children of the mist. The person who takes the liberty to live is superior to all the laws, by virtue of their relation to the lawmaker.

Henry David Thoreau—"Walking" (1861)

Thoreau wrote often about the virtues of life without regard for laws. His essay titled "Civil Disobedience" is an ode to this idea and may rival *Walden* in the important ideas it contains.

However, Thoreau was not simply clamoring for anarchy and lawlessness; his definition of law included living by the laws of nature governed by one's most inner desires.

We must be our own lawmaker if we are to be truly self-reliant.

Thoreau believed in the Concord of 1862 that fences and divided parcels of "improved" lands drove the natural wildness from us by imposing "laws which bind us where we did not know before that we were bound."

How do the expectations of others and our own beliefs make us seek to impose laws that we may obey? Do we really have to work this many hours? Do we really need to speak up to demonstrate how smart we are in any situation? Do others have to lose so that we may win?

Thoreau begins the essay "Walking" by encouraging readers to saunter. Walking about in the wild was his prescription for reclaiming one's own wildness and in doing so live by one's true nature not bound by self-imposed laws.

Today, reclaim your wildness—your child of the mist.

Challenge Question

What is one "law" you can begin to disobey? How can you make sauntering a daily habit?

_____

_____

February 21

Cumulative Rhythm

The rhyme and uniformity of perfect poems show the free growth of metrical laws, and bud from them as unerringly and loosely as lilacs and roses on a bush, and take shapes as compact as the shapes of chestnuts and oranges, and melons and pears, and shed the perfume impalpable to form.

Walt Whitman—Preface to Leaves of Grass *(1855)*

It is your idea, your promise, your innovation that will capture, not because of you, but perhaps in spite of you.

In this entry, Whitman compares all great works to music and declares that what makes music great is much like what makes any great work—a cumulative rhythm that allows it to be true.

But this is the very difficult thing about music and truth. If you believe that your idea must be shaped to meet a certain form, you are destined to limit the true power of your entrepreneurial journey.

If, however, you believe that your truth will one day ascend to make beautiful music, then you'll have the resiliency to keep at it and push through every less-than-perfect iteration.

Go about laying brick by brick, dropping seeds, in an organic fashion that only you can translate, and you may indeed stumble upon an idea, or even a brand that *"sheds the perfume impalpable to form."*

The outward form of your idea will come from your deeper internal truth.

It's okay if you're not sure of where your song is headed. Your heart knows the truth—keep working on your music.

Today, bring artistic intensity to every decision and choice you make. Simple!

Challenge Question

What's your absolute favorite work of music? Why?

_____

_____

February 22

Guruless

The true teacher defends their pupils against their own personal influence. They inspire self-trust. They guide their eyes from themselves to the spirit that quickens them. They will have no disciples. A noble artist, they have visions of excellence and revelations of beauty, which they have neither impersonated in character, nor embodied in words. Their life and teachings are but studies for yet nobler ideals.

Amos Bronson Alcott—"Orphic Sayings" (1840)

Many entrepreneurs seek the advice and mentoring of gurus and, in doing so, give away a great deal of their personal power.

Why is that?

What lack of self-trust makes us believe others know what is best for us? What fears stop us from defining our unique dream? Why is it safer to follow the advice of others than to expose ourselves to the criticism and rejection of our differentiating ideas?

Consider this as you seek the knowledge of others: the best teachers teach you how to teach yourself.

Challenge Question

What makes your dream truly unique?

_____

_____

Planning: Creativity

February 23

The Quality of Observation

In this way our hero got safely to college, / Where he bolted alike both his commons and knowledge; / A reading-machine, always wound up and going, / He mastered whatever was not worth the knowing.
James Russell Lowell—"A Fable for Critics" (1848)

One of the most common traits among successful entrepreneurs is curiosity.

It is an attribute that leads them to do things like read hundreds of books each year, identify new ways to think about long-established ideas, or change their minds when they discover something better.

Without the habit of curiosity, you won't ask questions, you won't worry away at all the little things that don't add up, and you certainly won't wonder about the extraordinary reasons you were put on this earth.

Questioning and exploring seemingly odd things—the social hierarchy of wolf packs, the engineering applications of matrices, how watersheds are formed—often leads to new and sometimes innovative ways to view what it is we do.

In *A Pattern Language*, a book about physical architecture, Christopher Alexander states:

> This is a fundamental view of the world. It says that when you build a thing you cannot merely build that thing in isolation, but must repair the world around it, and within it, so that the larger world at that one place becomes more coherent, and more whole; and the thing which you make takes its place in the web of nature, as you make it.

Consider Alexander's words in the context of your entrepreneurial journey and you just might conclude this curiosity thing has some merit.

Challenge Question

What counterintuitive subject could you explore today in the context of your journey?

_____

_____

Planning: Creativity

February 24

Fear and Doubt

Adhere to your own act, and congratulate yourself if you have done something strange and extravagant and broken the monotony of a decorous age. It was a high counsel that I once heard given to a young person,— "Always do what you are afraid to do."
Ralph Waldo Emerson—"Heroism," in Essays, First Series *(1841)*

Face the fear and just do it.

In addition to sounding a bit like a marketing slogan, that statement has become standard advice for entrepreneurs.

Before you push it aside as yet another thing you're supposed to do, sit with this idea—fear and doubt show up to tell you something. You can choose to ignore them, but they probably won't go away.

Learn to tune into your fears and doubts, witness them, study them, laugh at them, and then you just might become a bit more fully aware of your true path.

Steven Pressfield's *The War of Art*, the book-length version of today's reading, offers this nugget to chew on:

Are you paralyzed with fear? That's a good sign. Fear is good. Like self-doubt, fear is an indicator. Fear tells us what we have to do.

Challenge Question

What scares you the most about your journey? Why?

_____

_____

February 25

Analog Creative

For here there is no escape from the weight of a perpetual creation; all other forms and motions come and go, the tide rises and recedes, the wind, at its mightiest, moves in gales and gusts, but here is really an incessant, an indefatigable motion. Awake or asleep, there is no escape, still this rushing round you and through you. It is in this way I have most felt the grandeur,—somewhat eternal, if not infinite.
Margaret Fuller—At Home and Abroad; or, Things and Thoughts in America and Europe *(1856)*

This reading is Fuller's description of experiencing Niagara Falls for the first time, and yet it reads almost like a personal journey of self-discovery.

Our own creative output reflects how we take in the wonder of things both grand and "ungrand." Our journey as the self-reliance entrepreneur rests in bearing this weight of perpetual creation. That's what makes entrepreneurs so unique—and perhaps a little batty.

So how do you juggle the need to constantly remain creative without letting the weight of this notion turn into added stress?

Go analog. Today do something that requires your hands—not on a keyboard. Paint a wall, write in a journal with a pen, pickle some cucumbers, or sketch arbitrary objects in a park.

The power of random unplugged activities to free your mind to create is miraculous.

Challenge Question

What is your favorite writing instrument? (Don't know? Then research, test, and find it.)

_____

_____

February 26

Yes and No Are Lies

In writing, conversation should be folded many times thick. It is the height of art that, on the first perusal, plain common sense should appear; on the second, severe truth; and on a third, beauty; and, having these warrants for its depth and reality, we may then enjoy the beauty for evermore.

Henry David Thoreau—Familiar Letters *(1894)*

Here Thoreau is suggesting to Emerson that although the best writing seems simple and common sense, achieving this effect is not easy.

As a self-reliant entrepreneur, you can never stop looking for the truth in your vision, just as Thoreau felt he could never stop looking for the truth in nature. It's a bit of an epic journey even after you've "folded many times thick," as Thoreau proposes.

The most creative thing an entrepreneur can accomplish is the capacity to explain their vision in ways so practical that it is immediately recognizable to many.

And this is achieved maybe never fully—there will always be more questions, better questions to ask. The art of self-reliance depends on incessantly questioning and evolving your ideas. There is perhaps no true state of *done*.

Although that may indeed seem exhausting work, it's what you signed up for. It's the magic in the daily struggle.

In an unrelated journal entry, Thoreau emphasizes this idea further: "Yes and no are lies, [a] true answer will not aim to establish anything, but rather to set all well afloat."

Challenge Question

To what question about your journey does the answer frighten you most?

_____

_____

February 27

Unfinished Business

It was plain that I had worked myself out, pumped myself dry. So I knocked off, and went to playing billiards for a change. I haven't had an idea or a fancy for two days, now—an excellent time to write to friends who have plenty of ideas and fancies of their own, and so will prefer the offerings of the heart before those of the head.

Mark Twain—Mark Twain's Letters (1917)

Here's a known fact about entrepreneurs: they are more commonly starters than finishers. The dream gives way to the work once begun, and that's where boredom begins and interest wanes.

And it often gets worse the closer to completion. How many things have you let languish in your life for want of the final 10 percent?

Twain admits later in this letter that "My interest in my work dies a sudden and violent death when the work is done."

The self-reliant entrepreneur is a finisher.

Today, close something out that's been hanging around waiting for you to revisit it. Get it off your plate and you'll find yourself filling back up again with ideas and fancies of your own.

Challenge Question

What's one unfinished piece of business you should bring to a close?

_____

_____

Planning: Creativity

February 28

Your Sitting Place

*The green trees whispered low and mild; / It was a sound of joy! / They were
my playmates when a child, / And rocked me in their arms so wild! / Still
they looked at me and smiled, / As if I were a boy; // And ever whispered,
mild and low, / "Come, be a child once more!"*
    Henry Wadsworth Longfellow—Complete Poetical Works of Henry
                          Wadsworth Longfellow *(1845)*

There's kind of a weird thing about being an entrepreneur. Once you're
immersed in a business venture, you lose the ability to see many things that
are happening all around you and in your daily interactions with others.
You're so deep in the business that you're no longer able to see the path of
the business.

It's much as if you were to hike through a wilderness. Many things could
be going on all around you that would escape your notice as you pushed
through. Predators, highly attuned to their survival desire, would hide or run
without making a sound; trees would whisper "mild and low"; and the songs
of what seemed like a thousand little birds would go unheard.

That's just how it is—we're so determined to get to the summit or waterfall that we no longer see the miracles all along the path before us.

Outdoor guides and even hunters will tell you that the best way to capture nature is to sit and observe from the same spot day after day. Do this
and the patterns and happening of the entire territory, not just the map, will
openly reveal themselves.

Perhaps you did this as a child and have simply forgotten.

Find your sitting spot and visit it often. Wilderness is optional, but it
just might be the best option. Either way, develop the habit of "silent sitting
observation" as a way to remain outside of your business. You know—see the
forest *and* the trees. (You may have seen that coming.)

Challenge Question

Where can you go to find your sitting spot?

_____

_____

Author's note: This is Leap Year Day. A bonus entry three years out of four.

February 29
Positive Recharge

Thus it is that ideas, which grow up within the imagination and appear so lovely to it and of a value beyond whatever people call valuable, are exposed to be shattered and annihilated by contact with the practical. It is requisite for the ideal artist to possess a force of character that seems hardly compatible with its delicacy; they must keep their faith while the incredulous world assails them with its utter disbelief; they must stand up against all and be their own sole disciple, both as respects their genius and the objects to which it is directed.

Nathaniel Hawthorne—"The Artist of the Beautiful" (1844)

Today's reading seems like a downer now, doesn't it?

In a world that seems to want to keep anyone with a new idea for their life down, the secret to success may reside in what you choose to consume.

Now, I suppose this does include the food you eat, but it also applies to everything that comes your way.

We're constantly bombarded, whether or not we know it, by a steady stream of negative or even other people's view of what we could view as practical.

Today, and maybe every day, turn off the negative news, read books that inspire and encourage you, limit exposure to toxic people, listen to beautiful music, meditate with positive intentions, give someone a hug, get out in the woods.

You've only got so much positive stamina each day, so add some recharge routines to help your body keep going when your head starts to tell it otherwise.

It's hard enough to keep the faith without allowing yourself to be assailed by others wishing for you to wear their insecurities as you mold your dream.

Challenge Question

What positive, inspirational habit can you add to your daily recharge routine?

_____

_____

March

Henry David Thoreau (1817–1862)

If you have built castles in the air, your work need not be lost; that is where they should be. Now put the foundations under them.

—*Henry David Thoreau*

Source: Wikimedia

Henry David Thoreau was born in Concord, Massachusetts, in 1817. His early years were shaped by his education, first at Concord Academy and then at Harvard, and by his mother's love of nature.

After graduation, Thoreau met Ralph Waldo Emerson, who would become his dear friend and mentor. In 1840, Thoreau began contributing to *The Dial*, the transcendentalist journal that was edited by Emerson and Margaret Fuller.

His writing also began to take on a political bent. Thoreau was opposed to slavery and wrote about his viewpoint often. He published his essay, "Civil Disobedience," which became well-known and would later serve as an inspiration for activists like Dr. Martin Luther King Jr. and Mahatma Gandhi.

In 1845, Thoreau built a cabin and moved out to a piece of land near Walden Pond. During his two years there, he finished his first book, *A Week on the Concord and Merrimack Rivers*, which was not a popular success.

Following the cool reception to his first publication, Thoreau traveled around New England and Canada, revising what would become his second book, *Walden*. Based on his time living in the cabin, this book became a critical success in his lifetime and is still one of the most famous transcendentalist works today.

In the late 1850s, as the American Civil War approached, Thoreau again turned his attention to abolitionist causes, publishing essays and speaking out against slavery. He was also frequently ill in his later years; he contracted tuberculosis in the 1830s, and it recurred several times. His health continued to decline, and he died in 1862, at age 44.

March 1

The Bliss You Live

Is bliss, then, such abyss / I must not put my foot amiss / For fear I spoil my shoe? // I'd rather suit my foot / Than save my boot, / For yet to buy another pair / Is possible / At any fair. // But bliss is sold just once; / The patent lost / None buy it anymore.

Emily Dickinson—*"Life" from* Collected Poems *(1855)*

Sometimes these readings and reflections can seem a tad overly dramatic.

But think about this: have you known people who quit something that was meaningful to them only to never truly let it go? Some aspect of it ate away at their bliss endlessly. That's kind of serious, isn't it?

Self-reliant entrepreneurs understand their bliss and pursue it.

However, pursuing your bliss is not a license to do as you please; it's an admission that there's only one path for you and you have no choice but to give yourself fully to it.

In 1988, American mythologist and writer Joseph Campbell conducted a series of interviews for PBS, and upon airing, the term "Follow Your Bliss" became a catchphrase. In one segment Campbells states that "if you do follow your bliss, you put yourself on a kind of track that has been there all the while, waiting for you, and the life that you ought to be living is the one you are living."

Sure, you'll likely put your foot and head and hand and surely your heart along the way, but if bliss is redeemed just once, might it be worth it?

Challenge Question

What is the risk of not following your dream?

_____

_____

March 2
Feeling Beauty

*Only get rid altogether of your nonsensical trash about the beautiful, which
I nor nobody else, nor yourself to boot, could ever understand,—only free
yourself of that, and your success in life is as sure as daylight.*
Nathaniel Hawthorne—Mosses from an Old Manse *(1846)*

When asked about beauty, most turn to physical features or images, but what
makes you feel beauty? Is it happiness, kindness, soulfulness? Is it something
you strive for or something you sense in joyful moments?

Have you ever noticed a photo of someone who on the surface may not
have met with what would be seen as beauty by common societal standards?
And yet, there was something stunning about that person's expression, messy
hair and all.

Maybe beauty is something we do.

Today, make your beauty a gift to the world.

Challenge Question

What do you love most about your face? Seriously.

_____

_____

March 3

Choose Otherwise

Do not cumber yourself with fruitless pains to mend and remedy remote effects; let the soul be erect, and all things will go well. You think me the child of my circumstances: I make my circumstances.
Ralph Waldo Emerson—Self-Reliance *(1841)*

"I make my circumstances" is a statement easier made by some than others, but there's an essential element of truth in this argument.

Those born to poverty without the support of loving parents or the opportunity for education have fewer options from which to make their circumstances. Survival decisions make for different choices than say, career choices.

But to make your circumstances, in either case, is to suggest that all individuals have the power to see beyond their current limiting conditions.

The belief that you have this power doesn't change your situation, but it allows you to dream and, in doing so, multiplies your opportunities no matter your current plight. It frees those around you to dream, and it taps the collective capacity of the universe to help you build a story greater than your current one.

No doubt this task takes faith. Day to day, rock by rock, it might not seem possible. First, you must determine to make it so by making daily decisions that support a better set of circumstances.

In his highly quotable *7 Habits of Highly Successful People*, Stephen Covey illuminates this idea: "But until a person can say deeply and honestly, 'I am what I am today because of the choices I made yesterday,' that person cannot say, 'I choose otherwise.'"

Be a product of your choices rather than a victim of your circumstances.

Challenge Question

When was the last time you felt exceptionally free and alive? How did that make you feel?

_____

_____

March 4

Unreasonable Ambitions

I would not always reason. The straight path / Wearies us with its never-varying lines, / And we grow melancholy. I would make / Reason my guide, but it should sometimes sit / Patiently by the way-side, while I traced / The mazes of the pleasant wilderness / Around me. It should be my counsellor, / But not my tyrant. For the spirit needs / Impulses from a deeper source than it.

William Cullen Bryant—"The Conjunction of Jupiter and Venus" (1854)

The essential belief of every creative entrepreneur is that there's always a better way to do something, maybe everything. This goes without reason quite often and falls into the realm of, as Bryant described, "the mazes of the pleasant wilderness around me."

If you never look around the bend just to discover what's there, then your most original ideas may stay hidden forever.

Reason, of course, keeps us out of jail, prudently employed, and modestly goal oriented.

But achieving the impossible, implausible, or heaven forbid, unconventional, better way of doing something requires setting unreasonable ambitions buttressed with unreasonable actions. In fact, progress depends on it.

The only truly unreasonable act is to believe that everything is okay as it is.

Irish playwright George Bernard Shaw put it this way:

The reasonable man adapts himself to the world. The unreasonable one persists in trying to adapt the world to himself. Therefore, all progress depends on the unreasonable man.

Today, pledge to free yourself from the limitations of reason and give yourself permission to dream of things no reasonable person could.

Challenge Question

What's one limiting belief holding you back? Where did it come from?

_____

_____

March 5
Originality of Character

The position I early was enabled to take was one of self-reliance. And were all people as sure of their wants as I was, the result would be the same. But they are so overloaded with precepts by guardians, who think that nothing is so much to be dreaded for a person as originality of thought or character, that their minds are impeded by doubts till they lose their chance of fair, free proportions. The difficulty is to get them to the point from which they shall naturally develop self-respect, and learn self-help.

Margaret Fuller—Woman in the Nineteenth Century *(1845)*

Have your own thoughts about what you want from life ever frightened you because they seemed laughable?

Can you recall school classmates everyone made fun of because they were "different"? Maybe that was you.

Maybe you felt bad for those kids because they were bullied and made miserable, but they may have also been guarding what to them seemed the only way. They may not have defined it as self-reliance, but their "originality of thought and character" was something they had no choice but to live.

And it may have caused some pain, but it also may have turned into joy and self-reliance and, in many cases, success as only they could define.

Self-reliance requires freeing your mind of doubts. Self-reliance means you can't want everyone to like you. In fact, it may simply want you to like yourself.

Today, treasure your originality of thought and character and let it shine.

Challenge Question

Who is the most original person you've ever known?

_____

_____

March 6
In Dreams

Dreams are the touchstones of our characters. We are scarcely less afflicted when we remember some unworthiness in our conduct in a dream, than if it had been actual, and the intensity of our grief, which is our atonement, measures the degree by which this is separated from an actual unworthiness. For in dreams we but act a part which must have been learned and rehearsed in our waking hours, and no doubt could discover some waking consent thereto. If this meanness had not its foundation in us, why are we grieved at it? In dreams we see ourselves naked and acting out our real characters, even more clearly than we see others awake.
Henry David Thoreau—A Week on the Concord and Merrimack Rivers
(1849)

Dreams are a tricky topic for entrepreneurs. We are encouraged to dream bigger, but as Thoreau suggests, it is often our fears and failures that appear in our actual dreams at night.

But there also lies some truth, or at least perceived truth, in the things that haunt us most. Our reaction to insults or slights by others often reveals a seed of truth or—let's face it—a full-blown blind spot, if we would allow ourselves to learn from them.

So what are our dreams here to tell us? And no, not the one where you can't remember your locker combination sophomore year in high school.

Dreams could be here to show us that we are in charge of them if we choose to craft them intentionally. Thoreau also said, "Our truest life is when we are in dreams awake."

Today, take 15 minutes and dream with your eyes wide open. Heck, take 30 and dream about what your life could be if you had something uniquely meaningful to chase.

Challenge Question

What are you willing to give up to achieve your dreams?

_____

_____

March 7

To Inspire Another

There is a magic in free speaking, especially on sacred themes, most potent and resistless. It is refreshing, amidst the inane common-places bandied in pulpits and parlors, to hear a hopeful word from an earnest, upright soul. People rally around it as to the lattice in summer heats, to inhale the breeze that flows cool and refreshing from the mountains, and invigorates their languid frames.

Amos Bronson Alcott—"Orphic Sayings" (1840)

The success of an entrepreneurial vision often relies on attracting others who share or who are inspired by that vision.

Eloquently expressing that vision in ways that encourage and invigorate is central to the growth of any venture, no matter the ultimate measure of growth.

To inspire another to back a venture, join a team, or buy a product is the job of the entrepreneur stripped to its barest scope.

Certainly, a trained orator has some advantage is this regard, but the authenticity of belief and simplicity of passion inspires far more thoroughly than a practiced act ever can.

Speak freely and often. Tell people what you believe is true today, tell them where you want to go and how you want to make a difference, the audacious thing you know can be done. There is no need to convince.

Today, let people hear and feel your words and let them be inspired to act, join, and share.

Challenge Question

What do you ultimately wish to accomplish with this one life you've been given?

_____

_____

March 8
Your Own Day

Dead poets, philosophers, priests, / Martyrs, artists, inventors, governments long since, / Language-shapers on other shores, / Nations once powerful, now reduced, withdrawn, or desolate, / I dare not proceed till I respectfully credit what you have left / wafted hither, / I have perused it, own it is admirable, (moving awhile among it,) / Think nothing can ever be greater, nothing can ever deserve more / than it deserves, / Regarding it all intently a long while, then dismissing it, / I stand in my place with my own day here.
Walt Whitman—Leaves of Grass *(1855)*

It is somewhat ironic and telling of the nature of things that Whitman gives credit to the past when he himself would not be considered a great poet until he was also a dead poet.

Leaves of Grass was written at a time when America was still trying to find its "brand." To this point, what others said about America (mostly European) shaped its perception.

Fifty years later, Whitman would be called a prophet and the first truly American poet because he so often defined his uniqueness through conflict and contrast.

The self-reliant entrepreneur must often dismiss what has come before as a way to inform rather than direct, mesh rather than copy.

Today, stand in your own place with your own day here.

Challenge Question

How can you use conflict and contrast to make your idea/venture more potent?

_____

_____

March 9
Of Intense Light

The eye is the best of artists. By the mutual action of its structure and of the laws of light, perspective is produced, which integrates every mass of objects, of what character soever, into a well colored and shaded globe, so that where the particular objects are mean and unaffecting, the landscape which they compose, is round and symmetrical. And as the eye is the best composer, so light is the first of painters. There is no object so foul that intense light will not make beautiful.

Ralph Waldo Emerson—Nature *(1836)*

In both a metaphorical and physical sense, light is one of the most functional tools of the entrepreneur.

Often the basis of a business is to shine a light on a glaring need shared by a group of people.

Light creates beauty and provides utility. Light creates colors in nature, rendering the same mountain, seen over and over, ultimately unique in each day by cast, shade, and hue.

But where light provides its greatest service to the self-reliant entrepreneur is through the ability to create the conditions for nonjudgment.

Holding the intense light created by your passion allows you to rethink your relationship with narratives like good and bad, like and dislike, success and failure, fair and unfair.

By adopting nonjudgment as your primary manner of illuminating your world, you'll begin to stay focused only on what you can control in each day.

Today's job is to shine a light on how much you judge yourself, your thoughts, your ideas, your instincts, and your desires. Just witness and take note—that's the first step.

Challenge Question

What's one false belief about yourself that you must shed?

_____

_____

March 10

A Beautiful Noise

I would not always reason. The straight path wearies us with its never-varying lines, and we grow melancholy. I would make reason my guide, but it should sometimes sit patiently by the wayside, while I traced the mazes of the pleasant wilderness around me. It should be my counselor, but not my tyrant. For the spirit needs impulses from a deeper source than reason.

William Cullen Bryant—"The Conjunction of Jupiter and Venus" (1854)

Perhaps you know a person who approaches decisions with a methodical weighing of pros and cons. Making decisions, particularly those with the perceived and unpredictable risk associated with the entrepreneurial journey, requires both emotion and reason.

And emotion springs only from passion.

What entrepreneurs do in the freest sense is make passionate noise—but what a beautiful noise it is!

The Jewish author, philosopher, Holocaust survivor, and Nobel laureate Elie Wiesel famously noted that the opposite of love was not hatred, but indifference.

Making decisions purely on reason is a form of indifference, and your business deserves the opposite.

Call it intuition, gut feeling, or merely a sense about what only you know to be true, and you will be able to make choices that are uncomfortable. Pay close attention to that feeling because it's probably love.

Challenge Question

How can you bring more love to your entrepreneurial journey today?

_____

_____

March 11

Crazy for Yourself

I am come of a race noted for vigor of fancy and ardor of passion. People have called me mad; but the question is not yet settled, whether madness is or is not the loftiest intelligence—whether much that is glorious—whether all that is profound—does not spring from disease of thought—from moods of mind exalted at the expense of the general intellect.

Edgar Allan Poe—Eleonora (1842)

Have you ever tried to explain to others what you do only to be greeted with mild looks of confusion tinged with disapproval? Maybe it's a "Huh, that's interesting," which is a nice way of saying. "Huh, is that even a thing?"

Ah, but as Poe suggests entrepreneurs too come from *"a race noted for vigor of fancy and ardor of passion."* Maybe your parents, your spouse, or your high school buddies don't understand, because maybe you don't fully understand enough to articulate it just yet. All you know is that you possess a deep sense that you must do what you've set out to do.

Is it madness to lurch out on your own, or is it more so to show up and collect salary in the service of someone else's dream? Is it riskier to control your own destiny or to depend on the decisions of another to feed your soul?

Yeah, you're probably a little mad in somebody's definition, but all that is glorious springs from some form of madness.

Today, be crazy for yourself and no one else.

Challenge Question

Have you ever tempered your passion for something for fear others won't get it?

March 12
Resist Not Evil

Into his mind so long ago shone steadily the two thoughts, now so prevalent in thinking and aspiring minds, of "Resist not evil," and "Every person their own priest, and the heart the only true church."
Margaret Fuller—At Home and Abroad; or, Things and Thoughts in America and Europe *(1856)*

Today's reading is a tricky one; words like "priest" and "church" are charged with both meaning and emotion. Read another way, however, it might just be one of the best ways to introduce the more modern and practical notion that in your entrepreneurial journey you will discover "haters gotta hate."

Things like jealousy, a lack of knowledge, and insecurity fuel most forms of negativity, and you will experience it in many forms. You only need to decide how you deal with it.

The thing is, though, "haters" are amazing teachers. They can show you that you're on an amazing path, they can remind you to be less judgmental of others, and they can provide you with extra motivation to follow your heart—if you let them.

Today, you are free to follow your heart exclusively.

Challenge Question

How did it make you feel the last time someone insulted you?

_____

_____

March 13

Duty Bound

What I must do is all that concerns me, not what the people think. This rule, equally arduous in actual and in intellectual life, may serve for the whole distinction between greatness and meanness. It is the harder, because you will always find those who think they know what is your duty better than you know it.

Ralph Waldo Emerson—Self-Reliance *(1841)*

Duty is a word often used to entrap people into doing the work that others think should be done. Your only duty as a self-reliant entrepreneur is to do what *you* must do.

A phrase like this one, attributed to Robert E. Lee—"Do your duty, you cannot do more; you should never wish to do less"—can be applied as metaphorical shackles to keep people from striving for something that only they understand.

You can and should do your duty—that's not a bad word, but you get to define what your duty is.

Serving others through your entrepreneurial vision may be your duty, but so too may your greatness reside in tending to your own personal growth and health.

Raising two kids and paying a mortgage is a huge obligation and loving duty, but it may not be the complete duty. What you are committed to do can make room for what else you must do.

Challenge Question

What sense of duty is keeping you from chasing what you know you must do?

_____

_____

March 14
What's Difficult

He had discovered a great law of human action, without knowing it—namely, that in order to make a man or a boy covet a thing, it is only necessary to make the thing difficult to attain. If he had been a great and wise philosopher... he would now have comprehended that Work consists of whatever a body is obliged to do, and that Play consists of whatever a body is not obliged to do.

Mark Twain—The Adventures of Tom Sawyer *(1876)*

What if your work felt like play? That would be great, right? You could wake up excited and ready to go to the playground every day.

Or, you could change how you face difficulty. We've become so conditioned to go out of our way to have things be easy, convenient, comfortable, that we've forgotten what dealing with obstacles is supposed to teach us. We've somehow become weak and fragile.

It's not that you need to be slapped in the face or dunked in an ice pool each day—or maybe it is—but things worth doing, like inventing something that saves lives, *should* be difficult. What makes them hard, though, is when we lose the meaning in what we are doing.

Meaning is what makes us covet a thing not just when it's hard, but *because* it's hard.

It comes down to this: our real joy is ultimately defined by what we willingly struggle for.

Challenge Question

What is hard about what you do? What are you willing to do anyway?

_____

_____

March 15

Challenge Freedom

The love of freedom is one of those natural impulses of the human breast which cannot be extinguished. Even the brute animals of the creation feel and show sorrow and affection when deprived of their liberty. Therefore is a distinguished writer justified in saying, "Man is free, even were he born in chains."

William Wells Brown—Three Years in Europe; or, Places I Have Seen and People I Have Met (1852)

Brown wrote of the morally reprehensible practice of literal human slavery, the abolition of which became a central social issue for many of the transcendentalists.

Brown's unique point of view was one of both abolitionist and slave. Although I'm making no attempt here to draw any comparison to the freedom you enjoy, it is the last line that deserves context.

It is easy to feel helpless against our circumstances. Some challenges are indeed real, but most are simply made real by our relationship with them.

What we believe about the labels and tags we or others assign to us is what motivates how we behave. We can break free only when we become aware of the positive beliefs we have about ourselves and our circumstances and then move to supercharge those beliefs.

Today, consider this thought: what you believe makes you who you are.

Challenge Question

Where are you giving away your freedom?

_____

_____

March 16

See More Clearly

The wisest person preaches no doctrines; they have no scheme; they see no rafter, not even a cobweb, against the heavens. It is clear sky. If I ever see more clearly at one time than at another, the medium through which I see is clearer.

Henry David Thoreau—A Week on the Concord and Merrimack Rivers
(1849)

When all we can see is the ultimate course of success in achieving our audacious plans, everyday victories seem meaningless.

The medium clouds our view and puts obstacles in our way—at least that's how it feels—but growing science in the field of achievement suggests another somewhat counterintuitive culprit shields us from reaching our ultimate objective.

And in the words of Robert Brault, author of *Round Up the Usual Subjects*, "We are kept from our goal not by obstacles but by a clear path to a lesser goal."

This seems like a decent time to invoke a translation of Tao Te Ching—"The journey of a thousand miles begins beneath one's feet."

It's not a terribly sexy idea but to improve, start with one step, get just a little better today, and do the same tomorrow, and the next day. Use this practice over time and you will start to see more clearly the place at which you wish to arrive.

Challenge Question

What is one action you can take today that will lead you toward achieving your most important goal?

_____

_____

March 17
Being Nobody

I'm nobody! Who are you? / Are you nobody, too? / Then there's a pair of us—don't tell! / They'd banish us, you know. // How dreary to be somebody! / How public, like a frog / To tell your name the livelong day / To an admiring bog!

Emily Dickinson—*"I'm Nobody! Who are you?"* (1891)

The chase to be nobody may seem like advice for the slacker, but it may be the most spiritually advanced advice I can give you.

Who defines what being a somebody is anyway?

Freedom in life is achieved by letting go of all the things that define you as a somebody.

This notion probably freaks out your ego a little because, after all, striving to achieve some sort of status is a lifelong obsession for most of us.

But the really cool thing about being no one is that it allows you to be anyone—think about the power of that for a bit.

Challenge Question

What destructive pattern can you let go of on your way to becoming nobody?

_____

_____

March 18

Resist Much

To the States or any one of them, or any city of the States, Resist / much, obey little, / Once unquestioning obedience, once fully enslaved, / Once fully enslaved, no nation, state, city of this earth, ever / afterward resumes its liberty.

Walt Whitman—Leaves of Grass *(1855)*

As America's first counterculture movement, the transcendentalists were a rowdy bunch.

Thoreau's *Civil Disobedience* was perhaps the fullest telling of this movement, but in four little words Whitman gives the entrepreneur a mantra to live by—Resist Much, Obey Little.

This is our daily call to arms.

So, when you are told that your idea is foolish, resist much, obey little. When doubt tells you to turn back, resist much, obey little. When success suggests that now is the time to play it safe, resist much, obey little.

Challenge Question

Where will you place today's call to arms so that you may see it every day?

_____

_____

March 19

Struggle into Blossom

Plants of great vigor will almost always struggle into blossom, despite impediments. But there should be encouragement, and a free genial atmosphere for those of more timid sort, fair play for each in its own kind. Some are like the little, delicate flowers which love to hide in the dripping mosses, by the sides of mountain torrents, or in the shade of tall trees. But others require an open field, a rich and loosened soil, or they never show their proper hues.

Margaret Fuller—Woman in the Nineteenth Century *(1845)*

It's often surprising to see a plant or a tree shooting from an outcrop of rocks, seemingly thriving with little or no soil or sun as nourishment.

Ah, but that's not everyone—it may not be you.

Give yourself the environment that is rich in what you need. Surround yourself with people and mentors whose values you aspire to follow. Prune relationships, including clients, that drain you.

Tidy your desk each evening. Get better lights and chairs.

Don't hide your vision. Share your sense of purpose. Tell people how much you appreciate them. Be flexible with your work schedule and extend this to others.

Today, take a fresh look at the space around you and ask yourself if it makes you feel creative.

Challenge Question

What's one thing you could change for good about your work environment?

_____

_____

March 20
Conscious Ignorance

My desire for knowledge is intermittent, but my desire to bathe my head in atmospheres unknown to my feet is perennial and constant. The highest that we can attain to is not Knowledge, but Sympathy with Intelligence. I do not know that this higher knowledge amounts to anything more definite than a novel and grand surprise on a sudden revelation of the insufficiency of all that we called Knowledge before—a discovery that there are more things in heaven and earth than are dreamed of in our philosophy.

Henry David Thoreau—"Walking" (1861)

There is a concept in scientific research known as "thoroughly conscious ignorance." The idea is to remain conscious of the fact that there is a great deal more to know about something and that there is danger in casting your current knowledge as some form of wisdom.

Consider this additional passage from Thoreau's "Walking" for practical context:

Which is the best man to deal with—he who knows nothing about a subject, and, what is extremely rare, knows that he knows nothing, or he who really knows something about it, but thinks that he knows all?

We've all likely been on both sides of this equation. From the outside looking in, it's easy to see what thinking we know it all might be costing us.

James Clerk Maxwell, the physicist credited with coining the term, claimed that "Thoroughly conscious ignorance is the prelude to every real advance in science."

Stop looking for answers and focus on the questions that make you hungry for ignorance. All real growth comes from change and revision—from sympathy with intelligence.

Today, look at your world, your entrepreneurial path, and ask yourself what you think you know for sure.

Challenge Question

How is information robbing you of your curiosity? How do you know?

March 21
Material Freedom

To be in direct and personal contact with the sources of your material life; to want no extras, no shields; to find the air and the water exhilarating; to be refreshed by an evening walk or a morning saunter; . . . to be elated over a bird's nest or over a wild flower in the spring—these are some of the rewards of the simple life.

John Burroughs—Leaf and Tendril *(1908)*

The notion of living with less is quite popular in some circles.

But that, well, oversimplifies this idea. How much is enough is completely subjective.

The relationship we develop with the "sources of our material life" is a much fuller idea.

You should have material possessions that support you to live your true nature. Having too little, like having too much, draws energy and attention away from living your values. (Having said that, most of us have too much stuff.)

So how do make this determination and work toward the right balance? Start with love.

In *Simple Abundance*, author Sarah Ban Breathnach states it like this: "The key to loving how you live is in knowing what it is you truly love."

Today, think about the possessions that support your highest values—the ones you guard and protect the most.

Challenge Question

What material possession most enhances your life? Is this harder than you thought to answer?

_____

_____

March 22
On Letting Go

I was but too conscious of a vagrant fiber in myself, which too often thrilled me in my solitary walks with the temptation to wander on into infinite space, and by a single spasm of resolution to emancipate myself from the drudgery of prosaic serfdom to respectability and the regular course of things. This prompting has been at times my familiar demon, and I could not but feel a kind of respectful sympathy for those who had dared what I had only sketched out to myself as a splendid possibility.
James Russell Lowell—"On a Certain Condescension in Foreigners"
(1871)

What does *letting go* mean to you?

To achieve any form of freedom sometimes, we have to let go of our attachment to an ideal and trust that we're not in complete control of everything. That's not the same as giving up—it's an acceptance of the fact that something grander perhaps is waiting for us.

Everyone is weighed down by an attachment to one thing or another, and it's these things, these attachments, that keep us from getting what we want most.

It's not easy to identify what's holding us back, but it might be the "*drudgery of prosaic serfdom to respectability*"—or something like that.

Challenge Question

What are you gripping tightly to right now?

_____

_____

March 23

Sense of Wonder

So great a sight soon satisfies, making us content with itself, and with what is less than itself. Our desires, once realized, haunt us again less readily. Having "lived one day," we would depart, and become worthy to live another.

Margaret Fuller—At Home and Abroad; or, Things and Thoughts in America and Europe *(1856)*

In this reading, Fuller is describing her first visit to Niagara Falls.

How do we protect our sense of wonderment? As we experience each new thing in our journey, how do we guard against the common, unexciting, and expected—even in so great a sight? How do we remain in awe of the miraculous? How do we offer gratitude for these gifts?

Today, find a way to slow down a common experience and engage as many senses as possible—as in senses of wonderment. Maybe it's a place, a person, an event—live it fully and anew.

Challenge Question

What miraculous thing in your life has become unappreciated?

_____

_____

March 24
A Great Poem

Re-examine all you have been told in school or church or in any book, and dismiss whatever insults your own soul; and your very flesh shall be a great poem, and have the richest fluency, not only in its words, but in the silent lines of its lips and face, and between the lashes of your eyes, and in every motion and joint of your body.

Walt Whitman—*Preface to* Leaves of Grass *(1855)*

We have an obligation to live the one life we've been allowed as a great poem.

In an interview that appears in Mihaly Csikszentmihalyi's *Creativity*, former poet laureate Mark Strand states: "We're only here for a short while. And I think it's such a lucky accident, having been born, that we're almost obliged to pay attention."

Letting go of, or at least reexamining, everything we've been told in school, or church, or in any book takes a full set of guts, but questioning is at the heart of self-reliance.

Trust that your best advice will always come from within.

Challenge Question

What do you need to dismiss in your life right now?

_____

_____

March 25

Love to Live

Every person's position is in fact too simple to be described. I have sworn no oath. I have no designs on society, or nature, or God. I am simply what I am, or I begin to be that. I live in the present. I only remember the past, and anticipate the future. I love to live.

Henry David Thoreau—Familiar Letters *(1894)*

Today's reading is a full-throated appeal for mindfulness. But you've heard that before and, frankly, who has time for all that, right?

I live in the present. I only remember the past, and anticipate the future. I love to live.

Seems like a pretty simple prescription. This feels like a really good time to practice.

Find a comfortable seat, close your eyes, feel your body, take note of your breathing, and observe your wandering mind. That didn't take long, did it?

That's okay—admission is key.

Set an alarm every few hours today and just sit for a minute and breathe. Use these breaks to snap yourself back to the right now—the only place you can love to live.

Challenge Question

What future event has you worried?

_____

_____

March 26
Dear Truth

I have never been the slave of my own past, and truth has always been dearer to me than my own opinions.
Orestes Brownson—The American Republic *(1865)*

Our opinions, our view of the world are not the truth; they are simply what we currently see.

The truth lies in our seeking it, being open to it. It is not a thing once learned.

It is a continuous exercise blunted by the wants and fears that draw us to the comfort of the truth organized by others.

Today, get up and seek the truth and then come back tomorrow and see if it is merely an opinion. (Nobody said this was easy.)

Challenge Question

Can you think of an instance where you radically changed your opinion about something?

_____

_____

March 27

Lifting the Weight

The stigma gone, Hester heaved a long, deep sigh, in which the burden of shame and anguish departed from her spirit. O exquisite relief! She had not known the weight until she felt the freedom!
Nathaniel Hawthorne—The Scarlet Letter *(1850)*

Have you ever labored under a deadline, constantly procrastinating, making excuses, checking Facebook, only to determine that right now is the perfect time to tidy up your closet?

But then, April 14th rolls around (the day before your taxes are due). You put in the work and meet the deadline only to experience an amazing feeling of relief. A rich, physical lightness of being.

The problem is we don't realize how thoroughly our subconscious runs the show at times. How much weight it applies to anything it deems painful or even slightly uncomfortable.

Faced with even greater pain—not meeting a deadline and receiving a large fine—we gather the strength to finally wrest back control.

The key, of course, is to never allow yourself to lose control in the first place. Well, yes, that would be nice, wouldn't it? The solution lies in freeing up enough space for deep work. You can't accomplish your most important, most pressing, high-payoff work unless you permit yourself and your brainpower long runways of time to think and accomplish. Block out that time, or you'll never find it.

Today, identify that one most important thing on your to-do list and don't even think about anything else until you've completed it. Feel lighter already, don't you?

Challenge Question

What is your most important task today?

_____

_____

March 28
Your Tribe Is

The latch-key which opens into the inner chambers of my consciousness fits, as I have sufficient reason to believe, the private apartments of a good many other people's thoughts. The longer we live, the more we find we are like other persons. When I meet with any facts in my own mental experience, I feel almost sure that I shall find them repeated or anticipated in the writings or the conversation of others. This feeling gives one a freedom in telling their own personal history they could not have enjoyed without it.
Oliver Wendell Holmes, Sr.—Over the Teacups *(1872)*

Find your tribe. That's advice dished out these days to anyone starting something akin to an entrepreneurial venture.

And so it goes—you share your story, sometimes in a reserved manner, sometimes freely, in the hopes that others will acknowledge your unique contribution.

Do it long enough, however, and you are bound to encounter those who get you and perhaps, more important, feel that you get them.

Maybe that's your tribe, but then you look up and they seem so different from what you had imagined. More diverse, odder, perhaps a little abnormal even.

Management consultant and author Tom Peters advocates hiring what he calls freaks: "Highest accolades should go to those who have the guts to hire the Deviants." At some point, you'll discover how much you have in common.

Some come to this realization much earlier than others—*the longer we live, the more we find we are like other persons*—precisely because our "inner chambers" are far more connected than we could ever imagine. Encountering your tribe simply verifies this idea.

Challenge Question

Who should you ask to lunch today?

March 29

What Is Freedom, Then?

The shrine is vowed to freedom, but, my friend, / Freedom is but a means to gain an end. / Freedom should build the temple, but the shrine / Be consecrate to thought still more divine. / The human bliss which angel hopes foresaw/ Is liberty to comprehend the law. / Give, then, thy book a larger scope and frame, / Comprising means and end in Truth's great name.
Margaret Fuller—Life Without and Life Within *(1859)*

A lot of the appeal of running an entrepreneurial venture is that doing so affords you the freedom to earn far more than you would working for someone else.

But suppose material gain comes at the expense of others; this could mean those you boss around, but it might also mean your family. Does that really bring freedom? Freedom is, as Fuller states, "but a means to gain an end."

So, what is that end?

British author Henry James wrote this in 1903 of freedom's end:

Live all you can; it's a mistake not to. It doesn't so much matter what you do in particular so long as you have your life. If you haven't had that what have you had? . . . What one loses one loses; make no mistake about that. Still, we have the illusion of freedom; therefore don't be without the memory of that illusion.

That should do for today!

Challenge Question

How free are you to choose?

_____

_____

Planning: Freedom

March 30
Perfect Freedom

For a person to act themself, they must be perfectly free; otherwise they are in danger of losing all sense of responsibility or of self-respect.
Henry David Thoreau—Familiar Letters *(1894)*

You're perfectly free, right? In the civil sense, you have rights that allow you to go and say and, for the most part, do as you please.

But do you choose to find joy in a million little moments every single day? Are you free to be your wild self?

Thoreau wrote about "perfect freedom" as freedom that allows us to express our true nature. Freedom that resides in nature but that is missing in culture.

Today, go for a walk without a destination; saunter with an air of carelessness; experience perfect freedom again.

Challenge Question

What would bring you complete peace of mind?

_____

_____

March 31
Seeking Opinion

I have written freely from my own mind as I find it now formed; but how it has been so formed, or whence I have borrowed, my readers know as well as I. All that is valuable in the thoughts set forth, it is safe to assume has been appropriated from others. Where I have been distinctly conscious of borrowing what has not become common property, I have given credit, or, at least, mentioned the author's name, with three important exceptions which I wish to note more formally.

Orestes Brownson—The American Republic *(1865)*

Imagine how many artists, writers, and yes, entrepreneurs, fail to follow their hearts because of what others might say, how they might be judged, and even ridiculed.

Oh, and don't worry—you won't need to ask for others' opinions; they'll freely offer them.

But here's the hard part: it's natural to seek the advice of those who appear more successful or who seem to have arrived where you want to go. They may indeed have useful advice, but they aren't you.

Their path worked for them, and that's the only thing that's true.

Seeking and heeding the opinions of others is lazy, and it's an escape hatch—it allows you to put the brakes on your own dream because someone said it was right or wrong or hard or foolish. Believing that is easier than the alternative.

Today, witness your thoughts about opinions offered by others. You don't need to determine whether you agree or disagree, if you approve or disapprove. Simply reflect—is it true for you or not?

Challenge Question

Whose approval do you find yourself seeking most? Why does it matter?

_____

_____

April

Nathaniel Hawthorne (1804–1864)

To do nothing is the way to be nothing.

—*Nathaniel Hawthorne*

Source: Wikimedia

Born in Salem, Massachusetts, in 1804, Nathaniel Hawthorne was the only child of sea captain Nathaniel Sr. and Elizabeth Clark Hawthorne. His young life was shaped by a leg injury at age nine. This kept him inside for nearly two years, and it was during this time that he became deeply interested in reading and literature.

In 1821, he attended Bowdoin College. Upon graduation, he returned to Salem and worked various jobs as he wrote his first novel. Self-published in 1828, *Fanshawe* was not a success. In fact, later in life Hawthorne recalled the book and burned the remaining copies of it.

That first experience did not stop him from continuing to write, though, and during the 1830s he published several other works. He met Sophia Amelia Peabody in 1837, the woman he would later marry.

It was Peabody who introduced Hawthorne to the transcendentalist movement. Hawthorne became more involved throughout the 1840s, briefly joining Brook Farm, a commune centered around the ideals of the movement. He then moved to Concord in 1842.

In Concord, Hawthorne became friends with leading transcendentalists like Ralph Waldo Emerson, Henry David Thoreau, Margaret Fuller, and Amos Bronson Alcott.

In 1846, he returned to Salem. In 1850, he published *The Scarlet Letter*, which would become his first commercial success. He then moved again, relocating to Lenox, Massachusetts, and befriending his neighbor, Herman Melville, who would later dedicate *Moby-Dick* to Hawthorne.

The later years of Hawthorne's life were divided between Concord, where he and his family purchased the Alcotts' old home; Liverpool, England; and Italy. Hawthorne died in Concord in 1864.

April 1

Entrepreneur as Poet

Who sees the meaning of the flower uprooted in the plowed field? The plow-
man who does not look beyond its boundaries and does not raise his eyes
from the ground? No—but the poet who sees that field in its relations with
the universe, and looks oftener to the sky than on the ground. Only the
dreamer shall understand realities, though, in truth, their dreaming must
not be out of proportion to their waking!
Margaret Fuller—Woman in the Nineteenth Century *(1845)*

How is it that you describe what you do? Would you ever think of what you
do as poetry, a weaving of sights and sounds into an entrepreneurial field of
dreams? Perhaps no, but though you may never communicate using fanci-
ful words or rhymes, there is an art to raising your eyes from the work that
appears in front of you every day in an effort to observe the state of your
vision.

Your vision is connected in many ways to every other thing in the universe. You don't have to ascribe to a special brand of faith to witness this.
Simply observe what happens when you stop, step back, quiet yourself, and
listen.

Not for the noise, but for the silence.

Silence is often referred to as the absence of noise, but if you choose you
could begin today to see it as the unification of all sound, the joining of sound
and soundlessness that has the power to connect your vision to every particle
in the universe.

This connection is the ultimate goal of meditation, and when you begin
to seek silence in this way, you can see that the restlessness many experience
in attempting to meditate is born of the sounds of silence rather than the
unnerving still.

Challenge Question

What sound will capture your attention today?

_____

_____

Author's note: Today is my birthday, so, well, Happy Birthday to me!

April 2

The Light of Love

It is to the credit of human nature, that, except where its selfishness is brought into play, it loves more readily than it hates. Hatred, by a gradual and quiet process, will even be transformed to love, unless the change be impeded by a continually new irritation of the original feeling of hostility.
Nathaniel Hawthorne—The Scarlet Letter (1850)

In your entrepreneurial journey, there will always be a tremendous, raging conflict between your head and your heart.

Your head will ask, "Why is this so hard? Why don't people understand? Why must I go back and do this all over again today?"

Ah, but your heart, when given the proper space, will readily answer—what I must learn today to move forward, who I must meet today in support of the cause, and how I can greet each day with a fresh point of view.

This conflict will carry on until you decide which one to listen, obey.

The heart is seen romantically, philosophically, and metaphysically as the place where the flame of love is sparked and kept burning. Sure, love is often portrayed in the metaphorical sense or the greeting-card sense, but like love, the entrepreneurial flame is kept alive in our heartfelt passions—particularly in the times that seem darkest.

Your heart is your compass.

Passion, love for the day-to-day needs of your dream, requires incredible strength to hold and shape. Keeping the flame of love for your business alive will require you to step back and *"by a gradual and quiet process"* imprint what you love about your business firmly in your heart. Then, and only then, can you go about steadily getting very, very good at doing what you love.

Challenge Question

What do you love most about your entrepreneurial journey?

_____

_____

April 3

Because You Must

The great person knew not that they were great. It took a century or two for that fact to appear. What they did, they did because they must; it was the most natural thing in the world, and grew out of the circumstances of moment.

Ralph Waldo Emerson—"Spiritual Laws" (1841)

The most difficult objective of all is to set out to succeed.

There's an element of timing to all success, and many of the factors that come into play are not under your control.

The circumstances of this moment will determine to some extent what people call success, and it's our desire to bend to what we think we should or should not do in order to succeed that creates a great deal of entrepreneurial tension.

You know in your heart what you must do; forget *can't, won't, shouldn't*—those are for other people's lives.

Doing what you must is expressing who you are.

Your work today is to explore what you most want or need to do and be on the lookout for overwhelming pangs of doubt. The fear that expresses itself as "that's ridiculous" is telling you that you just might have found your must.

When you proceed because you must, success will always be on your terms.

Challenge Question

What's the one thing, the impact, you want to provide by your work?

_____

_____

April 4

In the Way We Empower

The power people possess to annoy me I give them by a weak curiosity. No one can come near me but through my act. What we love that we have, but by desire we bereave ourselves of the love.
Ralph Waldo Emerson—Self-Reliance *(1841)*

How much of your brilliance is censored through compromise?

Compromise when appropriate is not itself a problem; it's when you decide to concede some element of your dream based on the words of another or the norms of an industry that you give those words and norms meaning and the power to steal your self-reliance.

The following quote is usually credited to Eleanor Roosevelt: "No one can make you feel inferior without your consent." This quote has a great deal to do with self-esteem, a core trait of self-reliance, and it applies to the quality of nonconformity so needed to blaze your own path.

Today, try to spend some time around a small child and witness just how little validation the child needs from others to be certain that something is true.

Challenge Question

How are you conforming to the thoughts and wishes of others?

_____

_____

April 5

The Tinge of Red

*You don't know, perhaps, but I will tell you; the brain is the palest of all
the internal organs, and the heart the reddest. Whatever comes from the
brain carries the hue of the place it came from, and whatever comes from
the heart carries the heat and color of its birthplace.*
Oliver Wendell Holmes, Sr.—The Professor at the Breakfast-Table *(1860)*

Red is an emotional color; it's a color of extremes—love and hate, anger and
lust, danger and adventure. It is the color of stop signs and of the rising sun.

Red is also the color associated with the first, or root, *chakra*. The chakra
system originated in India thousands of years ago in the Hindu text called *The
Vedas*. According to healers, each of the seven chakras corresponds to specific
organs as well as physical, psychological, emotional, and spiritual states of
being, and they influence all areas of life.

There's not much scientific research that definitively links this life force,
prana, or spiritual energy, to physical well-being, but the idea is that when
your chakras are open, energy flows in ways that lead to a healthy mind
and body.

So in this sense red is not simply the color of the heart and of love. It is
attached to your base, foundation, or root physically and mentally. It is home
base for letting go of fear and feeling grounded.

Today, consider the extremes of your journey and the role of red in that.

Challenge Question

How will you see the color red today?

_____

_____

Discovering: Love

April 6

Darkness and Light

But there is no person, in whom humor and love, like mountain peaks, soar to such a rapt height as to receive the irradiations of the upper skies;—there is no person in whom humor and love are developed in that high form called genius; no such person can exist without also possessing, as the indispensable complement of these, a great, deep intellect, which drops down into the universe like a plummet. Or, love and humor are only the eyes through which such an intellect views this world. The great beauty in such a mind is but the product of its strength.

Herman Melville—"Hawthorne and His Mosses" (1850)

Many of the writers during the transcendentalist period were searching for a writing style that was no longer seen as some derivation of British literature. Less than a hundred years removed from the American Revolution, they sought to define an American style and, in doing so, were roundly criticized for the risks they took.

If you wear a mask to hide your true genius, to disguise the profound truths you must tell, to shield the parts you are not yet comfortable with, you will give us only a portion of your gift. The world must know your darkness in order to appreciate your light.

Challenge Question

What mask are you hiding behind?

_____

_____

April 7

In One Word

The cure for all the ills and wrongs, the cares, the sorrows, and crimes of humanity, all lie in that one word LOVE. It is the divine vitality that produces and restores life. To each and every one of us it gives the power of working miracles, if we will.

Lydia Maria Child—Letters from New York *(1843)*

How does one define the word love?

Ah, and a greater challenge—is it even appropriate to use in the context of business?

If indeed the cure for all or even some ills and wrongs is the goal of your journey, then perhaps expanding your relationship with the word love does make sense.

Not in the romantic sense, but in the humanity sense.

Do you know what makes you take risks, what creates connection, what inspires? These are all ideas that help entrepreneurial ventures soar, and they're all based on some sort of love.

Love takes courage. Love takes wisdom. Love take honesty. Love takes loyalty. Love takes . . . maybe it does have a place in business.

Challenge Question

What attribute of love is missing from your mission?

_____

_____

April 8

Making a Living

I wish to suggest that a person may be very industrious, and yet not spend their time well. There is no more fatal blunderer than they who consume the greater part of their life getting a living. All great enterprises are self-supporting. The poet, for instance, must sustain their body by their poetry, as a steam planing-mill feeds its boilers with the shavings it makes. You must get your living by loving.

Henry David Thoreau—"Life Without Principle" (1854)

As a burgeoning self-reliant entrepreneur, you likely have no objection to Thoreau's claim that you must get your living by loving, but imagine the mid-nineteenth-century reader. Nearly everyone today aspires to be some sort of entrepreneur, but hey, there was no Internet back then and the expectation was that you would toil away at something that served a purpose and fed your family. That you hated the existence it created was of little concern.

But consider Thoreau's last sentence carefully. Does it make any sense, with all the options available today, to simply go about what you do just to make a living—or must your venture also allow you to make a life worth loving? The difference amounts to simply trading your days for something to come or reveling in a self-supporting journey that feeds your soul now, in every present moment.

Oh, but you'll be tested every single day on this idea. Many days it will not feel more noble to starve than settle for a living that includes some bread? But then there will be those days when you see with impenetrable clarity that you are indeed making a living by loving.

Challenge Question

What role do you let loving play in your making a living?

_____

_____

April 9

Your Atmosphere

Who clothes with grace all duty; still, I know / Too well the picture has a another side, / —How wearily the grind of toil goes on / Where love is wanting, how the eye and ear / And heart are starved amidst the plenitude / Of nature, and how hard and colorless / Is life without an atmosphere.
John Greenleaf Whittier—"Among the Hills" (1869)

"Clothes with grace all duty"—that sounds like your to-do list today, doesn't it? No? Then perhaps, *"How wearily the grind of toil goes on."* Closer?

You simply can't afford to hate any aspect of what you do or you'll feed that hate. Dislike an exercise or yoga pose, and you can bet you'll make it harder. Hate the finance part of your business and you can bet you'll struggle collecting invoices. Embrace the things you dislike and eventually you'll sort of hate them less—not great, but still better. Being an entrepreneur allows you to live amidst the plenitude in some fashion, so how can the heart go wanting in any fashion?

You're in charge of how you interact with your environment, your atmosphere. Never forget that.

Challenge Question

What's one aspect of your work that you dislike today? How can you rethink your relationship with it?

_____

_____

April 10

Toil of Love

I had no time to hate, because / The grave would hinder me, / And life was not so ample I / Could finish enmity. / Nor had I time to love; but since / Some industry must be, / The little toil of love, I thought, / Was large enough for me.

Emily Dickinson—"Life," The Complete Poems of Emily Dickinson
(1855)

Great poetry is a most difficult form of writing. Imagine—in four lines or so, Dickinson covers love, hate, death, afterlife, and personal choice with no fat or fluff.

Life is short, and since you can't take love or hate (or enmity, mutual hatred) to the grave, you might as well choose the little toil of love since you must do something.

Now some might suggest that Dickinson is merely expressing a lack of passion in her own life, but here's the deal: love is just a choice and you get to define what it looks like to you.

Challenge Question

How does fear creep into your definition of love?

_____

_____

April 11

For Truth's Sake

I appeal from your customs. I must be myself. I cannot break myself any longer for you, or you. If you can love me for what I am, we shall be the happier. If you cannot, I will still seek to deserve that you should. I will not hide my tastes or aversions. I will so trust that what is deep is holy, that I will do strongly before the sun and moon whatever inwardly rejoices me, and the heart appoints.

Ralph Waldo Emerson—Self-Reliance *(1841)*

Asking someone to "love us for what we are" requires one significant act on our part: we must live fully who we are. The desire to have someone accept who you seem to be or, worse, who you've become to gain that acceptance is both a lot of work and somewhat dishonest.

To live fully who you are is the ultimate act of self-love—a prerequisite to self-trust and an evolving requirement in the attempt to gain any measure of self-reliance.

So today, set more boundaries, take better care of yourself, forgive others, pay attention to your thoughts, do what you need rather than what you want. Live fully who you are.

Consider a quote from Louisa May Alcott, for whom the struggle was very real—she was fighting prejudices, hatred, and the blindness of humanity: "Let my name stand among those who are willing to bear ridicule and reproach for the truth's sake, and so earn some right to rejoice when the victory is won."

What will you bear for truth's sake? Perhaps you're simply trying to bring more joy—start there.

Challenge Question

What act of self-kindness can you accomplish today? Without guilt?

_____

_____

Discovering: Love

April 12

Passion Without Perseverance

Passion, and passion in its profoundest, is not a thing demanding a pala-
tial stage whereon to play its part. Down among the groundlings, among
the beggars and rakers of the garbage, profound passion is enacted. And
the circumstances that provoke it, however trivial or mean, are no measure
of its power.

Herman Melville—Billy Budd, Sailor *(1924)*

Have you ever mistaken perseverance for passion?

Perseverance helps you do the hard stuff, try a new approach, even get back up time and time again.

Passion, though, is something you feel; it's the thing that gives your entrepreneurial journey power, no matter how insignificant or misguided it seems to others.

But here's the problem: you must have both.

You need a burning passion to make some difference, to make every new day an adventure, but you also need the perseverance to dig in and figure out how to get it all done—even the stuff you're not so passionate about.

Many businesses fail not due to a lack of passion but due to an inability of the business owner to figure out how to run the business. Getting the boring, dispassionate, mundane stuff done that must be done, the stuff that mostly just requires perseverance, grit, and patience. You may be supercharged about helping other business owners, but if you can't help yourself help your business run, what have you accomplished?

Today, consider both the things you're most passionate about and the things that will potentially take you down if you don't address them.

Challenge Question

What is the greatest vulnerability or gap that exists in your entrepreneurial journey today?

_____

_____

April 13

Creative Hate

If you love the good thing vitally, enough to give up for it all that one must give up for it, then you must hate the cheap thing just as hard. I tell you, there is such a thing as creative hate! A contempt that drives you through fire, makes you risk everything and lose everything, makes you a long sight better than you ever knew you could be.

Willa Cather—The Song of the Lark *(1915)*

Today's reading could easily be seen as a judgment of others—you know—"the ones who do contemptible work and who get on as well as you do." In fact, the character in *The Song of the Lark*, opera singer Thea Kronborg, is doing just that.

But judging things and others as good or bad or right or wrong is a bit of an assault on your self-reliance because it is based mostly in comparison to others. And you've probably already determined what a trap that is.

But for you, the self-reliant entrepreneur, to "*hate the cheap thing just as hard,*" you must look inward and ask where you've not remained true, where you've taken shortcuts, where you've gotten along just fine, where you've accepted mediocrity, where you've sold out.

You must be the source of your own "creative hate" when you haven't lived up to the impossibly high standards you've set for yourself. It's so much more work this way, but it will make you "*a long sight better than you ever knew you could be.*"

Challenge Question

Where have you not done your best work recently?

_____

_____

April 14

Homes in Hearts

From a very early age I have felt that I was not born to the common lot. I knew I should never find a being who could keep the key of my character; that there would be none on whom I could always lean, from whom I could always learn; that I should be a pilgrim and sojourner on earth, and that the birds and foxes would be surer of a place to lay the head than I. You understand me, of course; such beings can only find their homes in hearts.
Margaret Fuller—Memoirs of Margaret Fuller Ossoli *(1884)*

Raise your hand if you're an introvert.

Funny, but these days a lot more hands go up to that thought than ever before. Entrepreneurs are coming to realize this trait not as something to overcome but as a strength.

First off, let's define the word "introvert." It's not about shyness; it's about what brings you energy and what zaps it.

Swiss psychiatrist Carl Jung is credited with introducing the term. He defined introverts as those whose interest is generally directed inward toward their own feelings and thoughts.

More recently, through works like Susan Cain's *Quiet: The Power of Introverts in a World That Can't Stop Talking,* introverts are learning how to properly tap their tendencies as potent entrepreneurial tools. Cain writes:

> I also believe that introversion is my greatest strength. I have such a strong inner life that I'm never bored and only occasionally lonely. No matter what mayhem is happening around me, I know I can always turn inward.

The world of an entrepreneur is cast as a sometimes lonely struggle, but you were not born to the common lot and you possess the ability to turn inward and seek what you know to be true.

Today discover your home by looking inward to your heart.

Challenge Question

Have you ever asked people if they would call you an introvert or an extravert? What did you discover? (Try it.)

_____

_____

April 15

Truth in Arrogance

It takes two to speak the truth,—one to speak, and another to hear. How can one treat with magnanimity mere wood and stone? If we dealt only with the false and dishonest, we should at last forget how to speak truth. Only lovers know the value and magnanimity of truth, while traders prize a cheap honesty, and neighbors and acquaintance a cheap civility.
Henry David Thoreau—A Week on the Concord and Merrimack Rivers
(1849)

Being an entrepreneur requires humility, compassion, graciousness, fortitude, sincerity—and a dose of arrogance. Yes, something akin to a belief of superiority and exaggerated self-importance.

Now think about the most obnoxious, narcissistic, arrogant person you know—okay, we aren't talking about that person here.

A healthy touch of arrogance forces you to set the bar higher, and since you know you're right, you're going to find a way to grasp that bar.

A dollop of arrogance is what gives you access to the "*the value and magnanimity of truth.*"

Just a touch of arrogance pushes you through situations and experiences that might challenge a less secure human being's self-worth.

Arrogance is what allows you to respect what others stand for and accomplish because you possess an abundance of self-worth. (Just use this for good at all times.)

Challenge Question

What is something you know you are right about?

_____

_____

Discovering: Love

April 16

Joy with Duty

Thy symbol be the mountain-bird, / Whose glistening quill I hold; / Thy home the ample air of hope, / And memory's sunset gold! // In thee, let joy with duty join, / And strength unite with love, / The eagle's pinions folding round / The warm heart of the dove!
    John Greenleaf Whittier—"On Receiving an Eagle's Quill from Lake Superior," The Works of John Greenleaf Whittier, Vol. II *(1857)*

Can you do things well and with beauty and love at the same time?

One of the things that trips up entrepreneurs from the start is that they take stock or learn through some brief endeavor what they are good at and what they are not good at.

The problem is, few people are good at anything they have not practiced—at times for years.

How do you know what you're not good at doing? Can your dream afford for you to make that assumption? Sometimes doing something you love means you have to find something you're no good at, that you think you hate. Often that's where your passion is hiding.

You've never done what you are about to do—no one has—that's what makes it yours.

Figure out what's beautiful about what you love and get good at it.

Challenge Question

What's something you've tried and given up on?

_____

_____

April 17

The Work of Play

What I have done I have done because it has been play. If it had been work I shouldn't have done it. Who was it who said, "Blessed is the man who has found his work?" Whoever it was he had the right idea in his mind. Mark you, he says his work—not somebody else's work. The work that is really a man's own work is play and not work at all. Cursed is the man who has found some other man's work and cannot lose it. When we talk about the great workers of the world we really mean the great players of the world.

Mark Twain—*"A Humorist's Confession,"* New York Times Magazine
(1905)

It would be easy to read this passage as a call to abandon all but the thing you've created with your own hands. And, though there is much truth in the idea of controlling your destiny by controlling the means by which you make a living, the deeper meaning here is the focus on play.

An entrepreneur can be just as miserable in the thing they have created as the poor soul locked away in a cubicle a great distance from any source of meaning in their labor.

So, no matter your current circumstances this is a call for more play.

This may not mean skiing through a field of fresh powder or lounging on a boat at sunset—you know, the things you do when you're not working. It means play like conducting a piece of music you've never heard before, or solving a complex puzzle for which only you have the answer.

We alone create the boundary between work and play, and many of the tasks we call play are so because we make them so.

Philosopher and author Alan Watts said, "This is the real secret of life—to be completely engaged with what you are doing in the here and now. And instead of calling it work, realize it is play."

Challenge Question

How could you make more play in your work?

_____

_____

April 18

Do Great Work

The great person knew not that they were great. It took a century or two for that fact to appear. What they did, they did because they must; it was the most natural thing in the world, and grew out of the circumstances of moment.

Ralph Waldo Emerson—"Spiritual Laws" (1841)

You can set out to do great work, but you can never set out to be great. The first drives you to serve the latter to perform.

Do great work and in a century or two perhaps that greatness will be remembered. Work to be great and you'll be forgotten the moment you exit stage right.

Challenge Question

What must you be remembered for most?

_____

_____

April 19

Look with Hindsight

The unexpected favors of fortune, no matter how dazzling, do not mean very much to us. They may excite or divert us for a time, but when we look back, the only things we cherish are those which in some way met our original want; the desire which formed in us in early youth, undirected, and of its own accord.

Willa Cather—Song of the Lark *(1915)*

The wisdom of hindsight is that it's sort of accurate. Facts in hand, we are more equipped to assess potential pitfalls, opportunities, and outcomes.

Now, some might suggest there's little value in this; it's like using the answers to yesterday's crossword puzzle to complete it today.

The message is, always look with foresight to determine your ultimate outcome.

But there is much to be learned by taking stock of where you've actually arrived, no matter the intended destination or anticipated outcome.

The lesson in this is that often we arrive right where we are meant to be—no matter how hard we fight or fail to note along the winding path.

Look to your past with hindsight for the shiny little lights that mark the *"desire which formed in [you] in early youth"* to more fully understand why you are where you find yourself right now.

Challenge Question

What was one of your favorite things to do as a child?

_____

_____

April 20

In the Way We Empower

All are teachers and pupils in turn. We are equally served by receiving and by imparting. Those who know the same things are not long the best company for each other. But bring to each an intelligent person of another experience, and it is as if you let off water from a lake, by cutting a lower basin.

Ralph Waldo Emerson—"Uses of Great Men" (1849)

Seek the company, experiences, and best practices from outside of your tiny entrepreneurial bubble as much or more than you seek the validation of those who think just as you do.

Go to places that seem as though they possess little value, and you'll find just how much you don't know.

Experiencing the fear, stress, and excitement that comes from pushing outside where you're comfortable is reason enough, but you just might pick up new insights into how to do what you currently do in ways that had not occurred to you previously.

All art is some form of combination of elements—expand your palette.

Challenge Question

What's one seemingly random and unrelated group or event you could explore today?

_____

_____

April 21

Teach the World

The best part of the land is not private property; the landscape is not owned, and the walker enjoys comparative freedom. But possibly the day will come when it will be partitioned off into so-called pleasure-grounds, in which a few will take a narrow and exclusive pleasure ... To enjoy a thing exclusively is commonly to exclude yourself from the true enjoyment of it.
Henry David Thoreau—"Walking" (1861)

One of the more recent and somewhat controversial business practices is the no-holds-barred sharing of, well, everything. The digital and fully social landscape has made it much easier to do, but it's also a conscious choice to put into the world all that works, doesn't work, how you do it, what you learned, even metrics of success and failure.

You can dispute it as a business or even promotional practice, but there's little doubt that sharing in this manner demonstrates a belief that there is no scarcity in the world—that giving is just one part of receiving.

Today, freely share your gifts with the world, teach what you know, contribute what you have, and reap the true enjoyment of your abundance.

Challenge Question

What's a topic you know well enough to teach others?

_____

_____

Discovering: Love

April 22

Right to Do

From a healthy union of Affection and Thought flows Energy. When we do love to do that which we perceive it right to do, we cannot otherwise than embody it in earnest action. This is moral beauty.
Lydia Maria Child—"What Is Beauty?" (1843)

Today's reading could be a trap. To argue that moral beauty is to love to do what is right potentially suggests that someone other than yourself possesses the master list of what is right. It's the typical "they say" trick. Who are "they," anyway?

If you think about it, where do we get our sense of right and wrong? Initially we are taught by parents and teachers, and through experience and self-examination, we begin to develop our unique set of rules. Sure, some things are common sense, but some are simply socially nuanced.

To avoid this trap, you have to concede that ethics are up for interpretation—yours. You get to decide what moral beauty is.

It's an awesome responsibility and it comes with consequences, but if you are to love to do that which you perceive is right to do, then you have to be willing to be the author of your rule book.

Challenge Question

What is one experience in life that taught you a lesson about what was right for you?

_____

_____

April 23

Unstoppable Impact

No services are of any value, but only likeness. When I have attempted to join myself to others by services, it proved an intellectual trick,—no more. They eat your service like apples, and leave you out. But love them, and they feel you, and delight in you all the time.

Ralph Waldo Emerson—"Gifts," Essays: Second Series *(1844)*

The most potent way to think about any entrepreneurial venture isn't taught widely.

The classic start-up founder is urged to research and observe a gap in the market, find a way to fill this gap, and then explore cost-effective ways to reach this market. (All the better if you can work the word "lean" into a pitch deck.)

There's nothing wrong with this advice, but the most successful ventures of all time have found or happened upon something far more compelling. These companies, products, services, brands, missions have discovered a way to create a profound impact for everyone they draw into their universe.

So, the question is this: could you start or reshape a company by focusing solely on creating the greatest possible impact? Could you love everyone and everything about those you serve?

It might cause you to change your business plan, but it might just unleash a force of unstoppable impact on you and whatever you were meant to create.

Who knows—maybe it won't work. But don't you want to explore it?

Challenge Question

What measurable impact could you create for those you serve?

_____

_____

Discovering: Love

April 24

What We Do Well

Love sharpens the eye, the ear, the touch; it quickens the feet, it steadies the hand, it arms against the wet and the cold. What we love to do, that we do well. To know is not all; it is only half. To love is the other half.
John Burroughs—Leaf and Tendril *(1908)*

In case you haven't guessed by this point, the major theme running through this month is love.

So, do you love what you do? (Warning: The alternative isn't very fun.)

Love for what a person does isn't always the first thing that shows up. In fact, most entrepreneurs don't start out loving what they do or even understanding that they might love it because they don't do it well. They haven't realized a tangible return and are still swirling around trying to develop something akin to a meaningful relationship with this entrepreneur thing.

So it's the classic chicken-and-egg scenario: do you love what you do and so you do it well, or do you come to do something well and consequently fall in love with it?

The first part of the entrepreneurial journey is meant to teach, so it's okay if you haven't found love. But it's only half—to achieve a full sense of purpose, "to love is the other half."

It doesn't happen overnight, but it doesn't hurt to start looking for it.

Challenge Question

What's one aspect of your entrepreneurial journey you think you do well?

_____

_____

April 25

Your Unfinished Work

So long as we love life for itself, we seldom dread the losing it. When we desire life for the attainment of an object, we recognize the frailty of its texture. But, side by side with this sense of insecurity, there is a vital faith in our invulnerability to the shaft of death while engaged in any task that seems assigned by Providence as our proper thing to do, and which the world would have cause to mourn for should we leave it unaccomplished.
Nathaniel Hawthorne—"The Artist of the Beautiful" (1844)

Do you ever wonder if the world would mourn your loss because you did not complete what was your "proper thing" to do?

That's a lot of pressure, isn't it? But maybe that's the kind of leverage we need to get over our fear, bad habits, or lack of motivation.

If you don't fully commit to your dream, what will you leave incomplete in this world? Whose life will you not enrich because you were afraid to put yourself fully into the work you were meant to do?

This is not a call to embrace your mortality. You may be in your twenties and have it all figured out, or you may be in your sixties and wondering, "Is this all there is?" Or you may be somewhere in between wondering why your boat didn't come with much bigger paddles.

No matter; today you can choose to love life for itself. Either embrace your unfinished work of art or settle for living with the results defined by the dream of nobody in particular.

Challenge Question

What would make today amazing?

_____

_____

April 26

Ask for Help

We must not contend against love, or deny the substantial existence of other people. I know not what would happen to us. We have social strengths. Our affection towards others creates a sort of vantage or purchase which nothing will supply. I can do that by another which I cannot do alone. I can say to you what I cannot first say to myself. Other people are lenses through which we read our own minds.

Ralph Waldo Emerson—*"Uses of Great Men" (1849)*

It's easy to take all this self-reliance business to mean going it alone, singularly braced against the wind and cold as you trudge through the night. Kind of dramatic sounding, isn't it?

Well, that's not it at all. The success of any entrepreneurial journey relies on providing value to someone. That would seem like a hard thing to do if you simultaneously "deny the substantial existence of other people."

As you've likely already discovered that self-reliance requires substantial self-awareness and that no matter how often we turn inward, we require the reflection and interaction of others to help gauge where we are.

Simply put, you need the help of others to succeed and you should actively seek it. Remember the goal in all of this isn't to protect your ego; it's to allow you to serve your purpose.

If you refuse help and try to go it alone, you'll learn very little about those you hope to serve and even less about yourself. In the most practical business terms, asking for help is customer discovery—the practice of fully understanding the problems your prospective customers are trying to solve. And this isn't something you figure out by thinking about it. You go out there and ask for help. You live in your customers' shoes and use this interaction as a lens to help you discover your own mind.

Challenge Question

Who can you ask for help today?

_____

_____

Discovering: Love

April 27

A Worthy Opinion

If I could say I had done one thing for you that entitled me to your good opinion, (I say nothing of your love, for I am sure of that, no matter how unworthy of it I may make myself, you have always given me that, all the days of my life, when God Almighty knows I seldom deserve it,) I believe I could go home and stay there and I know I would care little for the world's praise or blame. There is no satisfaction in the world's praise anyhow, and it has no worth to me save in the way of business.

Mark Twain—Mark Twain's Letters *(1912)*

Which do you suppose you crave more: the world's praise, the unconditional love of those dearest to you, or the good opinion of those with whom you work on a day-to-day basis?

Careful! It's not as simple as it seems. Are these even different things?

It's a worthy question, a constantly evolving one, and one you'll perhaps struggle to balance throughout your entrepreneurial journey.

Come back to it often. There's no right or wrong answer.

Challenge Question

Whose good opinion do you find you seek most right now?

_____

_____

April 28

Communicating in Silence

The kindness I have longest remembered has been of this sort,—the sort unsaid; so far behind the speaker's lips that almost it already lay in my heart. It did not have far to go to be communicated. The gods cannot mis-understand, man cannot explain. We communicate like the burrows of foxes, in silence and darkness, underground. We are undermined by faith and love.

Henry David Thoreau—Familiar Letters *(1865)*

Communicating in silence is an art. But saying nothing at all is oftentimes the most potent way to say so very much.

We all know people who do this. They shine so brightly that they give off nothing but kindness and light. A long-time married couple can commu-nicate a chapter of caring with little more than a glance.

But as Thoreau points out, our words, be they filtered only by faith and love, can undermine.

What we underestimate in terms of communication is just how little our words matters.

In his essay titled "Social Aims," Emerson has this to add: "Don't say things. What you are stands over you the while, and thunders so that I cannot hear what you say to the contrary."

So, there's that.

Communicating in silence is mostly about who you are or who you are being at that moment.

Challenge Question

Are there any places where your words and actions are not aligned?

_____

_____

April 29

Force of Questions

The power which one's imagination has over their body . . . is a force which none of us is born without . . . If left to themselves, a person is most likely to use only the mischievous half of the force . . . ; and if they are one of these—very wise people, they are quite likely to scoff at the beneficent half of the force and deny its existence. And so . . . two imaginations are required: their own and some outsider's . . . The outsider's work is unquestionably valuable; so valuable that it may fairly be likened to the essential work performed by the engineer when he handles the throttle and turns on the steam; the actual power is lodged exclusively in the engine, but if the engine were left alone it would never start of itself.

Mark Twain—Christian Science *(1907)*

How much do you talk to yourself? Are you talking to yourself at this moment? Have you witnessed the impact or internal struggle of the two imaginations Twain refers to?

So, how do you use this power to push yourself out of the ruts and along the path?

The answer lies not in outside opinions, but in the internal questions you routinely ask yourself.

Studies have shown that questions have far more power to motivate and clarify than statements or affirmations.

So, "When will I make time to write?" is far better self-talk than "Darn it, I'm going to make time to write." Our brains must search for the answer, and that wrestling with the need to find an answer is what keeps us focused.

Questioning is the essential work you must turn into a daily ritual.

Today, give some thought to creating a series of questions you can lean on every time you feel a little unfocused or downright stuck in a rut.

Challenge Question

What question would motivate you today and every day?

_____

_____

Discovering: Love

April 30

A Portion of Thyself

Rings and other jewels are not gifts, but apologies for gifts. The only gift is a portion of thyself. Thou must bleed for me. Therefore the poet brings a poem; the shepherd, a lamb; the farmer, corn; the miner, a gem; the sailor, coral and shells; the painter, a picture; the girl, a handkerchief of her own sewing.

Ralph Waldo Emerson—*"Gifts,"* Essays: Second Series *(1844)*

Thou must bleed for me—wow, that doesn't sound good at all.

But how do you share your gifts? Not a logo'd pen or a coffee mug, I suspect.

In fact, how much of your work, your gifts are still hidden from the world? Are you waiting to be discovered, to have a literary agent, angel investor, or art critic tell the world about your brilliance?

You're not ready yet, right? The problem is you never are, so start sharing your gifts now. Don't bring apologies, bring you—unfinished as you are.

Start by giving those you encounter the gift of your presence or even a silent word of thanks for who they are.

Share, honestly and openly, who you are and receive who others are with equal vigor.

Challenge Question

What gift can you bring to the first person you meet today?

_____

_____

May

Walt Whitman (1819–1892)

*What is that you express in your eyes? It seems to me more than all the print
I have read in my life.*

—Walt Whitman

Source: Wikimedia

Walt Whitman was born in West Hills, New York, and raised in Brooklyn. There, he attended public school, but his love of literature blossomed as he began working in New York City printing offices in his teens.

As a young adult, he became a teacher. However, he left that behind in 1841 to become a full-time journalist. He founded a number of publications, most notably the *Brooklyn Freeman*, where he wrote openly about his abolitionist beliefs.

During the American Civil War, Whitman traveled to Washington, DC, to help his brother, who had been wounded in battle. He ended up staying there for 11 years, serving as a volunteer nurse and aiding many ailing soldiers.

He is best known, however, for his collection of poetry, *Leaves of Grass*, which he first self-published in 1855. The work would undergo numerous revisions over the next three-and-a-half decades. Six editions were published during his lifetime, and what began as a collection of 12 poems expanded, in its final iteration, to more than 300.

Leaves of Grass earned the attention and admiration of major transcendentalist figures, including Ralph Waldo Emerson, Henry David Thoreau, and Amos Bronson Alcott. Unfortunately, public opinion was not as favorable, and Whitman lived most of his life in relative poverty.

In 1873, he suffered a stroke, which left him partially paralyzed, and he passed away in his New Jersey home on May 26, 1892.

May 1

Fear the Storm

Lovely weather so far. I don't know how long it will last, but I'm not afraid of storms, for I'm learning how to sail my ship.
                    Louisa May Alcott—Little Women *(1868)*

Turns out that astraphobia is an abnormal fear of thunder and lightning.

Many entrepreneurs suffer from something akin to this, known more commonly as resistance. Some might call this a form of fear—of failure, of success, of being frowned upon by your parents, of being laughed at, of being told by your "friends" you're not good enough, of neglecting your family—and the list goes on.

Resistance is a mighty force.

It's the thing that stops you from jumping at an opportunity, sitting down and writing your book, opening up and consuming the countless courses you've bought.

It's the fear of storms—real and imagined.

But here's the thing: if you are afraid, if you don't at times feel like a fake, then you might not be on the right path. A total lack of fear in your undertaking will show up as indifference—and then who really cares what you're creating?

Use fear as a clear signal that you are on the right path, but kick the resistance it creates right in the teeth.

If you don't, you'll cheat not only yourself but the entire world of your gift.

Challenge Question

What do you fear and where could it lead?

_____

_____

May 2

Owned Impact

It is simpler to be self-dependent. The height, the deity of a person is to be self-sustained, to need no gift, no foreign force. Society is good when it does not violate me, but best when it is likest to solitude.

Ralph Waldo Emerson—Self-Reliance *(1841)*

Many people start businesses because they want to impact something, they want to right some wrong. Still more, however, start businesses because they don't have another option, they know how to do something, they figure it's a decent way to make a living, and they come to embrace the notion of impact.

The most potent outcome of being an entrepreneur is the impact that it provides you. In fact, the only way to change the world is to be that change in yourself first. You can't give something you don't possess.

Become self-dependent.

When you need nothing, owe nothing, become internally self-sustained, you can fully embrace the mark you plan to leave on others.

Today, sit quietly and alone and think for a moment about the impact that you're having, the impact you want to have, the impact that you need to have.

If you can start internally to be that impact, it will radiate externally.

Challenge Question

When is the last time something really had an impact on your life? Did anything change because of it?

_____

_____

May 3

Unsudden Heights

The heights by great persons reached and kept, / Were not attained by sudden flight, / But they, while their companions slept, / Were toiling upward in the night. / Standing on what too long we bore, / With shoulders bent and downcast eyes, / We may discern—unseen before— / A path to higher destinies.

Henry Wadsworth Longfellow—"The Ladder of St. Augustine" (1847)

We are little more than a collection of habits, practiced daily. Some with thought, some as a matter of unconscious routine—some propel, some create enormous friction.

It is this collection of habits that most deserves our attention. What we do today and every other day that moves us to a higher place.

The journey to find the truth in your life can most effectively be measured in days well lived, well practiced. Each new day offers limitless promise and can be stacked upon the next and scaled for as long as it takes to be done. (And you're never done.)

Forget the goal, the destination, the plan. Live this day well and then start tomorrow, when it is here, with the very same intention.

Put everything you have into the unit of a day and collapse into bed with the assurance that you lived today, you bore what was asked of you, and that was enough.

Challenge Question

What are you most thankful for right now?

_____

_____

May 4

The Force

I have difficulty to detect the precise person you are: and of course so much force is withdrawn from your proper life. But do your work, and I shall know you. Do your work, and you shall reinforce yourself. A person must consider what a blindman's-buff is this game of conformity.

Ralph Waldo Emerson—Self-Reliance *(1841)*

At an earlier point in this essay, Emerson states more plainly the following: "The objection to conforming to usages that have become dead to you is, that it scatters your force."

So let's tidy this up—Emerson felt that conformity takes a physical, mental, and spiritual toll on our lives and because there's only so much force to go around, we better stop squandering it.

Ah, but not so fast. It's easy to conclude that doing what others do or think you should do is some sort of giving in, but self-reliance means you get to decide and, for that matter, define what is and is not conformity.

But sometimes we accept the status quo as our path because we simply fail to question it.

Perhaps the point is that your force lies in the incredible lightness of being yourself. Wandering far off your path creates a burden you may not feel until it's lifted.

Let's check a few things: How often are you justifying your decisions? Does it seem like there's too much drama in your life? Are you finding it hard to start big projects? Are you clinging more and more to outside validation?

There aren't any right or wrong answers; there's just you and the force.

Challenge Question

What do you accept in your life because you fail to question the status quo?

_____

_____

May 5

Keep Thy State

At times the whole world seems to be in conspiracy to harness you with emphatic trifles. Friend, client, child, sickness, fear, want, charity, all knock at once at thy closet door and say—"Come out unto us." But keep thy state; come not into their confusion.

Ralph Waldo Emerson—Self-Reliance *(1841)*

This is one of the things they don't tell you about being an entrepreneur. It gets really noisy in there. Everything clamors at once, and there's a constant danger of the squeaky wheel simply running over you. (Have you ever wondered what happens to the nice, gracious wheel?)

You get to decide to come not into their confusion. And you must.

Let's face it: our own story is enough to handle.

Challenge Question

In whose melodrama are you needlessly staring?

_____

_____

May 6

No Vain Endeavor

One cannot conceive of a state of things so fair that it cannot be realized. Can anyone honestly consult their experience and say that it is so? Have we any facts to appeal to when we say that our dreams are premature? Did you ever hear of a person who had striven all their life faithfully and singly toward an object and in no measure obtained it? If one constantly aspires, are they not elevated? Did ever a person try heroism, magnanimity, truth, sincerity, and find that there was no advantage in them? that it was a vain endeavor?

Henry David Thoreau—Familiar Letters *(1865)*

This is the ultimate plea to elevate the journey over the destination, that we are better for the doing no matter the end.

This thought from Thoreau bears repeating: "*Did ever a person try heroism, magnanimity, truth, sincerity, and find that there was no advantage in them?*"

What if you fail? Would you arrive at a better place? What if you have less? Would you want what you already have more? What if you toil and lose? Would you not still be elevated?

The beauty of this point of view is that it begs you to color every little thing as a measure of winning.

Challenge Question

What is uniquely heroic about your journey?

_____

_____

May 7

Beautiful Compensation

It is one of the beautiful compensations of life that no one can sincerely try to help another without helping themself.
        Ralph Waldo Emerson—Essays: First Series *(1865)*

Today's reading goes directly to the heart of things like service, sacrifice, and selflessness.

Emerson, like many of the transcendentalist thinkers, fully subscribed to the idea that all human beings were interconnected by a force of energy that flowed through acts of giving and receiving.

And so, in effect, this reading can include a practical, and potentially self-serving, bonus idea. Giving isn't always the act of charity it's made out to be—it's often done in a self-centered fit, albeit an enlightened one.

Random acts of kindness, a belief in service for the benefit of others, a dedication to helping those in need—all very good things for those on the receiving end—compensate the giver just as fully.

Committing to a focus on helping another is the ultimate accounting hack.

Challenge Question

Who could you give a gift to today?

_____

_____

May 8

Make Enough Noise

Beat! beat! drums!—blow! bugles! blow! / Make no parley—stop for no
expostulation, / Mind not the timid—mind not the weeper or prayer, /
Mind not the old man beseeching the young man, / Let not the child's voice
be heard, nor the mother's entreaties, / Make even the trestles to shake the
dead where they lie awaiting the hearses, / So strong you thump O terrible
drums—so loud you bugles blow.
                          Walt Whitman—"Beat! Beat! Drums!" (1861)

Whitman's dramatic poem was a visual and auditory warning meant to describe the perils of the impending American Civil War.

He encourages those who would listen to carry out a mission to wake those who must wake—must heed the warning to never stop—never mind the pile of obstacles and excuses in your way.

While perhaps a tad overdramatic for our entrepreneurial journey, the commitment needed mirrors the type of single-minded determination extolled by the poet.

Make enough noise to silence your critics.

Challenge Question

When was the last time someone told you that you couldn't do something? How did you react?

_____

_____

May 9

The Lens of Others

To ascend one step—we are better served through our sympathy. Activity is contagious. Looking where others look, and conversing with the same things, we catch the charm which lured them. Napoleon said, "You must not fight too often with one enemy, or you will teach him all your art of war." Talk much with any one of vigorous mind, and we acquire very fast the habit of looking at things in the same light, and, on each occurrence, we anticipate their thought.

Ralph Waldo Emerson—Uses of Great Men *(1849)*

In order to expand, we need role models and examples or, as Emerson would have put it, exemplars.

These sources of inspiration are not here to teach us best practices or give us a template to duplicate, but as a way to see the world through new eyes. We need to study other entrepreneurs, even those we might study with envy, in order to "*catch the charm which lured them.*"

When you begin to study others in this manner, you are forced to drop the ego you may have attached to your brilliant idea and look to those who have succeeded in some dimension, not for answers but for questions.

The only way someone else can help you is to help you question what you believe.

Emerson further stated in this work: "I cannot tell you what I know: but I have observed there are persons who, in their character and actions, answer questions which I have not skill to put."

Let those you aspire to copy (although you have no idea why they are more successful than you) be a lens through which you can learn. Look not to them, but through them.

Challenge Question

What advice have you given to others that you are not yet ready to accept yourself?

_____

_____

May 10

Greater Miracles

From without, no wonderful effect is wrought within ourselves, unless some interior, responding wonder meets it. That the starry vault shall surcharge the heart with all rapturous marvelings, is only because we ourselves are greater miracles, and superber trophies than all the stars in universal space. Wonder interlocks with wonder; and then the confounding feeling comes.

Herman Melville—Pierre: or, The Ambiguities *(1852)*

Let's just start today by acknowledging the fact that we are *"superber trophies than all the stars in universal space."*

Everything we want and need on the outside occurs when we stir the inside with wonder. Every day, today, right now.

Silence invokes wonder.

Challenge Question

How could you create more whitespace and wonder in your life?

_____

_____

May 11

True Potential

Along the path of a useful life / Will heart's-ease ever bloom; / The busy mind has no time to think / Of sorrow, or care, or gloom; / And anxious thoughts may be swept away / As we busily wield a broom. // I am glad a task to me is given / To labor at day by day; / For it brings me health, and strength, and hope, / And I cheerfully learn to say,– / "Head, you may think; heart, you may feel; / But hand, you shall work always!"
Louisa May Alcott—Her Life, Letters, and Journals *(1889)*

To make something unnoticeable takes great skill. That may seem like an odd thing for an entrepreneur to consider given that we've spent so much time in this book talking about the grandness of your ideas.

But grandness is not simply show. Grandness is your commitment to your idea. More often than not, you will shape real success into something flat, plain, useful for sure, and unassuming, but yours uniquely.

Alcott's character extolled the virtues of being trained to do work with her hands, and this is advice every entrepreneur should consider, no matter the nature of the business. To craft something from hand is to perhaps unlock its true purpose.

Noted architect and wood craftsman George Nakashima spoke of the wood he worked with in this manner in *The Soul of a Tree*:

> Each flitch, each board, each plank can have only one ideal use. The wood-worker, applying a thousand skills, must find that ideal use and then shape the wood to realize its true potential.

Challenge Question

How will you realize your true potential?

_____

_____

Discovering: Commitment

May 12

Road to Greatness

A determination to excel is the sure road to greatness . . . It was that which has accomplished the mightiest and noblest triumphs in the intellectual and physical world. It was that which has made such rapid strides towards civilization, and broken the chains of ignorance and superstition, which have so long fettered the human intellect. It was determination which raised so many worthy individuals from the humble walks of society, and from poverty, and placed them in positions of trust and renown. It is no slight barrier that can effectually oppose the determination of the will—success must ultimately crown its efforts. "The world shall hear of me," was the exclamation of one whose name has become as familiar as household words.

William Wells Brown—Three Years in Europe; or, Places I Have Seen and People I Have Met *(1852)*

Be careful today. While the "*determination to excel is the sure road to greatness*" sounds like a quote to save to your Pinterest inspiration board, you might want to step back and analyze the heartache that could just as easily come with it.

Is it possible that a determination to succeed could hypnotize you into thinking you know how to succeed? The modern definition of determination is "the process of establishing something exactly by calculation." Does that sound like your entrepreneurial journey to date?

Sometimes, determination requires letting go, learning to focus only on the things you can control. When determination turns to struggle, your determination can simply give more energy to the fight.

If this is starting to sound a bit slackerish it's not—it's how you get unstuck, it's how you regain sight of your long-term goals, and it's how you find the truth in your journey.

Challenge Question

What are you hanging onto right now that you should let go of?

_____

_____

May 13

Everyone Pivots

The pilgrims were human beings. Otherwise they would have acted differently. They had come a long and difficult journey, and now when the journey was nearly finished, and they learned that the main thing they had come for had ceased to exist, they didn't do as horses or cats or angle-worms would probably have done—turn back and get at something profitable—no, anxious as they had before been to see the miraculous fountain, they were as much as forty times as anxious now to see the place where it had used to be. There is no accounting for human beings.

Mark Twain—A Connecticut Yankee in King Arthur's Court *(1889)*

And . . . there's no accounting for entrepreneurs, it seems.

Twain surely spent some time in Silicon Valley. What he's described in recounting the actions of the pilgrims is a classic pivot. You know the comical portrayal of the hoodie-wearing bros who proclaim, "Look, nobody wants what this, but we've got a great domain name and a killer logo so let's just pivot."

Now before you think this is an attempt to cast shade on the idea, know this: self-reliant entrepreneurs always pivot.

It's become trendy in start-up circles to use the term "pivot" as though it was created in the last decade or so, but it simply implies that you should question everything—always—and ask if there's a better way to do it. Try, measure, learn is a universal truth in business, and your willingness to change your mind is what keeps you both committed to your dream and self-reliant. (Don't forget the measure part or you'll feel the urge to pivot because you're bored.)

Challenge Question

What's one thing that's not working right now? Do you need it?

_____

_____

May 14

Question Facts

I am by the law of my nature a reasoner. A person who should suppose I meant by that word, an arguer, would not only not understand me, but would understand the contrary of my meaning. I can take no interest whatever in hearing or saying anything merely as a fact—merely as having happened. It must refer to something within me before I can regard it with any curiosity or care.
    Samuel Taylor Coleridge—Specimens of the Table Talk of Samuel
                                        Taylor Coleridge *(1836)*

There are no such thing as facts. On the surface, that's a mighty bold statement, so perhaps it could be helpful to think of it as more of a point of view.

The problem with listening for and accepting indisputable things as facts is that they most often simply validate what we already believe—and where's the growth in that?

The things we already know are only mildly important. It's listening for the things we don't know that allow us to discover something unimagined.

Our blind spots hide safely behind the things we know are true. What we are unaware of or reject controls us most.

Question everything.

Challenge Question

What's one thing you know is true?

_____

_____

May 15

For the Joy of It

Life is real! Life is earnest! / And the grave is not its goal; / Dust thou art, to dust returnest, / Was not spoken of the soul. // Not enjoyment, and not sorrow, / Is our destined end or way; / But to act, that each tomorrow / Find us farther than today.
   Henry Wadsworth Longfellow—Complete Poetical Works of Henry
                                   Wadsworth Longfellow *(1839)*

One the great challenges of the notion of entrepreneurship is that it frequently has us striving at succeeding or failing at one thing or another when the great promise of being an entrepreneur is the joy of being able to do something precisely for the joy of it.

If we are doing what we are meant to do, then there is no winning and losing, but only progress found in living today as today.

This may be all that our soul wants of us.

Challenge Question

Is there any aspect of your journey that is bringing you sorrow?

_____

_____

May 16

Intentional Procrastination

With patience wait till winter is o'er, / And all lovely things return; / Of every season try the more / Some knowledge or virtue to learn.
Louisa May Alcott—Her Life, Letters, and Journals *(1889)*

To everything there is a season—yeah, right, tell that to an entrepreneur.

Entrepreneurs are an impatient, maybe even impulsive, lot. The trait has its positive aspects—most notably, impatience inspires many entrepreneurs to create solutions rather than accept the alternative.

Some might suggest that urgency is the driving force in many an entrepreneurial adventure.

But sometimes the drive to go somewhere results in arrival at a mistaken location.

It takes tremendous self-awareness to know when to move and when to practice something akin to intentional procrastination. Procrastination gets a bad rap, but subtly applied it can provide the leverage you need to find the answer that is right for you at the present.

Challenge Question

What are you currently pushing that you should be observing?

_____

_____

May 17

Independence of Solitude

It is easy in the world to live after the world's opinion; it is easy in solitude to live after our own; but the great one is who in the midst of the crowd keeps with perfect sweetness the independence of solitude. The magnetism which all original action exerts is explained when we inquire the reason of self-trust.

Ralph Waldo Emerson—Self-Reliance *(1841)*

This self-trust that Emerson speaks of is a fleeting thing. It shows up when we honor our true feelings and emotions rather than shrouding ourselves in the validation of others. Self-trust, inner trust is not found outside ourselves.

Developing self-trust, however, requires that you slow down often enough to cultivate your innermost thoughts. Then, with compassion, you can enlist these thoughts when others decide to invite you into their drama. This is how you keep *"with perfect sweetness the independence of solitude."*

A lack of self-trust shows up physically too. Your body's subtle genius can tell you when something has challenged your opinion—it can come in the form of uninvited business advice or even someone cutting ahead of you in line. Your body isn't telling you that they are right; it's telling that you might be wrong.

And this is how we practice. The next time something happens *"in the midst of the crowd,"* tune in to how your body reacts (ranging from a tightening of the jaw to a punch in the gut). Let this be your training ground for letting go.

Develop a silent release phrase—something goofy like "I am glad that just happened"—so that you can connect these events with your ability to switch back into your realm of self-trust.

Oh, and by the way, meditate a lot.

Challenge Question

Who currently has the ability to push your pain buttons? What does it feel like when your body says no, what about yes?

_____

_____

Discovering: Commitment

May 18

Mind the End

Nothing is more clear than that every plot, worth the name, must be elaborated to its denouement before anything be attempted with the pen. It is only with the denouement constantly in view that we can give a plot its indispensable air of consequence, or causation, by making the incidents, and especially the tone at all points, tend to the development of the intention.

Edgar Allan Poe—"The Philosophy of Composition" (1846)

We can sum up Poe's reading today with this wise nugget: "begin with the end in mind."

But imagine if Poe was charged with writing a book that never ended or at least was intended to run for a good 20 or 30 years. How tidy would his denouement, his final scene be?

There's no doubting the wisdom of this "mind the end" advice, but entrepreneurs must remain both equally focused on the destination and detached from the details, allowing too for sweeping changes in the achievement. (Imagine the challenge for Poe's editors in that scenario.)

Let's call this required skill "detached focus."

You set your objective, but then you let go and get to work on what needs to be done today. In other words, you don't lose focus; you simply focus on the right things right now. If you set a goal of $1 million in revenue, you don't spend all day looking at your bank balance; you go about tilling the soil, planting the seeds, and building the irrigation canals, because a good gardening metaphor is always useful.

Focus on performing today's most pressing need.

Challenge Question

What's the most important thing you can accomplish today?

_____

_____

May 19

Your True Fans

The richest gifts we can bestow are the least marketable. We hate the kindness which we understand. A noble person confers no such gift as his whole confidence: none so exalts the giver and the receiver; it produces the truest gratitude. Perhaps it is only essential to friendship that some vital trust should have been reposed by the one in the other. I feel addressed and probed even to the remote parts of my being when one nobly shows, even in trivial things, an implicit faith in me.

Henry David Thoreau—Familiar Letters (1865)

Find your tribe, those who have unspoken faith in you, and build a commitment to making their lives better for having revealed this trust.

This is, in many ways, the ultimate commitment of self-reliance and self-trust. You can't take everyone with you, and you shouldn't try. In this socially connected world of wispy "connections," it bears reminding that a handful of true fans is the "richest gift."

Author Seth Godin sums up this call to action in his book *Tribes* beautifully:

> Yes, I think it's okay to abandon the big, established, stuck tribe. It's okay to say to them, "You're not going where I need to go, and there's no way I'm going to persuade all of you to follow me. So rather than standing here watching the opportunities fade away, I'm heading off. I'm betting some of you, the best of you, will follow me."

Challenge Question

Where are your true fans?

_____

_____

May 20

No Single Exception

The great poets are to be known by the absence in them of tricks, and by the justification of perfect personal candor. All faults may be forgiven of those who have perfect candor. Henceforth let no one of us lie, for we have seen that openness wins the inner and outer world, and that there is no single exception, . . . and that the soul has never once been fooled and never can be fooled.

Walt Whitman—Preface *to* Leaves of Grass *(1855)*

Even *The Conflicted Entrepreneur's Guide to Sort of Having Business Ethics* is likely to suggest that it's a bad idea to lie in business. (Don't worry; this book doesn't actually exist.)

While this should be a pretty open-and-shut discussion, it's not.

We can all agree that openness, transparency, and honesty are brilliant values, but as an entrepreneur you'll have them tested in an unimaginable range of circumstances.

And there's one test you may not have considered: the lies you tell yourself.

What? What are you talking about? That you really didn't want that project because the people would probably be a pain to work with, even though, you didn't put in the work you knew it would take to land it. That kind of thing.

There's a level of self-preservation that this sort of self-talk brings, but there's also a giant dose of cognitive dissonance—a notion that we experience mental discomfort when we attempt to hold two different and conflicting ideas simultaneously.

Your soul can't be fooled. Work it out.

Challenge Question

What lies are you telling yourself about your journey right now?

_____

_____

May 21

Have Your Experience

I try to judge things for myself; to judge wrong, I think, is more honourable than not to judge at all. I don't wish to be a mere sheep in the flock; I wish to choose my fate and know something of human affairs beyond what other people think it compatible with propriety to tell me.

Henry James—The Portrait of a Lady *(1881)*

The use of the word "judge" in today's reading leans more toward the idea of making choices and decisions that are right for you rather than considering something as right or wrong in general.

This is an important distinction for the self-reliant entrepreneur. We make a lot of decisions based on intuition, laced with fear, and are quite often hard pressed to explain them to others.

In the preface to a later work, *Lady Barbarina*, James offers this:

The thing of profit is to have your experience—to recognize and understand it, and for this almost any will do; there being surely no absolute ideal about it beyond getting from it all it has to give.

So, you see, go for it, make the decision that feels right. No one will die (probably), and you can always change your mind. Just have your experience.

Challenge Question

How do you tell the difference between fear and intuition?

_____

_____

May 22

On Purpose

Many people can choose the right and best on a great occasion, but not many can, with such ready and serene decision, lay aside even life, when that is right and best.

Margaret Fuller—Summer on the Lakes *(1844)*

If you've given your life over to your business, then it must be serving an incredibly fulfilling and useful purpose. Right?

Or is it possible that it's just a job that has found a way to consume you? This is okay if you've chosen it and right now it's where you want to be. But a far more insidious conclusion is that you got here or you're headed here without knowing how.

Or worse, why, and that's the point: without a deep connection to the purpose your business brings to your life, you'll continue to take on every noisy task that clamors for your attention—and that scales to infinity.

Today, recommit to the higher purpose your entrepreneurial journey provides.

Challenge Question

How does your life reflect the higher purpose your business serves?

_____

_____

May 23

Heart and Mind

We must earn our bread by the sweat of our brow, truly, but also by the sweat of our brain within that brow. The body can feed the body only. I have tasted but little bread in my life. It has been mere grub and provender for the most part. Of bread that nourished the brain and the heart, scarcely any.

Henry David Thoreau—Familiar Letters *(1865)*

Today's reading from Thoreau is a logical place to consider an overlap between science and spirituality.

One of the jobs of the heart is to send electrical signals to the brain telling it what chemicals to release. Many positive and negative physical and emotional states are triggered by this connection.

This is a bit of the science behind peace and happiness as well as stress and anxiety.

This is also why several minutes of slow, rhythmic breathing can immediately reduce stress and calm other emotions. It's in this moment that we send the highest quality signals to our brain.

But this messaging never turns off. All day long we are sending subconscious signals, including the self-loathing, self-doubting, self-sabotaging monologue going on behind the scenes. (Not you, but you probably know people like this.)

By routinely creating a state of what Rollin McCraty, research director at the Institute of HeartMath, calls coherence—the state when the heart, mind, and emotions are in energetic alignment—"we find that personal energy is accumulated, not wasted—leaving more energy to manifest intentions and harmonious outcomes."

Challenge Question

How does your heart feel right now?

_____

_____

Author's Note: Today's reflection is provided by my daughter, Mary Jantsch.

May 24

Anything or Nothing

Cautious, careful people, always casting about to preserve their reputation and social standing, never can bring about a reform. Those who are really in earnest must be willing to be anything or nothing in the world's estimation.

Susan B. Anthony—"On the Campaign for Divorce Law Reform" (1860)

Who are you, in your estimation? How do you evaluate your self-worth?

It's easy to fall into a place where you're comparing your work to that founder in the office next door that just got funding, to a social influencer with a huge audience, to that woman you went to university with who just started her own thriving business, to your siblings.

Screw that!

Are you a good person? Are you learning and growing? Are you there for people when they need you? Do you open up to others about both your success and failures?

Define the values and characteristics that are truly important to you. Rely on them. Entrepreneurs are known for creating their own path, boldly breaking the mold to solve a problem. So, don't revert back by then applying someone else's ideas or rubric for what success looks like.

Forge your own path and your own definition of success. Then, push yourself further by sharing both your ups and downs with the people around you. By being anything or nothing in the world's estimation, you can be the best you can in yours.

Challenge Question

Who in your life practices vulnerability and drops their guard, unworried about how it might impact their reputation and social standing? Tell them.

_____

_____

May 25

Involuntary Perception

We lie in the lap of immense intelligence, which makes us receivers of its truth and organs of its activity. When we discern justice, when we discern truth, we do nothing of ourselves, but allow a passage to its beams. If we ask whence this comes, if we seek to pry into the soul that causes, all philosophy is at fault. Its presence or absence is all we can affirm. Every person discriminates between the voluntary acts of their mind and the involuntary perceptions, and knows that to these involuntary perceptions a perfect faith is due.

Ralph Waldo Emerson—Self-Reliance *(1841)*

Intuition is meant to play a starring role in the life of the entrepreneur. Emerson felt that was the primary reason we need to pursue self-reliance. That human beings, empowered to follow their intuition, were essentially good and moral and that, left to decide their fate, would choose the right path.

The bonds of the "voluntary acts" of the mind, so often determined by the rules and dogma of others, of churches, of society, make it hard to break free and follow your heart. Our senses are overwhelmed with what the world expects of us, and so we work to figure out how to fit in and follow what's worked for others.

Go into any Facebook group of like-minded business folks and you'll see question after question concerning how to do this or that tactic associated with speaking or writing or marketing or whatever.

This activity is little more than a way to mask doing the work, getting better at your art, and following your involuntary perceptions. Admit this—you're not very good at what you do yet, and that's what needs your attention.

Your intuition knows what needs work.

Challenge Question

What aspect of your entrepreneurial journey needs practice?

_____

_____

Discovering: Commitment

May 26

To Speak Truth

We shall all do well if we learn so much as to talk,—to speak truth. The only fruit which even much living yields seems to be often only some trivial success,—the ability to do some slight thing better... What immense sacrifices, what hecatombs and holocausts, the gods exact for very slight favors! How much sincere life before we can even utter one sincere word.
Henry David Thoreau—Familiar Letters *(1865)*

You could read Thoreau's words and conclude that he was just in a bad mood that day, or you could view the tough love as an attempt to push us all.

Entrepreneurs are goal and deadline setters because we thrive on the push—the external stimulation. We check the boxes so we can post an Instagram story that shows we've done "*some slight thing better.*"

And of course, all the while we're missing the point—the entire point is to learn to speak truth before we run out of game.

Challenge Question

What truth are you avoiding speaking?

_____

_____

May 27

Your Special Place

Every individual has a place to fill in the world, and is important in some
respects, whether they choose to be so or not.
Nathaniel Hawthorne—Passages from the American Note-Books, Vol. 1
(1887)

Kind of tricky waters here—do successful entrepreneurs (you get to define that) ever choose to be important, or do they choose to be themselves and in doing so become important—to someone—most notably themselves?

Let's start by acknowledging the idea that you have a place to fill in the world through the words of the world's greatest cheerleader of being uniquely ourselves, Mister Rogers:

You've made this day a special day, just by being you. There's no person in the whole world like you, and I like you—just the way you are.

Kind of makes you feel warm and vulnerable all at the same time, doesn't it?

Go ahead, let yourself be vulnerable and you'll find that you'll immediately become more self-reliant and less dependent on what others think. This is when you'll start to do your most important work.

Or as Brené Brown, author of the *Power of Vulnerability*, sums it up: "Vulnerability is the birthplace of innovation, creativity and change." (For some further inspiration today, hunt down her TED Talk on the subject.)

Challenge Question

What's one thing you could share that makes you feel vulnerable?

_____

_____

May 28

True Genius

The imbecility of people is always inviting the impudence of power. It is the delight of vulgar talent to dazzle and to blind the beholder. But true genius seeks to defend us from itself. True genius will not impoverish, but will liberate, and add new senses. If a wise person should appear in our village, they would create, in those who conversed with them, a new consciousness of wealth, by opening their eyes to unobserved advantages
Ralph Waldo Emerson—Uses of Great Men *(1849)*

It is our job to learn to think for ourselves. Or as Emerson suggests, "True genius seeks to defend us from itself."

So much of what we witness under the banner of entrepreneurship is the bluster of those who want us to notice them, acknowledge their genius, +1 the fact that "they are humbled to be on so and so's top 1000 to follow on Twitter list."

It's pretty exhausting really, but time and again we fall for what they are selling.

Do you want to know how to tell if someone is the real deal—a great thinker that you should spend time with? They will maintain that you have the answers, not they.

True genius doesn't sell genius; it unlocks it in others.

Challenge Question

How can you show others that they have the answers?

_____

_____

May 29

Proportions Widened

But all great expression, which, on a superficial survey, seems so easy as well as so simple, furnishes, after a while, to the faithful observer, its own standard by which to appreciate it. Daily these proportions widened and towered more and more upon my sight, and I got, at last, a proper foreground for these sublime distances.

Margaret Fuller—At Home and Abroad; or, Things and Thoughts in America and Europe *(1856)*

Have you ever stood at the summit of a mountain observing the expansive world below?

The chief benefit of making the climb and seeing the view is that we are forever changed by what we've seen and perhaps now better prepared to act profitably when we are down among the trees and day-to-day tasks.

That's another way of saying we need global perspective in order to grasp the proper priorities to fill our days.

Or as René Demaul describes it in his classic, *Mount Analogue*:

What is above knows what is below, but what is below does not know what is above. One climbs, one sees. One descends, one sees no longer, but one has seen. There is an art of conducting oneself in the lower regions by the memory of what one saw higher up.

Back up and study why you are doing what you are doing today, and affirm that either it is sufficiently big enough or it's not. Act accordingly.

Challenge Question

What's one act you can take to help widen your perspective?

_____

_____

May 30

Sufficient Foreground

It is very gratifying to live in the prospect of great successes always; and for that purpose we must leave a sufficient foreground to see them through. All the painters prefer distant prospects for the greater breadth of view and delicacy of tint.

Henry David Thoreau—Familiar Letters *(1865)*

One of the initial lessons a landscape painter is taught is to create the horizon first as the placeholder of all perspective effects and then paint around that horizon.

Look up; where's your horizon? Are you busy creating what the plan called for while the horizon slides gently off in another direction?

Leave sufficient foreground so that you can see where you're going this week, this month, this quarter, and act accordingly.

Challenge Question

What new opportunity has appeared on your horizon? Think hard, it may not be apparent.

_____

_____

May 31

Greater People

Within the limits of human education and agency, we may say great people exist that there may be greater people. The destiny of organized nature is improvement, and who can tell its limits? It is for humans to tame the chaos; on every side, whilst they live, to scatter the seeds of science and of song, that climate, corn, animals, men, and women may be milder, and the germs of love and benefit may be multiplied.

Ralph Waldo Emerson—Uses of Great Men *(1849)*

The greatest contribution of the entrepreneurial journey is that we often leave some little corner of this world a better place for having done what we've done. But that's not our obligation; it's a happy side effect of being who and what we were meant to be.

If you believe, as has been suggested throughout this book, that we are all connected by a universal force, then as Emerson suggests, that "*to scatter the seeds of science and of song, that climate, corn, animals, men, and women may be milder, and the germs of love and benefit may be multiplied*" is both awesome and doable on a global level.

Our job, then, is to look for our true self in relationship to everything in the universe.

No matter how trivially you view your current situation, this is the impact of which you're capable.

Challenge Question

What impact on the world have you begun to sense you're having?

_____

_____

June

Louisa May Alcott (1832–1888)

*Keep good company, read good books, love good things and cultivate soul
and body as faithfully as you can.*

—*Louisa May Alcott*

Source: Wikimedia

Louisa May Alcott was born in Germantown, Pennsylvania, to social worker Abby May and philosopher and writer Amos Bronson Alcott. The family moved to Boston in 1843, and her father became involved in the transcendentalist movement. Alcott, therefore, spent her childhood surrounded by the likes of Ralph Waldo Emerson, Henry David Thoreau, and Theodore Parker.

The oldest of four girls, Alcott developed a love for writing at an early age. However, because her family was of modest means, she undertook many odd jobs in her teens and early adult years to help make ends meet.

She was finally able to focus on her writing in 1854, when she published her first book, *Flower Fables*. This book gained recognition, and she continued to write and publish her work.

When the American Civil War broke out, she decided to become a volunteer nurse. She left home but then contracted typhoid due to unsanitary hospital conditions. The illness required her to return to Boston, and she never fully recovered from the effects of typhoid.

Some good did come out of her time as a nurse. In 1863, she published the letters she had written home during the Civil War as a collection called *Hospital Sketches*, which brought her widespread attention.

In 1868, Alcott published *Little Women*, a story about four sisters, based on her own childhood. The book was instantly a major success and catapulted Alcott to international fame.

She continued to write throughout the rest of her life, and died in 1888, just two days after her father.

June 1

Firmly to Hope

Hope is the thing with feathers— / That perches in the soul— / And sings the tune without the words— / And never stops—at all— / And sweetest—in the Gale—is heard— / And sore must be the storm— / That could abash the little Bird— / That kept so many warm.
                    Emily Dickinson—"Hope is the thing with feathers" (1891)

Many people witness entrepreneurs who work through problem after problem only to come out on top and conclude that perseverance and commitment carried them.

The truth is that it was most likely hope.

Hope is what carries you beyond where most give up, because hope provides the faith that you can achieve your goal. It's not a wish or a desire, or even optimism; it's a belief that you will, perhaps must, overcome an obstacle or achieve a goal.

Today, connect with nature, for there is no better model of hope. Just start walking outdoors, lie in some grass, sit under a tree—let hope perch in your soul.

Challenge Question

What provides you with the hope to carry on when things get tough?

_____

_____

June 2

Castles in the Air

If you have built castles in the air, your work need not be lost; that is where they should be. Now put the foundations under them.
                                        Henry David Thoreau—Walden *(1854)*

Ideas are great, but ideas without execution are of little value. Or as the often misattributed quote goes, "Vision without execution is just hallucination."

Of course, the flip side of this can be just as devastating—all action without a plan.

But which is really better? If you have a great idea that you don't act upon you have little to show, but if you race ahead and take action without a plan at least perhaps something gets done.

Thoreau pleaded that we should live our lives today, have our adventures now, live in our castles in the air as a way to live as ourselves today rather than waiting to build the proper foundation so we can then live as we are meant to.

No one can map out a guaranteed plan of success, so in a way we are all guessing anyway. As Thoreau went on to suggest:

If one advances confidently in the direction of his dreams, and endeavors to live the life which he has imagined, he will meet with a success unexpected in common hours.

Meet with success and then do the practical thing—build a foundation under it.

Challenge Question

What are you missing by choosing to focus on the foundation for your vision?

_____

_____

June 3

On Being a Hero

The greatest obstacle to being heroic is the doubt whether one may not be going to prove one's self a fool; the truest heroism is to resist the doubt; and the profoundest wisdom to know when it ought to be resisted, and when to be obeyed.

Nathaniel Hawthorne—The Blithedale Romance *(1852)*

Do you ever consider yourself a hero or any aspect of your work heroic?

Of course, the common narrative associated with the concept of heroism makes this consideration seem a bit foolish, doesn't it?

Is it possible that you don't consider the work you do in the service of yourself or others something of a heroic journey because others might laugh at the notion?

Hawthorne's protagonist female characters, Zenobia Pierce, quoted in today's reading, and Hester Prynne in *The Scarlet Letter* broke the mold of the common portrait of women of that time and instead presented themselves as confident, strong-minded, self-reliant women. (Margaret Fuller, quoted throughout this work, became the real-life personification of this idea.)

For this, they were mercilessly criticized and laughed at (as was Hawthorne's work initially).

Were they being heroes or simply being true to who they were and what they believed? Hard to tell the difference, isn't it?

Challenge Question

What revolution do you need to start today?

_____

_____

June 4

No Apologies

My life is not an apology, but a life. It is for itself and not for a spectacle. I much prefer that it should be of a lower strain, so it be genuine and equal, than that it should be glittering and unsteady.

Ralph Waldo Emerson—Self-Reliance *(1841)*

The pursuit of purpose through persistent simplicity runs through much of the transcendentalist literature and lectures and is likely one of the most efficient paths to self-reliance.

And yet, we desperately seek to find the "why" in our journey so that we can define it in terms that sound glittering.

Consider this additional Emerson thought from his essay "The Over-Soul":

But the soul that ascends to worship the great God is plain and true; has no rose-color, no fine friends, no chivalry, no adventures; does not want admiration; dwells in the hour that now is, in the earnest experience of the common day.

So maybe you can stop searching for that grand purpose to describe your life, and then you can stop apologizing that you don't know what yours is.

Genuine and equal actions, feeling your purpose, rather than looking for it, is how you live today instead of some story about your past or future.

You don't need to justify your life—just rock it.

Challenge Question

What are you apologizing for right now?

_____

_____

June 5

Unlocking Solitude

To persons whose pursuits are insulated from the common business of life—who are either in advance of mankind or apart from it—there often comes a sensation of moral cold that makes the spirit shiver as if it had reached the frozen solitudes around the pole.
Nathaniel Hawthorne—*"The Artist of the Beautiful" in* Mosses from an Old Manse and Other Stories *(1846)*

Entrepreneurs are in many respects artists—or at least are prone to think like artists—for better or worse. Read the full text of "The Artist of the Beautiful" and you just might think Hawthorne was writing about you at times.

The life of an entrepreneur can be a lonesome one. You may work apart from others, live mostly in your head, and wrestle with the sensation that you are the only one who gets what you're trying to do.

Hawthorne's character Owen, the subject of today's reading, was indeed an artist. Throughout his journey he suffered from self-imposed isolation and bouts of depression—"a sensation of moral cold" (an office in the basement of your home can add to this feeling too).

Don't let this be you. Fight it. Get outside. Attend a conference. Meet a client face to face for a change. Get off social media for a week. Get an intern. Adopt a dog.

Oh, and just think how miserable the folks are who are stuck in jobs they hate.

Challenge Question

Who should you need to go see today?

_____

_____

Discovering: Security

June 6

Do You

Those love [truth] best who to themselves are true, / And what they dare to dream of, dare to do; / They followed her and found her / Where all may hope to find, / Not in the ashes of the burnt-out mind, / But beautiful, with danger's sweetness round her.

James Russell Lowell—The Vision of Sir Launfal *(1848)*

Truth in the abstract sense has little power to usher us forward. Everyone loves truth, right? What's not to like?

But truth as a way of life, brimming with passion, embodied, lived out in action, is something only you can do for yourself. So many of the readings in this book could be taken as advice for living, but they are not. That would be the height of irony. A book preaching self-reliance suggesting you simply need to rely on what you're reading is an absurd thought.

While that's a recipe for every self-help book ever written, it's the opposite of truth.

The only advice that matters is—do you. Be true.

Today, seek and find danger's sweetness in your own truth.

Challenge Question

What activity makes you feel as though you are most living your truth?

_____

_____

June 7

You Are Invincible

Nature still wore her motherly smile, and seemed to promise room, not only for those favored or cursed with the qualities best adapting for the strifes of competition, but for the delicate, the thoughtful, even the indolent or eccentric. She did not say, Fight or starve; nor even, Work or cease to exist; but, merely showing that the apple was a finer fruit than the wild crab, gave both room to grow in the garden.

Margaret Fuller—At Home and Abroad; or, Things and Thoughts in America and Europe *(1856)*

The example of self-reliance that exists in plain sight out our window is an often visited theme in the transcendentalist literature. Thoreau was the most overt; go live in the woods, simplify, and eat what you forage could sum up his relationship with nature. But Fuller and Emerson also used nature as both a metaphor for self-reliance and as a way to attempt to shed light on their belief that somehow we are all connected—something we might find more scientifically explained in the study of quantum physics today.

It's hard to read the passage from today's reading and not to imagine an entrepreneur in their struggle *"with the qualities best adapting for the strifes of competition."* But how often is it that how we think about our life is what creates the real competition?

If we begin with the notion that there is room for all our dreams to grow and that nature will provide the opportunity to those who ask, our job is to ask. Nature is a lesson in perfect grace. When you walk outside in the rain, that same rain falls on us equally.

You don't need anyone's permission to seek joy, happiness, gratitude, or anything else you feel you lack—use nature's perfect example of life to know that you are invincible right now.

So, stop shooting yourself in the foot, and go water your spot in the garden.

Challenge Question

When is the last time you sat and watched the trees sway in the breeze?

_____

_____

Discovering: Security

June 8

Spirit of Entrepreneurship

Business now takes the same place in the education of the people that was once held by war: it stimulates activity, promotes the intercourse of person with person, nation with nation; assembling all in masses, it elevates their temperature, so to say; it leads to new and better forms of organization; it excites us to invention, so that thereby we are continually acquiring new power over the elements.

Theodore Parker—Speeches, Addresses, and Occasional Sermons
(1852)

Comparing entrepreneurship to war may seem needlessly foolish because let's face it—war is hell.

There is, however, an energy contained in both that can instruct.

The most notable comparisons of business and war are drawn from the ancient work of Sun Tzu, *The Art of War.* Although many business writings citing the work focus primarily on the aspects of defeating the enemy, there is one quote that the self-reliant entrepreneur, who focused on preparing to never fight, might find most useful:

Unhappy is the fate of one who tries to win his battles and succeed in his attacks without cultivating the spirit of enterprise (entrepreneurship), as the result is waste of time and general stagnation.

We must make it our job to cultivate the spirit of entrepreneurship—to seek out change, to ask hard questions, to rise above mediocrity, to innovate, and to focus only on what we can control.

Our job is to take our journey seriously. To practice, sweat the little things, nurture and stay true to the elements that represent the best of our vision. To take our time and do it right the first time.

This is not a call for perfection; it's a call for sincerity.

Challenge Question

Where are you cutting corners and accepting mediocrity?

_____

_____

June 9

Don't Undervalue Yourself

Be polite and generous, but don't undervalue yourself. You will be useful,
at any rate; you may just as well be happy, while you are about it.
Oliver Wendell Holmes, Sr.—Elsie Venner *(1861)*

One of the greatest ways to undervalue yourself is to consume more than you create.

It's so easy to get in the habit of consuming, not just stuff but information that helps you undervalue yourself—low-quality content, streaming videos, social media, pretty much anything on BuzzFeed—your own negative thoughts?

Create, produce, innovate, build, write, sing, dance.

You're in control of your life. You may just as well be happy while you're about it.

Challenge Question

What's one source of information you can block from your life right now?

_____

_____

Discovering: Security

June 10

Risk Your Heart

[F]or of all writers [a poet] has the best chance for immortality. Others may write from the head, but he writes from the heart, and the heart will always understand him.

Washington Irving—The Mutability of Literature: A Colloquy in Westminster Abbey *(1885)*

Isn't it time to stop giving a damn about how many people share your great ideas in the places people turn today to share the sea of common drivel?

Leading with your heart requires that you risk your heart and demonstrate an amazing amount of vulnerability. Otherwise, it won't sell.

Being a self-reliant entrepreneur demands that you throw your heart and, what the heck, your soul, into the mix because this adventure is as much about what you get as what you give—and why would you wish to get anything less than immortality?

Challenge Question

Who is your favorite poet? If you don't have one, check out Billy Collins, poet laureate of the United States from 2001 to 2003.

_____

_____

June 11

Security in Optimism

What is good is effective, generative; makes for itself room, food, and allies. A sound apple produces seed—a hybrid does not. Is a person in their place, is constructive, fertile, magnetic, inundating armies with their purpose, which is thus executed.

Ralph Waldo Emerson—Uses of Great Men *(1841)*

Emerson believed in heroes. He was, it seems, to his core an optimist and an idealist.

Uses of Great Men opens with this thought:

It is natural to believe in great men. If the companions of our childhood should turn out to be heroes, and their condition regal it would not surprise us.

When do you suppose most people give up the notion of saving the world? Upon getting their first real job, taking on a mortgage, the moment they realize their lack of courage has caused them to overcommit to things they don't actually believe?

What is good, makes for itself room.

Idealism—the idea that you could in fact be the hero who produces something fruitful—gives you the confidence to do the things that if you knew better you would have never attempted.

There is security in optimism and idealism—cling to it.

Hey, if it doesn't work out, you've always got time to become pragmatic.

Challenge Question

How can you best turn your idealism into reality—even if you need to find it again?

_____

_____

June 12

No Speedy Limit

Here is this vast, savage, howling mother of ours, Nature, lying all around, with such beauty, and such affection for her children, as the leopard; and yet we are so early weaned from her breast to society, to that culture which is exclusively an interaction of person on person,—a sort of breeding in and in, which produces at most a merely English nobility, a civilization destined to have a speedy limit.

Henry David Thoreau—"Walking" (1862)

How can we reclaim a natural relationship with our mother? The metaphor of Mother Nature assumes the most positive attributes most associate with the unconditionally loving, graceful, and nurturing picture of someone you might call Mom.

This, however, isn't a reflection on family dynamics; it's a suggestion that nature and entrepreneurs are made for each other even as society has other plans.

Entrepreneurs need space to think and grow and solve problems.

David Strayer, a cognitive psychologist at the University of Utah who specializes in attention, conducted a study of Outward Bound participants and found that they performed 50 percent better on creative problem-solving tasks after three days of wilderness backpacking. Countless other studies suggest the science is clear—time spent in nature is good for you.

Do your planning outside; book a three-day company backpack. Dread the idea of lying on the damp, cold, hard ground, while all around you the coyotes yip, bark, and howl to each other? Okay, fine, go sit in the park today and swap energy with the soul of a tree.

Why create for yourself a speedy limit while this vast, savage, howling mother of ours is lying all around?

Challenge Question

When is the last time you had a big breakthrough in a conference room?

_____

_____

June 13

The Near at Hand

*Bees, like us human insects, have little faith in the near at hand; they expect
to make their fortune in a distant field, they are lured by the remote and
the difficult, and hence overlook the flower and the sweet at their very door.*
John Burroughs—"An Idyl of the Honey-Bee" (1895)

Burroughs, in this bit of introspection, is giving practical advice for the person looking to successfully locate a bee box in an effort to attract a colony to take up residence, but certainly he's hit upon something relevant for the entrepreneur.

To realize your dream as a self-reliant entrepreneur, you must learn to use these words: "No, thank you," or it could be "Thank you, no," or even just "No."

You've intentionally chosen the priorities you need to move your entrepreneurial journey forward, and yet you find yourself taking on projects and tasks for fear that you'll miss an opportunity—or worse, because you lack the courage to say no.

Scan your current accountabilities. What should you shed right now? What should you delegate? Uncommit to? What goals no longer make sense? Drop them; it's gonna be fine.

Self-reliance requires wicked self-care, and that starts with protecting the fragile focus you must rely on in order to stay true.

Say no to something today for the practice of it.

Challenge Question

What's one task you can delegate right now?

_____

_____

June 14

Seed of Faith

I only hope . . . that you are still happier than you are sad, and that you remember that the smallest seed of faith is of more worth than the largest fruit of happiness.

Henry David Thoreau—Familiar Letters *(1894)*

Genius, or the kind of obsession some associate with entrepreneurial vision, is often accompanied by personal demons.

Working in isolation to create something out of nothing can lead to a risk of depression. Not exactly a cheery topic, but one that has some data to back it up.

But a little madness goes a long way, too. In the words of Nassir Ghaemi, author of *A First-Rate Madness*:

Most of us make a basic and reasonable assumption about sanity: we think it produces good results, and we believe insanity is a problem.

Holding on to the smallest seed of faith is the answer. When we encounter any setback, it's not the setback that's the real issue—it is, of course, how we feel about it that gives it control.

Once again, we'll call on our friend meditation. Often how we feel about something is hardwired into our subconscious, and meditation unlocks the door between the conscious and subconscious.

Taking time to change how you think through a process that science proves rewires your brain and turns off the chemicals that cause stress is the magic tool for nurturing the seed of faith and reconnecting with why you're doing this all in the first place.

Start or end your day today, and perhaps every day, with 10 minutes of meditation and gratitude.

Challenge Question

What's something that always makes you smile? Why is that?

_____

_____

June 15

Ask Nature

Nature seems, as she often does, to have made a study for some larger design. She delights in this,—a sketch within a sketch, a dream within a dream. Wherever we see it, the lines of the great buttress in the fragment of stone, the hues of the waterfall copied in the flowers that star its bordering mosses, we are delighted; for all the lineaments become fluent, and we mould the scene in congenial thought with its genius.

Margaret Fuller—At Home and Abroad; or, Things and Thoughts in
America and Europe *(1856)*

Striving is perhaps the most counterproductive approach to entrepreneurship.

Nature never strives; it just does what it is meant to do. What if we grew like that?

There's a fascinating vein of science called biomimetics, or biomimicry. It is defined as the imitation of the models, systems, and elements of nature for the purpose of solving complex human problems.

Nature practices biomimicry, as Fuller describes in today's reading, so why can't we? You don't have to look far to find examples in everyday technology—locomotion, adhesives, structural design.

Although there are elements of sustainability to this notion, it's really more of a point of view. How as an entrepreneur can you take leadership lessons from nature?

How can you strive less and accomplish more? How can you consume less and produce more? How can you find ways to live with less and experience more joy?

Challenge Question

Want to have some fun? Visit Asknature.org, a database of innovation inspired by nature.

Discovering: Security

June 16

Joy Today

The pedigree of honey / Does not concern the bee; / A clover, any time, to him / Is aristocracy.
> Emily Dickinson—"Life," The Collected Poems of Emily
> Dickinson *(1855)*

Poems are funny animals. Ask 10 people to interpret Dickinson's words and you'll likely end up with 10 thoughts.

Perhaps one way to understand this in the literal sense is to first acknowledge that bees make honey as a way store food for when there are no flowers.

Factor that and the entrepreneurial lesson might be: have a plan for where you want to go, but let go and focus on today's joy. A clover any time is joy.

Challenge Question

What act would bring you joy today?

_____

_____

June 17

Something Regained

I, who cannot stay in my chamber for a single day without acquiring some rust, and when sometimes I have stolen forth for a walk at the eleventh hour of four o'clock in the afternoon, too late to redeem the day, when the shades of night were already beginning to be mingled with the daylight, have felt as if I had committed some sin to be atoned for,—I confess that I am astonished at the power of endurance, to say nothing of the moral insensibility, of my neighbors who confine themselves to shops and offices the whole day for weeks and months, ay, and years almost together.
Henry David Thoreau—"Walking" (1862)

How long will it take you to accomplish your most important (not most pressing) task today?

What if you were to give everything you had to that one task and then go for a very, very long walk? What do you suppose would happen? Would something cease, or would something be regained?

How much time do we spend today and every day doing things that only seem like they are important?

Challenge Question

What is your most *important* task today? Why does it matter?

_____

_____

June 18

Firsthand Experience

Have you reckon'd a thousand acres much? have you reckon'd the earth much? / Have you practis'd so long to learn to read? / Have you felt so proud to get at the meaning of poems? / Stop this day and night with me and you shall possess the origin of / all poems, / You shall possess the good of the earth and sun, (there are millions / of suns left,) / You shall no longer take things at second or third hand, nor look through / the eyes of the dead, nor feed on the spectres in books, / You shall not look through my eyes either, nor take things from me, / You shall listen to all sides and filter them from yourself.

Walt Whitman—Leaves of Grass *(1855)*

Success is gained through firsthand experiences and through self-examination in the midst of those experiences rather than following someone else's doctrine of their experience. Few ideas are more prevalent in the body of transcendentalist literature.

Whitman urges us not to take things at second or third hand but to "possess the origin of all poems" and the "good of the earth and sun" by experiencing them and considering them for ourselves.

Does this mean you must immediately go purchase *The Giant Book of Poems* and consume all 662 pages? No, probably not.

It may suggest you try something new today. Something you think you know about, but have never tried. Maybe it's yoga; maybe it's reading a poem.

Here's why this is important. To pursue self-reliance, you need to be good at not being good at things. You need to have total beginner mind to go with your total beginner skills so that you can feel what it's like to have an experience of something firsthand.

This is habit forming, and it's an amazing way to go through life—experience by experience.

Today, choose something you don't know anything about and experience it without someone else's handbook to guide you.

Challenge Question

If you could try anything new, what would it be?

_____

_____

June 19

Intellectual Consciousness

We welcome everything that tends to strengthen the fibre and develop the nature on more sides. When the intellect and affections are in harmony; when intellectual consciousness is calm and deep; inspiration will not be confounded with fancy.
Margaret Fuller—Woman in the Nineteenth Century *(1845)*

Intellectual consciousness is a fancy way of describing awareness. When our awareness is calm and deep . . . what happens then?

This may be Fuller's way of illustrating a mind-body connection. We have a conscious thought and it creates a feeling—perhaps inspiration. Or we see something we perceive as bad or negative for us and we feel frustrated. The only thing that changed in the world in either case was our thinking.

So, consciousness creates our reality, good or bad at some level.

When someone frustrates us, we react without much thought from the fight or flight mode, which pretty much doesn't have a deep and calm setting (and there is a physical sensation to go along with it).

Later we might think of how we could have handled the situation better. But how do you stay in that lovely deep and calm place long enough to tap the wisdom to resolve a situation in a manner that you control?

Everyone is different, so there's no easy answer. But if we start with the idea that we are all connected in some strange universal soup, then your inner self will attempt to resolve things in a way that works for everyone.

That may sound like a fairy tale come go time, but you are an inspired being so you'll figure it out.

Challenge Question

What's a pet peeve that always irritates you?

_____

_____

Discovering: Security

June 20

A Slow Walk

We should go forth on the shortest walk, perchance, in the spirit of undying adventure, never to return,—prepared to send back our embalmed hearts only as relics to our desolate kingdoms. If you are ready to leave father and mother, and brother and sister, and wife and child and friends, and never see them again,—if you have paid your debts, and made your will, and settled all your affairs, and are a free man, then you are ready for a walk.

Henry David Thoreau—"Walking" (1862)

You read a book like Tim Ferriss's *4-Hour Workweek* and become convinced that you can have it all.

But then you look up, realize that you needed the four-kid workweek or the four-bedroom house with a mortgage workweek version, and that maybe having an entrepreneurial dream isn't in the cards for you.

But is that simply a lie you're telling yourself because it's easier than actually following your heart?

No, you can't simply drop everything. That's a given.

This is certainly not a call to ditch your responsibilities and be you. Dreams take plans, dreams require flexibility, waiting, taking turns, starting small, prioritizing, being okay with where you are right now—but maybe your current employer or spouse is more supportive of the idea of you chasing a dream than you're allowing for.

So, maybe you're ready for the first tiny steps on a walk.

Challenge Question

What might you be blaming for not following your dream?

_____

_____

June 21

Exceeding Peace

Transfused through you, O mountain friends! / With mine your solemn spirit blends, / And life no more hath separate ends. // I read each misty mountain sign, / I know the voice of wave and pine, / And I am yours, and ye are mine. // Life's burdens fall, its discords cease, / I lapse into the glad release / Of Nature's own exceeding peace.
John Greenleaf Whittier—"Summer by the Lakeside," The Works of John Greenleaf Whittier, Vol. II *(1888)*

Today's reading, a poem by John Greenleaf Whittier, could be taken as an ode to nature, and a reading of the full text would reveal this to be true. The chosen passage for today's reading, however, speaks also of themes of kinship and relationship.

The premise of self-reliance at times gets treated as a call to go it fully alone. Search the term and you'll likely encounter a website or two telling you how to build your own home, make your own clothes, or render lard from pig fat.

All useful skills to be sure, but self-reliance is far more than that. Often the surest path to it is one that intersects with those who support and encourage your habit of self-examination.

These don't have to be people who agree with you or validate your every decision; in fact, they may prove more useful if they can call you out and push you toward the truth. Finding and spending time questioning others who, like you, wish to chart their own course may provide a potential shortcut to further self-discovery and "Nature's own exceeding peace."

If these friends be mountain friends, all the better.

Challenge Question

What would it take to create your own self-reliance community of rebels?

June 22

New Light

Science and art may invent splendid modes of illuminating the apartments of the opulent; but these are all poor and worthless compared with the common light which the sun sends into all our windows, which it pours freely, impartially over hill and valley, which kindles daily the eastern and western sky; and so the common lights of reason, and conscience, and love, are of more worth and dignity than the rare endowments which give celebrity to a few.

William Ellery Channing—Self Culture *(1897)*

There are many parts to every entrepreneur, and shining the common light that the sun sends into all of those windows is how you stay true to your values.

There are no business values, home values, relationship values, parenting values—only your common lights of reason, and conscience, and love.

Freely shine a very bright light of every part of that which is in your soul, and you'll show the world the complete brand that is you.

Today use this quote from John O'Donohue's wonderful *Anam Cara* as a central theme:

If you look at flowers early on a spring morning, they are all closed. When the light of the sun catches them, they trustingly open out and give themselves to the new light.

Challenge Question

What new part of yourself can you shine a light on today?

_____

_____

June 23

That Which Is Near

O thou sculptor, painter, poet! / Take this lesson to thy heart: / That is best
which lieth nearest; / Shape from that thy work of art.
Henry Wadsworth Longfellow—*"Gaspar Becerra,"* The Complete
Poetical Works of Henry Wadsworth Longfellow *(1845)*

One of the most compelling aspects of folk art is that the works are often made
from very common materials, many of which are on hand and reclaimed from
some former use.

The artist may not even consider themselves an artist or that they are
making art. They simply chose to fashion something out of what was near.

Consider this quote from folk art dealer Amelia Jeffers:

As society places a bigger emphasis and acceptance on individuality, folk art
should remain an appealing niche of the art and antiques market. It exem-
plifies characteristics like anti-establishment, creativity, and an autonomous
spirit.

Well, that sounds a bit like a tidy characterization of self-reliance, doesn't
it?

You are not a folk artist (unless you are), but there's an intriguing lesson
in the idea of bringing your "art" to life from a simple, humble, near idea
that only you can craft into something grand. Put like that, it sounds a lot
more exciting than visiting an art museum so that you can stare longingly at
someone's sculpture fashioned from the rarest of exotic wood. Don't suppose
one day that you will create your art; do it now.

Challenge Question

Are you an artist? Who says?

_____

_____

June 24

Love the Shade

Our friend has likened thee to the sweet fern, / Which with no flower salutes the ardent day, / Yet, as the wanderer pursues his way,/ While the dews fall, and hues of sunset burn, / Sheds forth a fragrance from the deep green brake, / Sweeter than the rich scents that gardens make. / Like thee, the fern loves well the hallowed shade / Of trees that quietly aspire on high; / Amid such groves was consecration made / Of vestals, tranquil as the vestal sky.
Margaret Fuller—Life Without and Life Within *(1859)*

An entrepreneur's show of extreme confidence, that thing that draws people and opportunities, is quite often a mask of deep-seated insecurity.

The greater the show of confidence, confidence that bleeds over into the realm of cockiness, the more disguised the feeling of lacking.

A telltale manifestation of this trait is the need to compete—incessantly about everything—with your team, with your loved ones, with your actual competitors.

No judgment if you're feeling uneasy reading this. Simply observe that this might be going on and look for ways to take note.

Insecurity will wreck what you expect out of life and control your beliefs and behavior in ways that will make joy in each and every day elusive.

Today, look for ways to love the well-hallowed shade. Look for ways to learn about the needs of others, to help others quietly aspire, to not compete.

Challenge Question

How do you feel physically when you get the urge to compete? Make note.

_____

_____

June 25

The Bended Tree

Power is in nature the essential measure of right. Nature suffers nothing to remain in her kingdoms which cannot help itself. The genesis and matura- tion of a planet, its poise and orbit, the bended tree recovering itself from the strong wind, the vital resources of every animal and vegetable, are demon- strations of the self-sufficing, and therefore self-relying soul.

Ralph Waldo Emerson—Self-Reliance *(1841)*

The self-reliant entrepreneur marries adaptability with self-belief to find solutions to problems and recover from setbacks.

Adaptability suggests the ability to change as needed, and it comes from a place of survival that's rooted in your need to do your own thing. What that thing is might not matter as much as the freedom to do it.

Many people are adaptable, but you are the bended tree that can recover itself from the strong wind, and that's what drives you to take on and figure out how to do things that are hard. That's what eventually allows you to string a bunch of hard-fought wins into something that looks like it's going to work after all.

Today, take stock in how you react to any situation that doesn't go as you expected.

Challenge Question

How adaptable are you? How do you know?

_____

_____

Discovering: Security

June 26

Master Your Craft

*The aim of the laborer should be, not to get their living, to get "a good job,"
but to perform well a certain work; and, even in a pecuniary sense, it would
be economy for a town to pay its laborers so well that they would not feel
that they were working for low ends, as for a livelihood merely, but for scientific, or even moral ends. Do not hire a person who does your work for
money, but one who does it for a love of it.*

Henry David Thoreau—*"Life Without Principle" (1854)*

Have you ever watched someone doing a job many would label as menial
and yet their posture and attitude belies this label? They look happy even,
and when asked will tell you how satisfying doing this simple job is.

Can you say that about your work? Maybe yes, often no. So, where does
that aura of contentment come from?

Do what you love and you'll never work another day in . . . don't worry,
we're not going there.

Perform well a certain work and you'll probably like doing it—that's the
start. But, continue to get better and you'll come to respect it as a craft, and
in that sense, it may ultimately bring you joy.

Mastery is the goal—look for it in others, teach it, practice it.

Challenge Question

What's the weakest part of your craft? What is it costing you?

_____

_____

June 27

Much Madness

Much madness is divinest sense / To a discerning eye; / Much sense the starkest madness. / 'Tis the majority/ In this, as all, prevails. / Assent, and you are sane; / Demur,—you're straightway dangerous, / And handled with a chain.
    Emily Dickinson—"Life," The Collected Poems of Emily Dickinson
                                                                    (1855)

Do you ever have those moments when you feel as though you're the only one who gets it?

Kind of like mainstream thinking just doesn't work for you?

Of course, you've probably kept your mouth shut. Or maybe you've been labeled as dangerous.

"Assent, and you are sane"—give in to mainstream and you'll be seen as sane. How's that for an entrepreneurial admonition?

The good news is, this simply means you're an entrepreneur. Your purpose is to rock the status quo—or else what's the point?

That can look a bit meandering and pointless at times to those who witness your madness, but changing your mind is how you change the world.

Challenge Question

When did you last change your mind for the good? And what did you learn?

_____

_____

June 28

In Your Power

In entering upon the great work before us, we anticipate no small amount of misconception, misrepresentation, and ridicule; but we shall use every instrumentality within our power to affect our object.
Elizabeth Cady Stanton—Declaration of Sentiments of the Seneca Falls Woman's Rights Convention *(1848)*

It is entirely possible that your entrepreneurial journey will make, or perhaps has already made, your life more difficult.

Generally, people fear change, and change is often the very thing that entrepreneurs seek most. For this reason, you must never give up, and you must refuse to compromise, even when it seems most natural to do either.

Let your desire to profoundly affect what you wish to see changed be your private form of rebellion, and draw consistency and stamina from that.

This is where your greatest power resides, and it is the safest place for you to dwell today.

Challenge Question

How could you acknowledge your personal power today?

_____

_____

June 29

Riding Flow

Place yourself in the middle of the stream of power and wisdom which flows into you as life, place yourself in the full center of that flood, then you are without effort impelled to truth, to right, and a perfect contentment
Ralph Waldo Emerson—"Spiritual Laws" (1841)

Do you recall, perhaps as a child, throwing sticks into a rushing river only to watch it go about its chosen path by riding the current to the path of least resistance? You could say it was this stick's destiny to flow in this fashion.

A natural element of flow is involved in the description of this idle amusement that applies not to the state of peaceful resignation but to the power in finding your truth. Your calling.

Emerson goes on to say further that if you place yourself in this stream "then you are the world. The measure of right, of truth, of beauty."

Fight the flow in your stream or you'll struggle. Sometimes you've got to struggle in order to place yourself back in the middle of your stream of power and wisdom.

Challenge Question

What's one area of your journey you struggle with? Why do you think that is?

_____

_____

June 30

Childlike Confidence

Trust thyself: every heart vibrates to that iron string. Accept the place the divine providence has found for you, the society of your contemporaries, the connection of events.

Ralph Waldo Emerson—Self-Reliance *(1841)*

Do you believe in your work?

Childlike belief—as though there's not a doubt that this is what you should be doing, not a care about what others are saying, and barely a notice of what others are doing. Remember when you could act that way?

Emerson acknowledged that we all possess this ability even if somewhere along the way we dismissed it:

Great men have always done so, and confided themselves childlike to the genius of their age, betraying their perception that the absolutely trustworthy was seated at their heart, working through their hands, predominating in all their being.

Today, even if just for a moment, think as you did as a child—would that child keep doing what you're doing? If not, well? If yes, then release the brakes and go for it.

Challenge Question

What is one thing you can rekindle with childlike confidence?

_____

_____

Discovering: Security

July

Emily Dickinson (1830–1886)

Forever is composed of nows.

— *Emily Dickinson*

Source: Wikimedia

The second of three children, Emily Dickinson was born in 1830 in Amherst, Massachusetts, to an established family. Her grandfather was a principal founder of Amherst College, and her father was a lawyer and, later, a state representative and senator.

As a young girl, she attended Amherst Academy, where she first became interested in both science and poetry. Upon graduation, she enrolled in the Mount Holyoke Female Seminary and attended for just one year before returning home.

Dickinson spent the rest of her life in Amherst, and though she had close relationships with her family and a handful of friends, she was known to be reclusive, particularly later in life.

Although she did not often venture from her home, she was a prolific writer. She sent countless letters, which often contained poems. She died at home in 1886.

During her lifetime, she was not well known. In fact, only 10 of her poems were published while she was alive. Upon her death, her family discovered 40 handbound books—today known as fascicles—which she'd assembled between the years 1858 and 1864. The books contained over 1,800 poems.

It was Mabel Loomis Todd, the mistress of Dickinson's older brother, who oversaw the posthumous publishing of her works. In the process, Dickinson's fascicles were disassembled and her punctuation was altered.

Although the initial edition was not faithful to Dickinson's original handwritten works, the collection was wildly popular. There were 10 subsequent editions published in less than two years. It was not until nearly a century later, in 1981, that Ralph W. Franklin undertook the process of reassembling the fascicles and publishing her poems as originally intended.

July 1

Meet Your Life

However mean your life is, meet it and live it; do not shun it and call it hard names. It is not so bad as you are. It looks poorest when you are richest. The fault-finder will find faults even in paradise. Love your life, poor as it is. You may perhaps have some pleasant, thrilling, glorious hours, even in a poorhouse. The setting sun is reflected from the windows of the almshouse as brightly as from the rich person's abode; the snow melts before its door as early in the spring. I do not see but a quiet mind may live as contentedly there, and have as cheering thoughts, as in a palace.

Henry David Thoreau—Walden *(1854)*

As you pursue your poetry, your art, you will be misunderstood by many, perhaps most.

The trick is to see your vision both as absolute truth for you and realize that there are no absolute truths. People all around you will see the world, not as it is but as they choose to see it.

This harsh reality applies equally to you. You get to choose how you see the world, you get to decide how remarkable your life has become, you get to determine how brightly the sun is reflected in your current setting.

All life is subjective.

Today, release the grip of absolute truths and simply meet your life and live it.

Challenge Question

When did you last find fault with something? How did it serve you?

_____

_____

Evolving: Failure

July 2

Not a Climb

Fame is a fickle food / Upon a shifting plate, / Whose table once a / Guest, but not / The second time, is set. / Whose crumbs the crows inspect, / And with ironic caw / Flap past it to the Farmer's corn; / Men eat of it and die.
Emily Dickinson—The Collected Poems of Emily Dickinson *(1890)*

In the climb to achieve some level of entrepreneurial fame, it's easy to fall into the trap of equating success with monetary, material, or social follower achievements.

Perhaps the real issue here is to first explore why we climb at all. If it is to achieve some accomplishment that we are certain will bring us happiness, then we may be doomed at the outset.

Happiness achieved in this manner never sticks—you never arrive at the summit, to stay with the climbing metaphor, you lurch on to one false peak after another, and along the way—you probably saw this coming—you miss the dazzling display of columbine and fireweed, the ruffling of Aspen leaves, and the young bull elk grazing in the meadow just off to your right.

Plenty of people will try to tell you how to get to the top of the mountain and why you must, but what we could all use is some advice on how to come back down. How to be grateful for the amazing things we've already achieved and the amazing people who have helped us along the way and those we have yet to meet who will do the same. (Thirty-two percent of Mount Everest and K2 [the second-highest mountain after Everest] fatalities occur during the descent.)

Happiness is a choice, not a climb.

Challenge Question

What have you already achieved that you are grateful for?

_____

_____

July 3

Measure Mindfully

Finish each day and be done with it. You have done what you could; some blunders and absurdities have crept in; forget them as soon as you can. Tomorrow is a new day; you shall begin it serenely and with too high a spirit to be encumbered with your old nonsense.

Ralph Waldo Emerson—letter to one of his daughters who was away at school, from James Elliot Cabot's Memoir of Ralph Waldo Emerson *(1883)*

You want to know how to put the past behind you? Experience something new each day.

Wake up expecting the miraculous today. And then, when some blunders and absurdities creep in, as they always do, deal with them and then move on. Why let today ruin a perfectly good tomorrow?

Find a way to put an end to your workday, something that tricks your brain into quitting. Something that draws a line in your to-do list. Perhaps it's to plan and forget tomorrow so that you can begin just as you did today: with a fresh and new experience.

Challenge Question

What does your workday-is-over routine look like?

_____

_____

July 4

After Work

The mass of humanity lead lives of quiet desperation. What is called res-ignation is confirmed desperation. From the desperate city, you go into the desperate country and have to console yourself with the bravery of minks and muskrats. A stereotyped but unconscious despair is concealed even under what are called the games and amusements of mankind. There is no play in them, for this comes after work. But it is a characteristic of wisdom not to do desperate things.

Henry David Thoreau—Walden *(1854)*

Few people, truly believe they are living anything as dramatic as some version of "quiet desperation."

No, today's version of this reading might substitute the words "quiet boredom" or "quiet reservation."

The tough thing about this idea is that you might be paying the bills, keeping your house in order, and smiling with the ones you love, but you might also be numb to the pain you're experiencing somewhere deep and hidden.

Our quiet desperation reveals itself in our incessant need to find some-thing that distracts us from the despair of boredom.

So how did we create all this boredom in a world brimming with possi-bility?

Is it possible you've achieved a level of comfort that somehow looks like the false mountaintop and you're reluctant to give up any ground?

Is it possible you've determined that this is pretty much as far as your talent, luck, and brains can take you?

Is it possible you've created a protective shield of bubble wrap around your mounting self-doubt?

Today, acknowledge quiet desperation by giving ground, by going home by another way, by looking in the mirror and asking yourself if you're settling.

Today, the desperate thing might be the truest thing of all.

Challenge Question

What's something you've "settled" for?

_____

_____

July 5

Seize Risk

For, so inconsistent is human nature, especially in the ideal, that not to undertake a thing at all seems better than to undertake and come short.
Harriet Beecher Stowe—Uncle Tom's Cabin *(1852)*

The entrepreneur is often seen as the ultimate risk taker—but only when the notion of risk is sorely misapplied. Careless, reckless, uncontrollable risk might be more closely aligned with seemingly steady employment.

Many entrepreneurs don't risk enough.

Risk stimulates your growth toward perfection. Not perfection in the sense of some sort of completeness, but the perfection that's aligned with living the life you were meant to lead, the service you were meant to render, the relief you were meant to contribute.

Stasis breeds mediocrity—your soul thrives on risk.

How are you rationalizing avoiding taking the risks you must take in order to fully realize your dream for fear of coming up short or some imagined version of failure?

Today, determine to remove your resistance to change; grab a risk, and experience taking it.

You can start very small—have a conversation you've been avoiding—have it and witness the growth bursting inside you.

Now, take that feeling and go knock down a wall.

Challenge Question

When is the last time you took a risk and failed? Did you learn or just fail?

_____

_____

July 6

Practiced Inconsistency

The other terror that scares us from self-trust is our consistency; a reverence for our past act or word because the eyes of others have no other data for computing our orbit than our past acts, and we are loath to disappoint them.

Ralph Waldo Emerson—Self-Reliance *(1841)*

A self-reliance point of view allows you to change your mind. Some might suggest it's part of the deal. Sticking steadfastly to an opinion or idea just because you always have, even if it no longer seems right to you, is the opposite of self-reliance.

If change is required for growth, as suggested by many, then occasional inconsistency is a must. Sure, if you can't be relied on to be there when needed you can erode trust, but that's different from being okay with changing your mind.

One of the reasons this idea is so hard for some to swallow is that our mind and body work against us subconsciously to retain the status quo. Neural pathways developed over time make us uncomfortable if we vary from our routines and prompt us to reach for the chips when watching TV.

Practiced inconsistency, shaking up our routines intentionally is one method to breaking up these pathways that want to keep us where we are. If you want to elevate your game, you must trust that remaining who you are, set patterns and all, might be the one thing holding you back the most.

Challenge Question

What one routine or habit you can totally shake up today? Coffee?

_____

_____

July 7

Relative Failure

But it is better to fail in originality, than to succeed in imitation. He who has never failed somewhere, that person cannot be great. Failure is the true test of greatness. And if it be said, that continual success is a proof that a person wisely knows their powers,—it is only to be added, that, in that case, they know them to be small.

Herman Melville—Hawthorne and His Mosses *(1850)*

The story goes that Sir James Dyson, of Dyson Vacuum fame, attempted 5,126 bagless vacuum prototypes that failed first. (A little more original than the overused Thomas Edison 10,000 failures example, right?)

That example sounds absurd, as does the current narrative espoused by some in entrepreneurial circles that praise failure as a badge of honor. There are even those who suggest you must fail in order to succeed.

That's a bit like suggesting you must go to the hospital in order to be sick.

What few seem to want to address—perhaps because it's kind of boring—are the endless stories of entrepreneurs who succeeded on their own terms in spite of no hard luck story.

The only real way to fail is hold back, not start, not bring your passion, not learn from what the universe tells you day to day.

You may experience failure at some point, but you don't have to go looking for it in order to find your greatness.

Challenge Question

What did you learn about yourself the last time you failed at something?

_____

_____

July 8

More Human

How life behind its accidents / Stands strong and self-sustaining, / The human fact transcending all / The losing and the gaining.
John Greenleaf Whittier—Among the Hills *(1869)*

The notion of self-transcendence, or seeking to exceed our previous achievements and extend our capacities, is very much aligned with the journey to self-reliance.

Self-reliance is ultimately obtained (ironically) not by being obsessed with the self, but by being more selfless. It is the ultimate manifestation of the principle that in order to receive it is better to give.

Viktor Frankl, author of *Man's Search for Meaning*, suggested this:

The more one forgets himself—by giving himself to a cause to serve or another person to love—the more human he is and the more he actualizes himself. Self-actualization is possible only as a side-effect of self-transcendence.

How could you be more human today?

Challenge Question

What area of your life would you wish to be so much fuller?

_____

_____

July 9

Learn to Struggle

If I wished to see a mountain or other scenery under the most favorable auspices, I would go to it in foul weather, so as to be there when it cleared up; we are then in the most suitable mood, and nature is most fresh and inspiring. There is no serenity so fair as that which is just established in a tearful eye.

Henry David Thoreau—The Maine Woods *(1864)*

There's a lyric in Bob Dylan's "Brownsville Girl" that adds color to this idea: "Strange how people who suffer together have stronger connections than people who are most content."

This isn't an invitation to struggle, but you're going to. Suffer and learn how to become stronger from it. Then when the storms move away, take in the petrichor—the smell in the air around the time when rain falls on dry, stony ground (the word is derived from the Greek *petra*, meaning stone, and ichor, which is the divine fluid, the blood of the gods).

Sounds kind of fun when you look at it that way.

Challenge Question

Who do you want to be right now?

_____

_____

Evolving: Failure

July 10

Perceived Strength

Our strength grows out of our weakness. The indignation which arms itself with secret forces does not awaken until we are pricked and stung and sorely assailed. A great person is always willing to be little. When they are pushed, tormented, defeated, they have a chance to learn something.
Ralph Waldo Emerson—"Compensation," Essays: First Series *(1841)*

There is so much that is counterintuitive to this practice of self-reliance.

How can there be strength in our weakness? To acknowledge this, you must believe that it applies to our ability to accept only what some might perceive to be a weakness as our greatest strength.

Because perceived weakness is a societal fabrication and little more.

You may possess amazing writing skills and a complete lack of accounting skills. You should master your writing (strength) and have the good sense to admit someone with different gifts than you should do your accounting (weakness).

Admitting this is a strength, but so too is your ability to listen intently, admit that you don't have an answer to something, ask for help, lead by learning, take calculated risks, and thank those who make your journey possible. All things some might see as signs of weakness.

Let the "*indignation which arms itself with secret forces*" awaken in your inner strength.

This is, by far, the greatest power of self-reliance.

Challenge Question

What is your greatest weakness? Is it?

_____

_____

July 11

Battles Lost

With music strong I come, with my cornets and my drums, / I play not marches for accepted victors only, I play marches for / conquered and slain persons. / / Have you heard that it was good to gain the day? / I also say it is good to fall, battles are lost in the same spirit / in which they are won.
                    Walt Whitman—Leaves of Grass *(1855)*

History will always label some as victors and some as losers; that's just the score-keeping system whether we're speaking of politicians, athletes, or, yes, entrepreneurs.

Your story likely has a long way to go before being measured as such, but you will encounter many on your way up or down engaged in the same heroic struggle as you. Comparing your success, your victories, or your failures serves no one.

Whitman provides a tender embrace to the defeated because the difference between what someone calls success or failure may hinge on the slightest whims of good fortune and fate.

Fully accept and embrace where you are now. Mind your own biscuits* and make decisions that will move you in the direction you want to go. (*Credit: Kacey Musgraves)

Challenge Question

From whose success can you draw inspiration?

_____

_____

July 12

No Expectations

All who strive to live for something beyond mere selfish aims find their capacities for doing good very inadequate to their aspirations. They do so much less than they want to do, and so much less than they, at the outset, expected to do, that their lives, viewed retrospectively, inevitably look like failure.

Lydia Maria Child—Letters of Lydia Maria Chile *(1882)*

One of the more habitual practices of entrepreneurs is self-denigration.

We are either not saving the world hard enough or we are leaving too much on the table by not realizing the full potential of our market.

This constant pressure to do everything eats away at our ability to do anything. And then one day we look back and our lives, *"viewed retrospectively, inevitably look like failure."*

How we filter anything is through the lens of our expectations. What do you expect to accomplish on your entrepreneurial journey?

In so many ways, it is this future expectation that robs us from adding up what we've done to date to equal success. Expectations, how things are going to go, are our greatest source of stress, because if our slated path is not as planned we immediately experience failure.

What if you could let go of expectations and simply do what your heart says to do today? Yes, it might mean changing your perspective and focusing on what you truly intend to accomplish and not so much on how it gets accomplished.

Think about all the little, meaningless tasks that you think must be done a certain way. How much energy does that burn?

When we hold rigidly to our expected path, we fall into the realm of trying to control things we can't and we close the door to the fact that there are infinite and perhaps even better ways to get what we want.

Today, let go and see how much easier almost everything is.

Challenge Question

What are you holding onto that you need to let go of?

_____

_____

July 13

Not Very Busy

They make a great ado nowadays about hard times; but I think that the community generally take a wrong view of the matter. This general failure, both private and public, is rather occasion for rejoicing, as reminding us whom we have at the helm,—that justice is always done. If our merchants did not most of them fail, and the banks too, my faith in the old laws of the world would be staggered . . . It is not enough to be industrious; so are the ants. What are you industrious about?

Henry David Thoreau—Familiar Letters *(1865)*

British scholar C. Northcote Parkinson coined the phrase, "Work expands to fill the time available for its completion." The proverb is so accurate it became known as Parkinson's law.

Busy? What are you busy about?

Here's the problem with busy in the words of the Roman philosopher Seneca:

No one pursuit can be successfully followed by a man who is preoccupied with many things . . . since the mind, when distracted, takes in nothing very deeply, but rejects everything that is, as it were, crammed into it. There is nothing the busy man is less busied with than living: there is nothing that is harder to learn.

Our constant multitasking makes it impossible to have a deep, meaningful relationship with anything, including ourselves.

Busy is a habit, that's all it is. Your job is to break it and take back what means the most to you. Your job is to figure out what's meaningful in each day, and it's probably not scanning Facebook. Then, of course, your job is to stop doing about 80 percent of your busy work. (Get your email batched a couple of times a day; check out adios.ai.)

So, today, if someone asks how you are, tell them, "Not very busy."

Challenge Question

What does downtime look like for you?

_____

_____

Evolving: Failure

July 14

Failing Judgment

Filled is Life's goblet to the brim; / And though my eyes with tears are dim, / I see its sparkling bubbles swim, / And chant a melancholy hymn / With solemn voice and slow. // . . . And he who has not learned to know / How false its sparkling bubbles show, / How bitter are the drops of woe, / With which its brim may overflow, / He has not learned to live.

Henry Wadsworth Longfellow—"The Goblet of Life," The Complete Poetical Works of Henry Wadsworth Longfellow *(1845)*

Perhaps today's reading could be summed briefly as this: we all have our part to play and we will experience our share of both joy and sorrow.

Accepting things as they are without judgment is one of life's greatest challenges. If you were to assess the one characteristic that the happiest people in the world share, it might be this:

> Be content with what you have; rejoice in the way things are. When you realize there is nothing lacking, the whole world belongs to you.
>
> *Lao Tzu*

Challenge Question

When's the last time you placed yourself squarely in someone else's shoes?

_____

_____

July 15

Entrepreneurial Guilt

The bird may burst the silken chain which bound him, / Flying to the green home, which fits him best; / But, O, he bears the prisoner's badge around him, / Still by the piece about his neck distressed. / He ne'er can breathe his free, wild notes again; / They're stifled by the pressure of his chain.
Margaret Fuller—Life Without and Life Within *(1859)*

Guilt, living in the past, dreading the unknown of the future—these are entrepreneurial chains that can stifle your wild notes.

Guilt? What guilt?

You're not spending enough time working on your business. You're spending too much time. You're neglecting your family. You're not contributing enough to the finances. And then of course, if you're a parent of young children—what were you thinking?

Life is full of choices. The key is to make choices that feed your soul. If you're wondering what the heck that means to you, it's probably your downtime choices.

Taking downtime and taking it seriously, without guilt or judgment, is how you recharge to be sure, but it's also how you start releasing the chains of guilt. It's how you build the muscle memory required to work when you work and play when you play.

Today, it's time to train your brain to let go of your entrepreneurial guilt.

Challenge Question

What would you like to spend more time doing?

_____

_____

Evolving: Failure

July 16
Hope Guides

For a little while, hope made a show of reviving—not with any reason to back it, but only because it is its nature to revive when the spring has not been taken out of it by age and familiarity with failure.
Mark Twain—The Adventures of Tom Sawyer *(1876)*

Today's passage occurs inside the familiar plot line that finds Tom Sawyer and Becky Thatcher lost in MacDougal's Cave.

The scene was analyzed by some as a symbol of self-reliance creeping into the literature of the time. Previous works may have used the character's peril as a way to provide a lesson on God's punishment, salvation, or even prayer.

Twain chose to have Tom keep his wits and rely on adult behavior, hope, and self-trust to save himself and Becky. (Sure, the male character saved the damsel in distress when he could have just asked for directions before they got lost, but that's another story.)

The cave and darkness and even scant use of candles to light the dark are pretty easy metaphors for the entrepreneur's life of sporadic peril.

But hope, mercifully, has a habit of reviving, and without that, eventually our failed attempts and losses would accumulate to the point of miserable.

Hope is not a strategy, but hope creates strategy, hope moves you in the direction of your goals, hope burns like a candle in the pitch black. Even with very little to back it, hope guides.

Hope keeps sight of the next objective.

Challenge Question

When is the last time you relied on hope when you felt like giving up? Did it serve?

_____

_____

July 17

Exceptional Trust

We learn of our contemporaries what they know, without effort, and almost through the pores of the skin ... But we stop where they stop. Very hardly can we take another step. The great, or such as hold of nature, and transcend fashions, by their fidelity to universal ideas, are saviors from these federal errors, and defend us from our contemporaries. They are the exceptions which we want, where all grows alike.

Ralph Waldo Emerson—Uses of Great Men *(1849)*

Do our friends hold us back? Maybe, at times. Sometimes unknowingly and sometimes out of fear, they cling tightly and push aside any thought that might cast them as being left behind by us. And of course, our family members are our first and most ferocious contemporaries.

In your journey toward self-reliance, you will not leave anyone or anything behind, you will not adopt narcissistic pursuits, you will develop ruthless self-trust. You will come to believe that you and, likely you alone, know what's best for you.

If those around you have not developed or even considered trusting themselves at this level, you will experience their doubt and fear as part of your journey. Don't stop where they stop.

You can experience their support and love as well, but if someone wants only what's best for you they won't hold you back; they will push you, lift you up, trust you. Sure, they'll also tell you when you have food in your teeth and when they see you self-destructing, but often they'll bring you new and even bigger ideas. They'll stretch your capacity, and they'll listen—especially when the chips are down. They'll mentor you but won't tell you what to do. Oh, and you'll trust them.

If this is not what you have, this is what you need to find. This is what will defend you from your contemporaries. How will you know them? You will know them by *"their fidelity to universal ideas."*

Challenge Question

Who do you need in your life right now? Name them.

_____

_____

July 18

Time with Yourself

We are made happy when reason can discover no occasion for it. The memory of some past moments is more persuasive than the experience of present ones. There have been visions of such breadth and brightness that these motes (particles of dust) were invisible in their light.

Henry David Thoreau—Familiar Letters *(1865)*

What are you capable of being? How can you live well today? How can you grow and cultivate the soul? How can you experience more present moments?

One of the many spiritual practices promoted by the transcendentalists was solitude. Some drew their inspiration for such from the Stoics and the eastern religious traditions of China and India.

Thoreau was the poster child for solitude, as that was the state in which he wrote most of *Walden*. So, are you ready to hit that cabin for a couple years to figure this all out?

As nice (or scary) as it might sound, retreating is likely not an option for you. But seeking solitude in small sips is a practice that will strengthen your self-reliance.

Spending time with yourself alone is where you'll find your life.

Alone means alone; when you read a book or listen to music, you are in conversation with the author or artist. Meditate, journal with pen and paper, sit in your car in the garage for five minutes, end your workday in silence, take an entire day once a month or an entire weekend once a quarter and practice solitude.

In *Walden*, Thoreau came to describe his solitude in soulful terms:

Sympathy with the fluttering alder and poplar leaves almost takes away my breath; yet, like the lake, my serenity is rippled but not ruffled. These small waves raised by the evening wind are as remote from storm as the smooth reflecting surface.

Challenge Question

How will you start your solitude practice?

_____

_____

July 19

Our Beautiful Art

We must know, as much as possible, in our beautiful art, yours and mine,
what we are talking about—and the only way to know is to have lived and
loved and cursed and floundered and enjoyed and suffered.
Henry James—Portrait of a Lady (1881)

To be fair, Henry James probably doesn't belong in this book. He was a brilliant writer, one of the best ever, but he was a newborn when Emerson penned *Self-Reliance*. (He was also decidedly transatlantic.)

Perhaps you were asked to read *The Portrait of a Lady* or *The Turn of the Screw* in high school or college. If so, then maybe you recall how layered and complex James's characters are. He spent more time inside the minds of his characters than on the external trappings of the day.

And that's where entrepreneurs must live as well. To gain the experience of being *"loved and cursed and floundered and enjoyed and suffered."* Not to simply live through it, but to witness it, be a part of it, and learn from it.

This is where we gain humility and strength, and this is what turns us more deeply inward to where we discover we can endure so much more than we believe we are capable of. Because this is the place where we realize just how good our life is.

Challenge Question

What suffering in your life can you make peace with today?

_____

_____

Evolving: Failure

July 20

Your Best Work

All I can say is, that it is an honest book, a sincere book, and contains my best thoughts on the subjects treated. If well received, I shall be grateful; if neglected, I shall endeavor to practise resignation, as I have so often done.
Orestes Brownson—The American Republic *(1865)*

Can you say this about your work? That it's honest and sincere and that it contains your best thoughts?

That's all we have to do, and then we have to release it and sleep well. Brownson was referring to his written works, but it's no stretch to see yourself adopting this point of view. But if your first attempt is not well received, you're not allowed to "*practise resignation.*" In fact, resignation can go pound sand.

So, why include this reading?

Maybe we need an occasional reminder that there will be times when you think you've done your best, but the world greets it a collective who cares. That's not the time to sulk, to mutter under your breath. No, that's the time to get up and figure it out. Run around the block screaming if you like, but then come look at your challenge with a fresh point of view.

Do that, and then like Thoreau you can exclaim:

I did not wish to live what was not life, living is so dear; nor did I wish to practise resignation, unless it was quite necessary. I wanted to live deep and suck out all the marrow of life, to live so sturdily and Spartan-like as to put to rout all that was not life . . .

Today, you get to make resignation quite unnecessary. (Unless, of course, it is a resignation from a job you hate—then do it!)

Challenge Question

In what areas of your life are you not applying the best of you?

_____

_____

July 21

Slow and Sure

There are very few individuals, let them be doing ever so well in the world, who are not always straining every nerve to do better; and this is one of the many causes why failures in business so frequently occur among us. The present generation seem unwilling to "realize" by slow and sure degrees; but choose rather to set their whole hopes upon a single cast, which either makes or mars them forever!

George Pope Morris—The Little Frenchman and His Water Lots *(1839)*

It's pretty amazing that this was written in 1839. Close your eyes and this could have been written yesterday.

The condition is real—straining every nerve to do better is still today one of the reasons businesses fail, or at least fail to bring joy.

Slow and sure degrees, each and every day—that's what builds success.

Challenge Question

Where could you slow down and go deeper?

_____

_____

July 22

Exert Your Talent

Suppose that a writer who has reached and passed the natural limit of serviceable years feels that they have some things which they would like to say, and which may have an interest for a limited class of readers,—are they not right in trying their powers and calmly taking the risk of failure? Does it not seem rather lazy and cowardly, because they cannot "beat their record," or even come up to the level of what they had done in their prime, to shrink from exerting their talent, such as it is, now that they has outlived the period of their greatest vigor?

Oliver Wendell Holmes, Sr.—Over the Teacups *(1872)*

It would be easy to assume that Holmes is simply making a case for an aging entrepreneur to keep contributing, but one can outlive *"the period of their greatest vigor"* in their still young mind as well.

Many entrepreneurs, after experiencing a moment of success or a window of fame faded, find it harder to carry on or reboot than before they had tasted anything like success.

Once you've had money, it's harder to be poor until you realize how much happier you were before you felt entitled to something. That's the problem with success; it can leave you feeling like you deserve more.

And when it doesn't come, you can either curse the dark or turn on another light and get out there and kick some more butt—see, this time you'll appreciate it so much more.

You've got so much to give. Doesn't matter if you're young or old, new at this or a grizzled veteran of failure, exert your talent—the world needs you.

Challenge Question

What are you going to try this time? When?

_____

_____

July 23

Show Up, Show Up, Show Up

Genius is often only the power of making continuous efforts. The line between failure and success is so fine that we scarcely know when we pass it—so fine that we are often on the line and do not know it. How many a person has thrown up their hands at a time when a little more effort, a little more patience, would have achieved success. As the tide goes clear out—so it comes clear in.

Elbert Hubbard—Electrical Review *(1895)*

In words sometimes attributed to comedian and director Woody Allen, "Eighty percent of success is showing up."

Now, showing up consistently is an awfully easy thing to suggest. Just ask any overnight success icon, and they'll tell you that's precisely what they did. The part we miss, however, is that most overnight success stories take years to write.

We don't get to see the continuous effort, the patience, the wins and losses, the point at which they finally decide, "You know, this is going to work."

If you're struggling with showing up, don't throw up your hands and discard what you've accomplished to date as a failure—look for the passion that drove you to start.

The thing it takes to get you to show up long enough to find your ultimate success is to discover and cling to that one little piece of something that you're most passionate about—the purest nugget of joy. Many times you can even restart or pivot your idea by clinging to the reason you started in the first place—that might be enough.

Entrepreneurs find that they fall in love with their business once they discover some aspect of it that brings them joy. That's your job today.

Challenge Question

What aspect of your business brings you the greatest joy?

_____

_____

Evolving: Failure

July 24

The Meaning of Happiness

Happiness in this world, when it comes, comes incidentally. Make it the object of pursuit, and it leads us a wild-goose chase, and is never attained. Follow some other object, and very possibly we may find that we have caught happiness, without dreaming of it; but likely enough it is gone the moment we say to ourselves, "Here it is!" like the chest of gold that treasure-seekers find.

Nathaniel Hawthorne—Passages from the American Notebooks, Vol. II
(1851)

As an entrepreneur, you'll find that choosing to chase happiness means that most of the time you won't be what people would call *happy*. You'll be busy pushing your life, and your family, and your health aside so that you can try to be happy.

That sounds kind of crazy when you read it, doesn't it?

What many entrepreneurs have found, is the thing that actually makes them feel happy and fulfilled isn't what some call happiness or even success; it's the feeling that what they are doing has meaning.

Without meaning or purpose in your work, happiness is reduced to pleasure seeking.

Let's revisit Viktor Frankl's *Man's Search for Meaning*:

Success, like happiness, cannot be pursued; it must ensue, and it only does so as the unintended side effect of one's personal dedication to a cause greater than oneself . . . Happiness must happen, and the same holds for success: you have to let it happen by not caring about it.

Wow, happiness happens by not caring about it. Can you live with that?

Today, dig deep and uncover, or at least come to terms with, what a meaningful life would look like for you.

Challenge Question

What cause, greater than yourself, are you dedicated to? Why?

_____

_____

July 25

The Razor's Edge

We take everything heartily and naturally in the right way,—for even mishaps are like knives, that either serve us or cut us, as we grasp them by the blade or the handle.
James Russell Lowell—Literary Essays: A Moosehead Journal *(1890)*

The metaphor of the knife or razor's edge certainly applies to the inherent risk involved in seeking to become a self-reliant entrepreneur.

The epigraph from W. Somerset Maugham novel *The Razor's Edge* contains this translation from the ancient text of the Katha Upanishads:

Rise, wake up, seek the wise and realize. The path is difficult to cross like the sharpened edge of the razor (knife), so say the wise.

That sort of sums up this journey, doesn't it? Merely accepting the reality that we must grow is hard enough, but we're also asked to choose perhaps the hardest path in order to achieve that growth. To kick fear to the curb and risk failure, or something like being cut to pieces.

Oh, and let's add this to the mix: by taking this risky path, you may arrive at a destination, but you will probably never arrive at "the" destination. And you must be okay with this.

On this trek you will need to embrace continuous learning and unlearning, acceptance and rejection, and wonder, lots of wonder, about the light and the dark and the celebration of magic that you find out there on the road.

Challenge Question

What's the goofiest thing that's happened to you on your entrepreneurial journey? Does it make you smile?

_____

_____

Evolving: Failure

July 26

Judge Not Success

They talk of short-lived pleasure—be it so— / Pain dies as quickly: stern, hard-featured pain / Expires, and lets her weary prisoner go. / The fiercest agonies have shortest reign; / And after dreams of horror, comes again / The welcome morning with its rays of peace;
William Cullen Bryant—"Mutation: A Sonnet," Poems of William Cullen Bryant *(1824)*

Pain and pleasure, agony and ecstasy, failure and success—these pairs of seeming opposites also bear striking similarities.

We judge the first of each pair as a negative experience while we claim to be seeking the second of each pair as our eventual path to happiness.

The problem with judging pretty much anything as good or bad is that it's mostly a form of self-judgment.

In her book *The Judgment Detox*, Gabrielle Bernstein defines judgment as "the separation of oneness and the truth within us." She further offers that "judgment is a signal of a wound that needs to be healed."

Ironically, our judgment of what defines success may be the very thing that hinders our journey toward it.

The first step on the path to nonjudgment is to appreciate how often we automatically judge everything in our environment as either right and wrong and, in doing so, limit our own options for success.

You don't have to judge anything; simply be open to what you feel and move on. Drop your limiting beliefs and *"welcome morning with its rays of peace."*

Challenge Question

What's one thing you frequently pass judgment on? How can you drop it?

_____

_____

July 27

Getting Unstuck

When, in the progress of a life, a person swerves, though only by an angle infinitely small, from their proper and allotted path (and this is never done quite unconsciously even at first; in fact, that was their broad and scarlet sin,—ah, they knew of it more than they can tell), then the drama of their life turns to tragedy, and makes haste to its fifth act . . . These departures,—who have not made them?—for they are as faint as the parallax of a fixed star, and at the commencement we say they are nothing,—that is, they originate in a kind of sleep and forgetfulness of the soul when it is naught.

Henry David Thoreau—Familiar Letters *(1894)*

Do you ever have a sense of "stuckness"? While feeling stuck can imply non-movement, it's equally available to the person who *"swerves, though only by an angle infinitely small, from their proper and allotted path."*

Quite often we feel stuck when we don't seem to be moving in the direction of our desires, but for the most part stuckness lives in our past. We get stuck when we stick to worn habits, patterns, and routines from our past.

Even as we realize that this past sediment doesn't serve, we cling to it rather than learn from it so as to remain firmly rooted in the present.

If you ever get frustrated with something that doesn't work, that always goes a certain way, that turned out just about like you thought it would, there's a good chance the past is powering your reality and keeping you stuck.

Close your eyes right now and take a few slow breaths. Now, slowly open your eyes and focus on the first thing that meets your eyes. That's real, that's here, that's now. Do this whenever you start to feel the past creeping up on you and then snap back to the present—the only place you can solve your problems.

Challenge Question

What's the most frustrating habit or activity that makes you feel stuck?

_____

_____

July 28

Truth Prevails

Truth, crushed to earth, shall rise again; / The eternal years of God are hers; / But Error, wounded, writhes with pain, / And dies among his worshippers.
    William Cullen Bryant—The Battle-Field—Poems of William Cullen Bryant *(1824)*

Martin Luther King Jr. quoted this passage from Bryant's poem during his time as a civil rights leader. He used the poem to compare truth to victory and error to defeat. (King often quoted Emerson, Lowell, Thoreau, and Longfellow.)

The truth always prevails—it may take a while, but it will exist.

Now the issue with this is that it's both twofold and double edged. (How's that for some metaphors?)

You must follow your truth, but the truth will always follow you.

The truth is what's in your heart, but the truth is, you'll probably have to work really, really hard to discover it.

The truth is, you instinctively know what you want, but the truth is, you'll have to be willing to admit you know nothing at times.

The truth is, many ventures fail, but the truth is, failure might be your greatest teacher.

Challenge Question

What would you regret not doing, being, or having in your life?

_____

_____

July 29

Soul Care

*No thinking being lives who, at some luminous point in their life of thought,
has not felt lost amid the surges of futile efforts at understanding, or believing, that anything exists greater than their own soul.*
                                        Edgar Allan Poe—"Eureka" (1848)

A great many of the works I've cited in this book are considered literary classics, yet many of the authors of these works also focused on
developing rich spiritual practices that are today perhaps considered
commonplace.

They encouraged journaling, meditation, walking in nature, reading,
and simple living as ways to develop the soul and forge a path to divine
living. They questioned the common religious dogma of the time and elected
to put themselves in charge of finding and caring for their soul.

Call it your soul or whatever you like—humbly discovering the dignity
of our personal nature is possibly all we were set on this earth to do.

It is this element of self-reliance that led many of these authors to champion and lead social reforms such as women's rights, the abolition of slavery,
and education reform.

Entrepreneurship is lauded as an economic driver and job creator, but
the societal contribution of entrepreneurs is often undervalued.

Entrepreneurs who make self-reliance a lifelong chase often include
social reforms as a driving force behind their ventures. This can come in
the form of an innovative way to approach an underserved population or
through an internal culture that prioritizes personal growth and diversity in
the workplace.

A self-reliant entrepreneur is a gift to society and a force for good.

Challenge Question

What is the number one way you feed your soul?

_____

_____

July 30

Step Aside

Amid the seeming confusion of our mysterious world individuals are so nicely adjusted to a system, and systems to one another and to a whole, that by stepping aside for a moment a person exposes themselves to a fearful risk of losing their place forever.

*Nathaniel Hawthorne—*Twice-Told Tales *(1837)*

Do you ever feel as though you're getting left behind? Or that if you fight through the fear and take a leap you'll never recover if you're wrong?

There is safety in safety yet rarely greatness or even much joy.

Your place is probably not where you are right now. Your job is to find that place, to break the system that wants you to stay in line even as your heart longs to step aside, even if just for a moment.

Think of your life as an experiment and, as Emerson said, *"The more experiments you make the better."*

Challenge Question

What sort of outrageous experiment could you try today?

_____

_____

July 31

Encounter with Reality

I am not afraid that I shall exaggerate the value and significance of life, but that I shall not be up to the occasion which it is. I shall be sorry to remember that I was there, but noticed nothing remarkable,—not so much as a prince in disguise; lived in the golden age a hired man; visited Olympus even, but fell asleep after dinner, and did not hear the conversation of the gods.

Henry David Thoreau—Familiar Letters *(1894)*

Be present or you'll miss your life. You'll miss your shot at being anything close to a self-reliant entrepreneur. Every self-help book and self-care blog and self-improvement podcast is telling us this.

So why are we still missing it?

You see, those external forces, work, the Internet, social media, kids, your nonstop brain aren't the problem at all. It's how your brain thinks about and processes or automates them that's the problem.

And that's the power of the present moment, those external forces of the past or even tomorrow's aren't there.

Staying present takes a ton of practice. We've spent years practicing the opposite, so that makes sense, right?

Maybe you could set up hourly alarms as a reminder to snap back into the present, create a twice daily mindfulness ritual—something as simple, yet goofy, as paying attention to every step you take on your way to the restroom.

Your automated brain—the same one that tells you to breathe without you needing to pay attention—is working against you, and you have to find ways to de-automate or tame the forces.

Of course, meditation is an amazing way to train your brain to be here in the same room with the rest of your body.

Challenge Question

What typically distracts you from being present? Technology of some sort?

_____

_____

Evolving: Failure

August

Herman Melville (1819–1891)

I know not all that may be coming, but be it what it will, I'll go to it laughing.
— *Herman Melville*

Source: Wikimedia

Born in New York, Herman Melville was one of seven children. His father was a grain trader who attempted to transition, unsuccessfully, into the fur trade business. He lost all the family's money and then died shortly thereafter, leaving a 13-year-old Melville and his siblings to enter the workforce in order to support themselves.

Melville worked a handful of odd jobs for nearly a decade before stumbling into a life at sea in 1839. He first served as a captain boy on a merchant ship and then transitioned into whaling.

These years were filled with adventure, including a crew mutiny, capture by cannibals in French Polynesia, and a jail break. When he returned home in 1844, the stories he had accumulated from his own life and from fellow sailors he met along the way became the basis for his early works.

His first story, *Typee*, met with positive reviews in both the United States and Europe, as did his next three stories, *Omoo*, *Redburn*, and *White-Jacket*.

This encouraged him to begin work on the manuscript that would become *Moby-Dick*. Unfortunately, when it was published critics and readers did not respond favorably. This was a turning point for Melville, who continued to write but never achieved critical success again in his career.

Melville grew increasingly depressed and discouraged with his literary prospects. In 1863 he moved back to New York and got a job as a customs inspector, which he held for the next 20 years of his life.

He turned his focus to poetry in his later years. But he was never recognized for his later writings in his lifetime and died in relative obscurity in 1891.

August 1

Our Individual Nature

Each season brings a world of enjoyment and interest in the watching of its unfolding, its gradual harmonious development, its culminating graces—and just as one begins to tire of it, it passes away and a radical change comes, with new witcheries and new glories in its train. And I think that to one in sympathy with nature, each season, in its turn, seems the loveliest.

Mark Twain—Roughing It *(1872)*

The unfolding of seasons aligns well with the life of the entrepreneur. Discover, evolve, blossom, regenerate—developments that occur naturally with the changing light and temperatures—mimic the eventual change that must come with entrepreneurial growth.

And that's our task—to recognize that each season, in its turn, seems the loveliest—that's the art of entrepreneurial life.

Frederic Henry Hedge argued for something he called "The Art of Life" in an 1840 edition of *The Dial*:

The work of life, so far as the individual is concerned, and that to which the scholar is particularly called, is self-culture,—the perfect unfolding of our individual nature.

To many who subscribed to this belief of "self-culture," it was the purpose of life. Impractical as it may feel to pursue today in a life full of "go get 'em," it may indeed be the secret to happiness and personal power.

There is in this life for us an infinite changing of the seasons. Take them one at a time. And know that every season will be worth living, perhaps even lovelier than the last, when every day is worth living.

Challenge Question

What is your favorite season? Why?

_____

_____

August 2

Prove Yourself Wrong

Suppose you should contradict yourself; what then? It seems to be a rule of wisdom never to rely on your memory alone, scarcely even in acts of pure memory, but to bring the past for judgment into the thousand-eyed present, and live ever in a new day.

Ralph Waldo Emerson—Self-Reliance *(1841)*

One of the better rules of self-reliance is you get to change your mind—you can even contradict yourself. Now, as Emerson suggests, this frightens some, but how silly is it to hold on to something that no longer serves?

Consistency breeds trust, but when it no longer serves, it's simply a lie. In how many areas of your life can you afford to hang on to a lie?

You don't have to stick with your big idea, you don't have to keep that client, you don't have to remain in an unprofitable business partnership.

The point of all of this is not to prove ourselves right, but to prove ourselves wrong. If today you have all the answers, how are you going to grow?

Just in case you need a little more Emerson on this topic, he goes on to say, "*A foolish consistency is the hobgoblin of little minds . . .*"

Fundamentally what Emerson is suggesting is nothing less than integrity.

Challenge Question

What's one thing you need to change your mind about?

_____

_____

August 3

It Will Require Work

Lives of great men all remind us / We can make our lives sublime, / And, departing, leave behind us / Footprints on the sands of time; / Footprints, that perhaps another, / Sailing o'er life's solemn main, / A forlorn and ship-wrecked brother, / Seeing, shall take heart again. / Let us, then, be up and doing, / With a heart for any fate; / Still achieving, still pursuing, / Learn to labor and to wait.
Henry Wadsworth Longfellow—"A Psalm of Life" (1838)

Let's start with this today: no matter what you choose to do, if you choose to get good at it, it will require work. Sorry, there's no way around it; it will require a lot of work. Some jobs are more demanding than others, but it's all pretty much uphill, particularly if you're just getting started.

Feeling pumped now?

Here's the trick if you want it to *not* feel like work: don't bother trying to figure out what you love; figure out what you have to give, how you can serve, how you can make someone's world a little better.

There's nothing terribly grand about this idea. It's actually rather practical.

Imagine what a messed-up world we would live in if everyone got to choose what they thought they would love to be. We would have way too many best-selling authors, inspirational speakers, and celebrity game show hosts, wouldn't we?

Everyone is unique, and there's probably a unique way we are supposed to use this fact to inform how we show up in the world. That's your job; figure that out and get really good at it.

You might even get famous, not by seeking fame but by becoming famously good at serving someone.

Challenge Question

What is your greatest skill? How can you use it to serve?

_____

_____

Evolving: Resilience

August 4

Suffering Strengthens

They say that "time assuages,"— / Time never did assuage; / An actual suffering strengthens, / As sinews do, with age. / / Time is a test of trouble, / But not a remedy. / If such it prove, it prove too / There was no malady.
Emily Dickinson—*"Life,"* The Collected Poems of Emily Dickinson
(1855)

The hard part about reading Emily Dickinson is that often you must find truth in what can only be seen as a large dose of bitterness. (Oh, and for the record assuage = heals.)

"That which does not kill you only makes you stronger" could be a quick way to sum up today's reading, but then she suggests that suffering in some way must strengthen if it is real.

Such a downer, right?

But what if we could see this as something more like smoldering wisdom? Something that drives us to find a way to survive and thrive without the manufactured construct of time? Perhaps our suffering is what creates our resilience, our determination, and our self-trust when properly harnessed.

When taking the Old English definition of sinews to mean "source of power," this is the money line:

An actual suffering strengthens,
As sinews do, with age.

Challenge Question

What have you gained from suffering at some point in your life?

_____

_____

August 5

The First Dozen Times

Let me suggest a theme for you: to state to yourself precisely and completely what that walk over the mountains amounted to for you,—returning to this essay again and again, until you are satisfied that all that was important in your experience is in it. Give this good reason to yourself for having gone over the mountains, for mankind is ever going over a mountain. Don't suppose that you can tell it precisely the first dozen times you try, but at 'em again, especially where, after a sufficient pause, you suspect that you are touching the heart or summit of the matter, reiterate your blows there, and account for the mountain to yourself. Not that the story need be long, but it will take a long while to make it short.

Henry David Thoreau—Familiar Letters *(1857)*

In your entrepreneurial journey there lives a progression toward "*the heart or summit of the matter.*" It may at times take the disguise of progress, contraction, or more likely a plateau, and it will involve repetition, endless repetition, to get it right.

Thoreau loved the mountains, and even in this letter to a friend he used their image to speak of the pains involved in his creative writing process.

With repetition comes muscle memory. Repetition allows us to better know ourselves, to better understand our value. With repetition comes simplicity. Repetition allows us to chisel away the parts that serve to weigh us or our ideas down.

Repetition—some might call it practice—allows us to move from that uncomfortable space where our creativity is bred to that comfortable space where our creativity is grasped.

And this is when we can share it with the world—as we continue to practice and evolve still further.

It may take you no time at all to find your story, but it will take repetition to make it short.

Challenge Question

What aspect of your art needs practice? How will you get it?

_____

_____

Evolving: Resilience

August 6

From Sitting Still

The great fact was the land itself, which seemed to overwhelm the little beginnings of human society that struggled in its sombre wastes. They felt that people were too weak to make any mark here, that the land wanted to be let alone, to preserve its own fierce strength, its peculiar, savage kind of beauty, its uninterrupted mournfulness.

Willa Cather—O Pioneers! (1913)

The theme of land runs throughout *O Pioneers!*. It's present in pretty much every chapter but not simply as a setting—more like a character, perhaps a protagonist meant at times to destroy and at times lift up.

In the same fashion that the characters in the story occupy the land, we as entrepreneurs occupy a market, an industry, a community, a little corner of a dream. In that space, and in conjunction with nature, we are meant to carve out something.

Alexandra Bergson, the superstar farmer in *O Pioneers!*, admits in the end that she succeeded by bending her will to the will of nature:

> The land did it. It had its little joke. It pretended to be poor because nobody knew how to work it right; and then, all at once, it worked itself. It woke up out of its sleep and stretched itself, and it was so big, so rich, that we suddenly found we were rich, just from sitting still.

It is our giving in to our landscape, unforgiving as it may be, moody as it may turn, that will deliver the ultimate prize. You have limited resources, energy, and, let's face it, control over what happens. Sit still more and focus on fixing problems and the market will come to you.

Challenge Question

What problem do you solve? Who would pay for that?

_____

_____

August 7

Get What You Need

Discontent is the want of self-reliance: it is infirmity of will. Regret calamities if you can thereby help the sufferer; if not, attend your own work and already the evil begins to be repaired.
                    Ralph Waldo Emerson—Self-Reliance *(1841)*

Emerson may have liked this lyric from the Rolling Stones: "You can't always get what you want, but if you try sometime you might find you get what you need."

Be content and you're on the road to self-reliance. Not complacent, but happy with right now while preparing to make a big fat dent in your space—that's content.

Go through life discontented and you'll constantly seek happiness in and from things outside of your control.

Challenge Question

How are you using your gifts to contribute to something?

_____

_____

August 8

Indestructibly Content

In a word, the whole human race [is] content, always content, persistently content, indestructibly content, happy, thankful, proud, no matter what its religion is, nor whether its master be tiger or housecat. Am I stating facts? You know I am. Is the human race cheerful? You know it is. Considering what it can stand, and be happy, you do me too much honor when you think that I can place before it a system of plain cold facts that can take the cheerfulness out of it. Nothing can do that. Everything has been tried. Without success. I beg you not to be troubled.

Mark Twain—*"What Is Man?"* (1906)

What do you first think of when you hear the word content? Sounds okay, doesn't it?

Nothing wrong with being "indestructibly content," right?

You can become content with anything—the hole in the ceiling you no longer even notice, the job that isn't so bad, the relationship that lacks anything close to its original spark.

So, yeah, nothing wrong with content—until it morphs into settling for less. Into taking a dispassionate stroll through each day. Into an unlit path on the road to disdain.

It's not your fault, though. Your time is coming. You need to think it through a little longer. Besides, playing small is kind of noble. Plus, successful people just seem greedy. And your favorite Netflix show is on tonight anyway. (A little sarcasm here might be just what Twain ordered.)

Yikes, kind of in your face today, but maybe a push is just the right thing.

It's not about wanting more; it's about being more. It's never "as good as it gets" unless you allow it to be.

You're not meant to be content. You're meant to brew your unique happiness potion and then drink it in deeply each and every day.

Challenge Question

Where are you settling for someone else's vision of happiness? Why?

_____

_____

August 9

Amen! of Nature

Why should we be more shy of repeating ourselves than the spring be tired of blossoms or the night of stars? Look at Nature. She never wearies of saying over her floral pater-noster. In the crevices of Cyclopean walls,—in the dust where men lie, dust also,—on the mounds that bury huge cities, the wreck of Nineveh and the Babel-heap,—still that same sweet prayer and benediction. The Amen! of Nature is always a flower.
  Oliver Wendell Holmes, Sr.—The Autocrat of the Breakfast-Table *(1858)*

Have you ever stumbled upon a single flower somehow blooming spectacularly in the slightest crack in the sidewalk? No doubt that flower would have had it much easier were it placed in fertile soil, but still it blooms where it was seeded.

And to those who pass, it is surely a welcome gift.

Flowers don't decide to bloom; they bloom because it is their nature to do so.

The Amen! of Nature is always a flower.

No matter where you find yourself today or how far along the path you consider yourself right now, you can always be a gift to someone else. There's no faster way to advance your cause than to change how you view what you're here to do in this stage of your journey.

You may not like where you are right now. It may not seem like progress to you. But consider these words from poet Maya Angelou:

If you don't like something, change it. If you can't change it, change your attitude about it.

In your grace lies your resilience.

Challenge Question

Who can you be a blessing to today?

_____

_____

August 10

Puddle Backward

If I think of my woes I fall into a vortex of debts, dishpans, and despondency awful to see. So I say, "every path has its puddle," and try to play gayly with the tadpoles in my puddle, while I wait for the Lord to give me a lift.
Louisa May Alcott—Her Life, Letters, and Journals *(1889)*

So perhaps you're wondering if you are on the right path because there's a great big puddle on your path. You can't curse the puddle; you can only laugh at it and promise to move forward.

Ever watch how a three-year-old deals with puddles? So much joy is yours to bring.

What's the puddle here to teach you? Maybe it's a lesson in perseverance. Or maybe it just wants you to have a little more fun.

Here's the thing about problems: they are rarely here to stay, rarely as bad as we believe at first, and often exist mostly because of the way we think about them.

Want to solve your most vexing problem? Walk through the puddle backward.

Sounds silly, but most of our problems remain our problems because we miss the obvious solutions by overthinking things. Break it down, read it backward, and the obvious solution might just be, well, obvious. (And more fun to discover!)

Challenge Question

What problem do you need to solve? How can you look at it backward? Is it really even a problem?

_____

_____

August 11

Remove All Obstacles

It is not always those who have the best advantages, or the greatest talents, that eventually succeed in their undertakings; but it is those who strive with untiring diligence to remove all obstacles to success, and who, with unconquerable resolution, labour on until the rich reward of perseverance is within their grasp. Then again let me say to our young men—Take courage; "There is a good time coming." The darkness of the night appears greatest just before the dawn of day.

William Wells Brown—Three Years in Europe; or, Places I Have Seen and People I Have Met *(1852)*

Perseverance is a powerful tool for the would-be and the experienced entrepreneur alike.

The first step in building the grit to persevere is to make sure that your objectives are worth your perseverance. It's all a big fat balancing act—what are your relationships, health, and happiness worth anyway? Check? You've got this then.

Just know that however you've got it dialed in, there will be times you want to quit. But resilience isn't about finding heroic mental stamina; it's about taking the next step even though all you want to do is lie on your back and lazily toss and catch a baseball several thousand times (for illustration purposes only; you may or may not have ever done this—it's kind of soothing though, but . . . where were we?).

To "*strive with untiring diligence to remove all obstacles to success*" is the answer. Remove all obstacles, one at a time, step by step.

Cope by blowing off steam, taking every obstacle for what it's worth, letting go of timelines, celebrating everything.

Sometimes a worthy goal is as small as making it to another sunrise. To bring a fresh pair of eyes to the obstacle. To win because you showed up.

Challenge Question

What is your definition of perseverance?

_____

_____

Evolving: Resilience

August 12

Opposite Ends of the Same Stick

We must be something in order to do something, but we must also do something in order to be something. The best rule, I think, is this: If we find it hard to do good, then let us try to be good. If, on the other hand, we find it hard to be good, then let us try to do good. Being leads to doing, doing leads to being.

James Freeman Clarke—Dictionary of Burning Words of Brilliant Writers *(1895)*

Today's passage reads a bit like a classic puzzle, but it might also define the meaning of entrepreneurial life.

Clarke, like so many writers of the era, boldly suggested that success was both defined and achieved by who you are being, not what you are doing. Of course, again the puzzling part: what you are doing then becomes so much more useful to others in spite of your efforts that success comes without even trying. No matter where you point it, doing and being are opposite ends of the same stick.

Focus on being great and you'll improve your chances of doing great. Do great and you'll come to be great.

Challenge Question

Are you currently doing great or being great? How do you know the difference?

_____

_____

August 13

Study Out of Doors

You must walk like a camel, which is said to be the only beast which ruminates when walking. When a traveler asked Wordsworth's servant to show him her master's study, she answered, "Here is his library, but his study is out of doors." Living much out of doors, in the sun and wind, will no doubt produce a certain roughness of character,—will cause a thicker cuticle to grow over some of the finer qualities of our nature, as on the face and hands, or as severe manual labor robs the hands of some of their delicacy of touch. So staying in the house, on the other hand, may produce a softness and smoothness, not to say thinness of skin, accompanied by an increased sensibility to certain impressions.

Henry David Thoreau—Walking *(1861)*

Homo sapiens are the only species on Earth that get up on two legs and walk for long distances. Thoreau and other transcendentalists turned walking, or sauntering as Thoreau referred to it, into a spiritual practice.

They didn't invent this practice to be sure, but they molded it into a bit of an art that would have them referred to as "peripatetic philosophers," a nod to these nomadic tendencies.

Walking is medicine. Not just to fight the ravages of the modern sitting life, but for thinking, innovating, discussing, studying, rehearsing, reviewing, writing, examining, relaxing, and reconnecting with yourself and others. The physical act is partly to credit for the restorative powers of walking—but join it with the outdoors element and ease that contemplative sauntering implies and you have what borders on a miracle drug.

Thoreau's *Walking* is worth a full read, as is *Wanderlust: A History of Walking* by Rebecca Solni if you wish to add walking—not as a form of transportation, but as a way to experience your true nature—to your self-reliance toolbox.

Challenge Question

If you could choose to walk anywhere in the world, where would it be?

_____

_____

August 14

Greet the Dawn

I know of no more encouraging fact than the unquestionable ability of a person to elevate their life by a conscious endeavor. It is something to be able to paint a particular picture, or to carve a statue, and so to make a few objects beautiful; but it is far more glorious to carve and paint the very atmosphere and medium through which we look, which morally we can do. To affect the quality of the day, that is the highest of arts.

Henry David Thoreau—Walden *(1854)*

Perhaps one of the greatest gifts we as human beings are granted is the gift of a new day.

No matter how bleak or hopeless today might seem, there's always tomorrow.

It's no secret that the most successful men and women claim that their success lies in their morning rituals. While we are each granted the gift of the new day, some take full advantage of this natural rhythm to greet the dawn as an opportunity to set the quality of their entire day.

This "*highest of arts,*" as Thoreau calls it, takes practice and persistence, but the payoff regarding focus and productivity makes it a worthy investment.

To develop your morning ritual(s), look first to your most important priorities and feed these before all else.

For entrepreneurs, this often includes finding a centering thought for the day, exercise, planned nutrition, and connection with the highest vision for their life.

You are the master of the "*very atmosphere and medium through which we look,*" and how you start today will likely determine how you live the day.

Challenge Question

What's one positive practice that you can add to your morning routine?

_____

_____

August 15

Have a Little Faith

Happy they themselves who call / To risk much, and to conquer all; / Happy
are they who many losses, / Sore defeat or frequent crosses, / Though these
may the heart dismay, / Cannot the sure faith betray.
Margaret Fuller—Life Without and Life Within *(1859)*

You're not in control of your business—you'll never be, not fully anyway.
There are simply too many elements over which you have no control.

Letting go in the face of this constant uncertainty requires faith.

Just getting up and walking out the door requires a level of faith, but
running a business, dreaming a big dream, not hyperventilating every single
day of your entrepreneurial life, that requires amazing faith.

But faith in what? Maybe it's a god, but maybe you're a god.

Faith in yourself, faith in your power to manifest through focused attention, faith in your ability to witness miracles, that's the faith you possess.
That's the faith the universe offers you. It's there for everyone.

Faith like this isn't about wishing something will happen; it's about
knowing it will happen. Maybe not as you mapped it out on the whiteboard,
maybe not because you're in complete control, but in time, in your way, as
you knew it would.

Today, let go more; have a little faith.

Challenge Question

What do you need to give up controlling? Do you have the faith to do it?

_____

_____

Evolving: Resilience

August 16

Nature's Gift

Let us draw a lesson from nature, which always works by short ways. When the fruit is ripe, it falls. When the fruit is dispatched, the leaf falls. We judge a person's wisdom by their hope, knowing that the inexhaustibleness of nature is an immortal youth.

Ralph Waldo Emerson—"Spiritual Laws" (1841)

Time and again the transcendentalists turned to mystical descriptions of nature for lessons in their writings.

Subsequent nature authors such as Edward Abbey, Aldo Leopold, and John Muir credit Thoreau and Emerson's influence in their writing.

Emerson's essay titled "Nature" includes these words: "In the woods, we return to reason and faith."

They did not, however, stop at the promotion of nature as something merely to be appreciated. They believed that all human beings are connected and that nature played the role of catalyst for this connection.

Okay, before we start exploring biospheres and self-regulating ecosystems, consider this huge generalization: few people have ever not felt better, stronger, more present, from going and sitting in a forest for a while.

Nature's greatest gifts are those that allow us simplicity, patience, effortlessness, sustainability, and perhaps hope. Who knows? They might help.

Today, go have a sensory experience in nature and just witness what happens.

Challenge Question

When you go outdoors next, what do you see, hear, feel, smell, taste, and sense?

_____

_____

August 17

Extreme Self-Care

In America, we hurry—which is well; but when the day's work is done, we go on thinking of losses and gains, we plan for the morrow, we even carry our business cares to bed with us, and toss and worry over them when we ought to be restoring our racked bodies and brains with sleep. We burn up our energies with these excitements, and either die early or drop into a lean and mean old age at a time of life which they call a person's prime in Europe. We bestow thoughtful care upon inanimate objects, but none upon ourselves. What a robust people, what a nation of thinkers we might be, if we would only lay ourselves on the shelf occasionally and renew our edges!

Mark Twain—The Innocents Abroad *(1869)*

Entrepreneurs beat themselves up pretty routinely. Sure, being an entrepreneur takes a mental toll, but it's physically and spiritually draining as well. That's the part few acknowledge.

Running a business is an extreme sport. If you're going to make it, you have to adopt a mindset of extreme self-care.

For some, self-care feels selfish. But let's face it: if the car breaks down, you're not getting to where you're going. So think of it as preventive maintenance if you must. If you're out to save the world, self-care is the most selfless option.

Self-care requires forming new habits. It requires intention.

Mind—defriend the negative (whatever that looks like), read for inspiration each day, ask someone how their day is going and listen, meditate (duh), fix something that's been bothering you

Body—put on SPF 45 facial lotion before leaving the house, stretch for five minutes every hour, develop a love of exercise, take dance breaks, learn about aromatherapy, take 15-minute naps.

Spirit—get more laughter (Dilbert works well), send a random thank-you note every day, identify animal shapes in the clouds, buy the best quality, make a tiny connection with a stranger.

Challenge Question

How will you add a self-care routine to your journey?

_____

_____

August 18

Enough Already

People acting gregariously are always in extremes; as they are one moment capable of higher courage, so they are liable, the next, to baser depression, and it is often a matter of chance whether numbers shall multiply confidence or discouragement. Nor does deception lead more surely to distrust, than self-deception to suspicion of principles. The only faith that wears well and holds its color in all weathers is that which is woven of conviction and set with the sharp mordant of experience.

James Russell Lowell—Abraham Lincoln *(1864)*

Today's reading is mostly about telling the truth, a practice that serves entrepreneurs in particular. Not much debate about that, but if the habit of your life has been untruthfulness you will find it difficult to suddenly act with a level of sincerity necessary to build trust.

So, there's that, but a closer examination of the reading reveals an even deeper truth: we deceive ourselves more often than we deceive others. Sure, you can do both, and at the same time, but lying to yourself is perhaps more destructive than lying publicly in the marketplace.

Today untruths, broken promises, overstated claims in the name of commerce are found out, but the little falsehoods we hold in our soul simply fester and contaminate our capacity to shine.

Things like "I can't (because I'm afraid to try)," "I'll ship when my product is perfect," "I'm not smart enough, well off enough, young enough, old enough, experienced enough, connected enough, talented enough, free enough . . ."

Yeah, well, bullshit—enough already!

Challenge Question

How are you deceiving yourself? How are you going to fix this?

_____

_____

Evolving: Resilience

THE SELF-RELIANT ENTREPRENEUR

August 19

Law of Choice

Every excess causes a defect; every defect an excess. Every sweet hath its sour; every evil its good. Every faculty which is a receiver of pleasure has an equal penalty put on its abuse. It is to answer for its moderation with its life. For every grain of wit there is a grain of folly. For every thing you have missed, you have gained something else; and for every thing you gain, you lose something. If riches increase, they are increased that use them. If the gatherer gathers too much, nature takes out of the man what she puts into his chest; swells the estate, but kills the owner.

Ralph Waldo Emerson—"Compensation" (1841)

Isaac Newton's laws of motion were published over one hundred and fifty years prior to Emerson's essay, but it is easy to assume that Emerson was familiar with them. Most notably Newton's third law translated to read: "To every action there is always opposed an equal reaction."

Though Greek philosophers dating to Aristotle had pondered this notion in philosophical context, Newton validated it in the physical world, therefore giving those who subscribed to the theory that the physical and quantum worlds are interconnected reason to explore Emerson's more metaphysical approach.

While there are certain laws dictating our fate, our destiny is still ours to choose. And choose we must—every single day. When luck opens a door, we have to choose to run through it as our very best self in order to turn it into an opportunity. We are essentially a bundle of the choices we make each day, and those choices either propel us with momentum toward our honest path or they add friction and drag to an equation that doesn't care what choice we make.

Make choices consciously, eliminate the things you know are keeping you from being the best version of yourself, take your life and your business in your own hands.

Challenge Question

Who are you at your very best? Now go make choices as that person.

_____

_____

242   Evolving: Resilience

August 20

Define Success

Do not be too timid and squeamish about your actions. All life is an experiment. The more experiments you make the better. What if they are a little coarse and you may get your coat soiled or torn? What if you do fail, and get fairly rolled in the dirt once or twice? Up again, you shall never be so afraid of a tumble.
    Ralph Waldo Emerson—Journals of Ralph Waldo Emerson *(1909)*

What if you do fail? What's your backup plan?

So much chatter about failure, how it's good for you, how you should expect it, welcome it, learn from it. Nope, failure sucks.

Here's another question.

What if you succeed, wildly, what then?

What's your plan for when things go better than you could have ever imagined?

No one lets themselves consider that notion, but you should.

Challenge Question

How do you define success? How do you define your success?

_____

_____

August 21

The Following Journey

Hark ye yet again,—the little lower layer. All visible objects, man, are but as pasteboard masks. But in each event—in the living act, the undoubted deed—there, some unknown but still reasoning thing puts forth the mould-ings of its features from behind the unreasoning mask. If man will strike, strike through the mask!

Herman Melville—Moby-Dick: or, the Whale *(1851)*

At some point, people will follow you. Your mission will become their mission. That's how this entrepreneurial thing works. At first, it may be because you've proven you have a good idea. And then it's because they grasp your story. Eventually someone, or many someones, may want to join you on this journey—be led and fulfilled by the purpose you hold in your heart.

This is the part where we should recall that *Moby-Dick* is centrally about revenge. Ahab proclaims that everything happens for a reason, and his reason is to seek revenge at all cost—no matter that there is little money to be made in the quest. He calls his men to "chase him round Good Hope, and round the Horn, and round the Norway Maelstrom, and round perdition's flames . . ." (perdition being hell—*Wrath of Khan* fans may recognize this line).

The point here is that people will follow you. But will you lead them on a journey worth pursuing? Are you even certain you know what purpose, what impact, you've chosen to have and to hold? Fate will arrive and help you achieve your goal, be it for something good or for something offensive, it doesn't really care—so lead you will.

Create your vision, the values you've based this vision on, and the principles you intend to follow as you chase your vision. And then start sharing your vision with the world.

Challenge Question

What values have you based your entrepreneurial vision on?

_____

_____

Evolving: Resilience

August 22

Keep Grubbing

There is a sudden hoist for a meek and lowly scribbler, who was told to "stick to teaching," and never had a literary friend to lend a helping hand! Fifteen years of hard grubbing may be coming to something after all; and I may yet "pay all the debts, fix the house, and keep the old folks cosey," as I've said I would so long, yet so hopelessly.

Louisa May Alcott—Her Life, Letters, and Journals *(1889)*

Your day is coming. So, maybe you're not rich or famous yet. But you're making a difference, even if it's just in your own life. Heck, maybe you are rich and famous too.

You're willing to take risks to paint the life you want. You're open to the fact that you might fail. And dang it, people like you.

You've carved out time to learn new things. You're thankful for what you have right now. You no longer feel the need to explain yourself. You've stopped worrying about balance; you're more worried about fully living.

Yes, you've got a chip on your shoulder, too. You've still got something big to prove, but you know all this "hard grubbing" is going to pay off.

Want to know the ultimate way to determine whether you're making progress? More of two kinds of people might start showing up in your life—people who want to build you up and people who want to hold you back.

Once you get clear on where you are headed and start working toward it, the right people will take note and want to work with you. You'll also start hearing from those who envy what you're doing. It's okay, just smile; it means you're making progress. Let it go and keep doing you.

Challenge Question

Who wants to build you up? Who wants to hold you back?

_____

_____

August 23

Radical Humility

Noise proves nothing. Often a hen who has merely laid an egg cackles as if she had laid an asteroid.

Mark Twain—Following the Equator *(1897)*

Here's a common entrepreneurial balancing act. The world needs to know that you're kind of a big deal, because then more people will want to—buy from you, write about you, work for you, talk about you, invite you . . . but then that turns into the . . . "Humbled to be named to the top 1,137 entrepreneurs in Poughkeepsie to follow on Twitter" status update.

That's not humbled; humbled is what you get when someone calls you out on how ridiculous that post is. But that's the celebrity-seeking times we live in, right?

Self-reliant entrepreneurs don't spend time thinking less about themselves; they just spent less time talking about themselves. They spend more time listening, asking for help, testing their theories, praising others, and most important, admitting when they are wrong.

This Emerson quote gets at the value of humility: "Practice radical humility. Those who master the art of humility cannot be humiliated."

Self-reliant entrepreneurs can't be humiliated.

Today, practice not taking credit for anything—and please, no humble brags on Facebook.

Challenge Question

What is your definition of humility?

_____

_____

August 24

Beyond First Impressions

He must always make a deep impression; but to suppose the world at large capable of a right estimate of his different powers, would be forming a judgment against every-day proof. However deep may be the first effect of genius upon us, we come slowly, and through study, to a perception of its minute beauties and delicate characteristics. After all, the greater part seldom get beyond the first general impression.

Richard Henry Dana—"Kean's Acting" (1850)

The Kean in "Kean's Acting" quoted here is Edmund Kean, a British Shakespearean stage actor of the era. The reading comes from a theatrical review of the celebrated actor's work, but it contains an important element of human nature and how we develop relationships and appreciation for the art of others.

Rarely do we choose to go beyond first impressions.

First impressions, first meetings, first sales calls, first interviews, are where people decide if we are likable, trustworthy, maybe even smart enough for the task. But it only dents the shell and holds little lasting value for either party.

Networking events are first-impression mixers.

You were meant for something much deeper. You were meant to show the world your "*minute beauties and delicate characteristics.*"

So how do you do this? Do real stuff with people, share experiences, find tribes with shared passions and nothing to gain, seek out diversity—this is where you'll find profound connections and common bonds. (They exist online and offline alike.)

This is where the greater part gets beyond the first impressions, and this is where you will serve your purpose.

Challenge Question

What gets you revved up? Where can you find others who think like that?

_____

_____

August 25

Unfinished Parts

The tops of mountains are among the unfinished parts of the globe, whither it is a slight insult to the gods to climb and pry into their secrets, and try their effect on our humanity. Only the daring and insolent, perchance, go there.
Henry David Thoreau—The Maine Woods *(1864)*

While writing *The Maine Woods*, a work Thoreau would not finish before his death, he hiked up a mountain in Maine called Ktaadn (Katahdin), which today also marks the northern terminus of the Appalachian Trail in Baxter State Park.

While this passage honors the indigenous ideology that the god Pomola, said to live on Ktaadn, would punish those who climbed, it's also serves as a marvelous metaphor for the self-reliant entrepreneur.

We are after the unfinished parts of the globe, and though there may be risks in gaining such heights, we are just daring and insolent enough to go there.

Do you really care what people think? Do you need permission to act boldly? Are you okay outside the cherished comfort zone? Are you fine being bad at something in order to get good at something? Can you say yes even if you're not sure how? Do you break a few rules and enjoy it?

On tops of mountains, as everywhere to hopeful souls, it is always morning.
Thoreau, Walden

Challenge Question

Where is one place you can get far outside your comfort zone today?

_____

_____

August 26

Happiness of Life

The happiness of life is made up of minute fractions—the little soon forgotten charities of a kiss or smile, a kind look, a heartfelt compliment, and the countless infinitesimals of pleasurable and genial feeling.
Samuel Taylor Coleridge—"The Friend. The Improvisatore" (1828)

One of the easiest things to do in business—and this goes for life in general—is to take things for granted.

You accomplished this much, so more is coming. You built this all by yourself. Your clients should appreciate your work more fully. Your team should just work more hours. Your spouse could be a little more understanding.

Until one is no more—and suddenly you wonder how you got to this point, but by then maybe you've squandered some of the "happiness of life."

Just turn to Facebook for a couple of minutes and witness the trivial pain and genuine suffering of the entitled masses subjected to travesties such as a 30-minute flight delay or a slower-than-usual barista. Lord!

What are you taking for granted? It's amazing that you can fly from San Diego to Kansas City in under three hours and that you can afford a $4 cup of coffee. Let's shut up all the whining already.

Let's hold dear the *"charities of a kiss or smile, a kind look, a heartfelt compliment."*

Warning: This is not new news ahead—it's just the secret to happiness.

Please, take 10 minutes at the start of each day and thank the world for everything you have and—what the heck—do it again tonight.

And who knows, maybe while you're waiting through that 30-minute flight delay you'll strike up a conversation with someone who wants to invest in your brilliant entrepreneurial journey.

Challenge Question

Can you write down all the little things you are thankful for today? This is not a yes or no question—do it.

_____

_____

August 27

Adversity's Opportunity

Something pulled in her—and broke ... But when the sun rose in the morning, she was far away. It was all behind her, and she knew that she would never cry like that again. People live through such pain only once; pain comes again, but it finds a tougher surface.

Willa Cather—The Song of the Lark *(1915)*

Adversity will come. It's only a matter of time and you can either dread it or make peace with it and mature. Adversity breeds resilience, and you're gonna need that.

But adversity also allows you to grow and appreciate the need to grow in order to achieve.

I'm not saying you should go looking for adversity; it's just that when you meet it, meet it as part of the recipe.

Hikers, when first taking up a trek, look to the steep climb with fear. Once they've gained the skill and conditioning required to make the climb, they go looking for greater climbs with greater anticipation.

And that's how it is with adversity: it's conditioning, it's an opportunity to get tougher, it's a means to understand how strong you are now.

You don't overcome adversity as much as you learn how to accept its lessons. You lose a job; do you solve the problem by getting another job, or do you receive it as an invitation to make your side hustle a front and center I'm-all-in hustle?

Sometimes we need a big dose of adversity to shake us awake and force us to embrace the life we were supposed to live. Of course, a good cry never hurt anyone either.

Challenge Question

What's one thing you've overcome and gotten stronger because of it?

_____

_____

Evolving: Resilience

August 28

High-Quality Leisure

*Society never advances. It recedes as fast on one side as it gains on the other.
It undergoes continual changes; it is barbarous, it is civilized, it is christian-
ized, it is rich, it is scientific; but this change is not amelioration. For every
thing that is given, something is taken.*

Ralph Waldo Emerson—Self-Reliance *(1841)*

Few would argue that advances in communications and technology have given us the ability to do things that our parents and grandparents could have only dreamed of. But at what cost?

No, the technology is not to blame; it's our use of technology that is per-haps to blame for diverting our freedom and with it our happiness.

We've allowed our use of technology to marginalize activities such as solitude, conversation, reflection, mindfulness, and deep thought.

Consider this warning from Cal Newport's *Digital Minimalism*:

It's now possible to completely banish solitude from your life. Thoreau and Storr worried about people enjoying less solitude. We must now wonder if people might forget this state of being altogether.

But as with any addiction, there is a detox.

Step one is to consider what void we are filling with the constant need for technological stimulation. What's missing? What needs deadening?

The key to changing any habit or addiction once you discover its source is to fill up the space with something else entirely.

We've lost control of the joy in life by giving it away to time spent on junk. Newport suggests we can regain that joy by "engaging in activities that serve no other purpose than the satisfaction the activity itself generates" or what he refers to as "high-quality leisure."

Today's task: find something to join, someone to lunch with; take up woodworking or a musical instrument you've always wanted to play.

Challenge Question

What high-quality leisure activity (hobby) can you explore today?

_____

_____

August 29

Why We Must Sail

I find the great thing in this world is not so much where we stand, as in what direction we are moving: To reach the port of heaven, we must sail sometimes with the wind and sometimes against it,—but we must sail, and not drift, nor lie at anchor.
Oliver Wendell Holmes, Sr.—The Autocrat of the Breakfast-Table *(1858)*

Many entrepreneurs lie somewhere on a spectrum of behaviors that some find hard to appreciate. It is not uncommon for entrepreneurs to look for things that are broken in order to fix them. But if they are not broken, they'll just paint over them to fulfill the need to keep doing something, always, moving, ooh, here's another great idea . . .

The tendency to *"sail sometimes with the wind and sometimes against it"* is both a blessing and perhaps a disease.

It's a blessing because nothing happens until something is imagined, made, tested, fixed, packaged, shipped, promoted, and sold. It's a disease because we like new projects, new ideas, new directions, new technologies, and we grow tired of what we start right at about the 70 percent finished point.

Perfect is not the enemy of the entrepreneur; distraction is.

Think about your most important projects right now. What's the end game for each? What's the long-term value? How do they support the big picture? How much team buy-in and support do you have? Are you still excited about the prospect of completing them?

Sail, do not drift or lie at anchor—you were built to be at sea, but maybe you should create a map before you commence.

Challenge Question

What completed project are you most proud of? What difference did it make?

_____

_____

Evolving: Resilience

August 30

Believe in Simplicity

I do believe in simplicity. It is astonishing as well as sad, how many trivial affairs even the wisest man thinks he must attend to in a day; how singular an affair he thinks he must omit. When the mathematician would solve a difficult problem, he first frees the equation of all incumbrances, and reduces it to its simplest terms. So simplify the problem of life, distinguish the necessary and the real.

Henry David Thoreau—Familiar Letters *(1894)*

In each and every day, you will be presented with the necessary and real, but you'll also get a face full of the useless and ambiguous, all of it seemingly urgent.

So how do you go about sorting out what deserves your focus from what fills up your day?

The trick here is to first make the firm decision about that which is a priority above all else. In order to simplify, then you can choose to do less, have less, consume less—but above all else, you must stay focused on your stated priority objectives.

Setting priorities and establishing a habit of tackling them before, let's see, checking Facebook, relining the drawers in your desk, or cleaning out your inbox, is the key to simplicity in body, mind, and spirit. All this other stuff amounts to little more than you hiding from the truth of what deserves to get done.

Priorities unattended weigh you down. You know what produces value and payoff, and by swirling around and giving attention to *"trivial affairs,"* you increase the mental and physical strain of being an entrepreneur.

Create your three to four highest priorities, check in with them first thing every day, and advance them before you do anything else. Then perhaps you'll wonder if you even need to consider doing anything else—and that's the key to entrepreneurial simplicity.

Challenge Question

For the next 90 days, what are your top three or four priorities? What will you gain by focusing on them?

_____

_____

August 31

You Cannot Fail

You cannot put a fire out; / A thing that can ignite / Can go, itself, without a fan / Upon the slowest night. / / You cannot fold a flood / And put it in a drawer,— / Because the winds would find it out, / And tell your cedar floor.

      Emily Dickinson—"Power," The Complete Poems of Emily Dickinson
                                   (1855)

What would you attempt to do if you knew you could not fail? Powerful question, right? (There's an Etsy print and t-shirt if you need the extra motivation.)

This question became a popular Silicon Valley start-up slogan, but its roots go back to a popular Christian televangelist from the 1970s, Robert Schuller.

But you can't put a fire out—you can't fail.

You're not your circumstances, or even your past and current experience. You are a fire, a thing that can ignite again and again.

As long as you're doing something worth doing—and you get to define "worth doing"—you cannot fail.

Challenge Question

What would you attempt to do if you knew you could not fail? What goals would you be setting for yourself if you knew you could not fail?

_____

_____

September

Edgar Allan Poe (1809–1849)

There is no exquisite beauty . . . without some strangeness in the proportion.
—Edgar Allan Poe

Source: Wikimedia

Edgar Allan Poe was born in Boston in 1809. His parents, both working actors, died before Poe reached the age of three.

He was sent to Virginia to be raised by John Allan, a wealthy tobacco exporter. Allan took Poe in, but was not particularly kind or generous to him. When Poe matriculated at the University of Virginia at Charlottesville in 1825, he could attend for only one year because Allan refused to pay tuition.

Their relationship deteriorated, and Poe relocated to Boston and joined the army. While there, he published his first collection of poetry, *Tamerlane and Other Poems*, in 1827. He continued to write as he served in the military and was honorably discharged in 1829.

Over the next few years, Poe moved frequently. He first settled in New York, and then moved to Baltimore, where he reconnected with his aunt, Maria Clemm, and her daughter Virginia. In Baltimore, he began to gain attention for his writings, and eventually he was tapped to serve as editor for *The Southern Literary Messenger*.

He took the job, moving to Richmond, Virginia, with his aunt and cousin, whom he would later marry. During this time, he continued to write his own stories and poetry but became best known as a literary critic. He earned his living over the next decade editing various publications.

His wife fell ill and died of tuberculosis in 1847. This marked another period of upheaval in Poe's life, where he traveled around the East Coast, giving lectures and readings.

In 1849, as he was preparing for his second marriage, he stopped in Baltimore while en route to Philadelphia. There, he disappeared for several days, turning up semiconscious in a local bar. He was brought to the hospital and died three days later; no one knows what happened to Poe in the last days of his life.

September 1

Unearth the Complexity

The art of art, the glory of expression and the sunshine of the light of letters is simplicity. Nothing is better than simplicity . . . nothing can make up for excess or for the lack of definiteness. To carry on the heave of impulse and pierce intellectual depths and give all subjects their articulations are powers neither common nor very uncommon.

Walt Whitman—Leaves of Grass *(1855)*

Whitman was not the only author to extol the virtues of simplicity. Thoreau famously penned the phrase "Our life is frittered away by detail . . . simplify, simplify."

An entrepreneur's life is often filled with detail—in fact, the very act of bringing something that did not exist until you took the action to make it so suggests a life of complexity.

And yet, when unchecked complexity turns to excess, turns to perplexity, turns to "stuckness." Nurturing simplicity is the path back to center.

The source of a great deal of our complexity is found in the internal struggle to manifest our ideas. Yes, crazy town is real.

We often self-complicate, where simplicity would suffice, when we feel the need to defend our point of view, demonstrate that we are right, or grasp rigidly to details over desired outcomes, settling for perception over reality.

The good news is that self-reliance means that you never need to be right in the eyes of others. You never have to explain or defend your point of view. You can bask, always, in the sunshine of the light of your simplicity. Awesome, isn't it?

Today's challenge is to unearth the source of complexity in your entrepreneurial journey. Look for a chance to let go of defending your point of view, pass up the opportunity to explain why you are right, and pay close attention to the subtle shift in just how free you feel in that moment.

Challenge Question

What's one thing you are making more complex than it needs to be? What's one thing you could delegate today?

_____

_____

Evolving: Congruence

September 2

Congruence

No person for any considerable period can wear one face to himself and another to the multitude, without finally getting bewildered as to which may be the true.

Nathaniel Hawthorne—The Scarlet Letter *(1850)*

Quite often the very thing that leads many to strike out on their own is an attempt to bring their business and personal lives in alignment—the corporate culture they had entered and adopted no longer feels congruent with their personal goals.

Congruence by definition implies sameness, agreement, harmony, or compatibility—all concepts made wholly real by following an entrepreneurial vision.

So, it's terribly ironic then that when the amazing, fresh opportunity afforded the entrepreneur is coupled with the day-to-day pressure to build a business, people are easily pushed further and faster out of congruence than when they started. Remember playing crack the whip at the ice-skating rink as a kid? Kind of feels like that.

This looks like working more hours than is healthy or necessary, promoting products and services you don't use or believe in, asking others to do things you are unwilling to do, or worse, wearing one face to yourself and another to your team, your employees, and your loved ones.

In geometry, when stating that two triangles are congruent, you might use a congruence statement that looks something like $AB \cong LM$, $BC \cong MN$, $AC \cong LN$.

In your entrepreneurial quest, it's even more complex.

Challenge Question

How is your life a reflection of the gift you need to bring to others, and how is it not?

_____

_____

September 3

Truth in Grace

Rather than love, than money, than fame, give me truth. I sat at a table where were rich food and wine in abundance, and obsequious attendance, but sincerity and truth were not; and I went away hungry from the inhospitable board.

Henry David Thoreau—Walden *(1854)*

Thoreau concludes his oft-quoted work with a call for truth.

Entrepreneurs are in a sense the ultimate truth seekers—searching for a higher truth in their calling that is perhaps not found for them in places like religion or science or even the trappings of wealth.

Thoreau's ultimate source of truth was nature In it he believed resided a truth with the power to create change, to bring peace, to connect with our soul, and to foster the interconnectedness of all forms of life. All from a hike—not a bad ROI.

A truth that lives in the everyday miracles found hiding in plain sight all around us. A truth found by living in awe of the simple gifts revealed in the natural world, which although often taken for granted, still unveil their blessings freely.

Today's suggestion: go outside and take photos of a handful of miracles and place them as present reminders of your truth in grace.

Challenge Question

What would claim as your spirit animal?

_____

_____

Evolving: Congruence

September 4

Into Silence

What are the great faults of conversation? Want of ideas, want of words, want of manners, are the principal ones, I suppose you think. I don't doubt it, but I will tell you what I have found spoil more good talks than anything else;—long arguments on special points between people who differ on the fundamental principles upon which these points depend.
Oliver Wendell Holmes, Sr.—The Autocrat of the Breakfast-Table *(1858)*

Defending one's position is a clear signal of a lack of trust—not in the person subjected to your defense, but in yourself.

Assuredness in a point of view sounds a lot like silence.

Yes, today's call is to be still and listen.

This isn't a knock on your ability to share or even the fact that you have brilliant ideas to share. It's just that when we choose to listen more, some beautiful things can happen.

In conversation, the economy of our words gives space for others to feel heard and valued. It invites people to find themselves and see you as a source of energy that allows rather than prescribes.

Listening draws ideas, relationships, stories, information, and clues that let you better understand the impact you have on others.

For most, but particularly entrepreneurs, this advice requires biting your tongue and reining in your natural inclination. But if you can allow yourself to embrace this habit and practice it, you'll never give it up.

Today, try to speak only when spoken to and then listen with your entire body. Observe how silence feels and take note of your urges to burst out talking. But more important, bask in the transformation of those who experience your active listening.

If you have a lot you need to say, then write it down. Of course, the sneaky little trick in this advice is that writing forces you to listen to yourself and observe just what you sound like.

Challenge Question

Who will you listen to today?

_____

_____

September 5

Tend Your Field

There is a time in everyone's education when they arrive at the conviction that envy is ignorance; that imitation is suicide; that they must take themselves for better, for worse, as their portion; that though the wide universe is full of good, no kernel of nourishing corn can come to us but through the toil bestowed on that plot of ground which is given to us to till.

Ralph Waldo Emerson—Self-Reliance (1841)

On the surface, this passage could rest as the thesis for self-reliance and a call for independence unencumbered by the opinions, successes, and analysis of others.

But that would miss what is perhaps the much deeper meaning: that envy robs you of the opportunity to realize the innermost aspirations of your soul.

Suicide is an intentionally harsh metaphor, but it displays how deeply Emerson felt about the fact that you can only be the miraculous you and that trying to be something other than that is, at best, a distraction and, at worst, or as he states later in the essay, like living as "a shadow on the wall."

Today, note how often the information, content, and messages you take in fan the flames of envy.

Then, take stock of the gifts and goodness in your life. Let's go to work on your singular field of corn.

Challenge Question

What is the most unique and original part of you?

_____

_____

Evolving: Congruence

September 6

In Solitude

I think a little solitude every day is good for me. In the quiet I see my faults, and try to mend them; but, deary me, I don't get on at all. I used to imagine my mind a room in confusion, and I was to put it in order; so I swept out useless thoughts and dusted foolish fancies away, and furnished it with good resolutions and began again. But cobwebs get in. I'm not a good house-keeper, and never get my room in nice order.

Louisa May Alcott—Her Life, Letters, and Journals *(1889)*

Who has time to sit, alone, in a room, with only their thoughts? And, as long as we're being honest, let's also admit this—it's scary as hell. (Why do you think solitary confinement is considered a harsh punishment?)

Silence is disquieting because society has deemed it abnormal, and our brain knows this. Our subconscious brain in particular feels the loss of control in solitude and cues up a tantrum.

But once you absorb all the silent shouting in extended moments of solitude, you just might slip into a place where the pulsing discontent we all feel in our versions of the entrepreneurial storm begins to quiet.

A moment of solitude here and again is great, but the nature of solitude required for repair lies somewhere between Walden and a weekend retreat.

An hour might feel like too much, but after a while an entire day will feel too short. We need attachment and detachment alike, but you just might become more self-reliant, and you won't care what people think about your need for solitude.

Although you can do your time anywhere you find solitude, outdoors in nature offers unique opportunities to engage the senses in ways that leave your frightened brain no choice but to give in.

Challenge Question

How do you feel when you're alone? What is this telling you?

_____

_____

September 7

Well-Held Beliefs

The most familiar sheet of water viewed from a new hilltop, yields a novel and unexpected pleasure. When we have travelled a few miles, we do not recognize the profiles even of the hills which overlook our native village . . . We do not commonly know, beyond a short distance, which way the hills range which take in our houses and farms in their sweep. As if our birth had at first sundered things, and we had been thrust up through into nature like a wedge, and not till the wound heals and the scar disappears, do we begin to discover where we are, and that nature is one and continuous everywhere. It is an important epoch when a person who has always lived on the east side of a mountain, and seen it in the west, travels round and sees it in the east. Yet the universe is a sphere whose center is wherever there is intelligence.

Henry David Thoreau—A Week on the Concord and Merrimack Rivers
(1849)

What's your go-to reaction when you confront a point of view that runs counter to your well-held beliefs? Defriend, run, shut down?

Here's the problem: some of our beliefs are based on our own ignorance or hand-me-down ignorance—a simple lack of knowledge or understanding—and that's an issue. Beliefs are not facts, sorry.

If you've never traveled around and seen the east side, how can you hold the view that the west is the best? In making the trip, you may find that you change your opinion or strengthen your argument—either way, it's a worthwhile endeavor if you're open to it.

We don't consider both sides of an argument in hopes of changing someone else's mind; we do it in hopes of awakening ours.

Hey, you don't have to look both ways before you cross a busy street, but it's often a pretty good idea.

Challenge Question

When did you first start believing _____? Have you ever questioned this belief or sought to learn more about it?

_____

_____

September 8

Sacred Integrity

Nothing is at last sacred but the integrity of your own mind. Absolve you to yourself, and you shall have the suffrage of the world.
                    Ralph Waldo Emerson—Self-Reliance *(1841)*

Emerson believed that every person had a God-given destiny and that our primary job in life is to remain true to that.

Nice work if you can get it, right?

And like so much of this work and your work, it is deeply personal. It has to be, or else this whole self-reliant bit would be cookie cutter.

Live true to yourself, follow your deepest calling, and you *"shall have the suffrage of the world"*—literally the world will vote for you to succeed. (Okay, maybe that's figuratively speaking, but it's still great.)

Challenge Question

In what critical ways are you living the life people expect you to live? What are you going to do about that?

_____

_____

September 9

Ignore Everything

The voyage of the best ship is a zigzag line of a hundred tacks. See the line from a sufficient distance, and it straightens itself to the average tendency. Your genuine action will explain itself and will explain your other genuine actions. Your conformity explains nothing. Act singly, and what you have already done singly will justify you now.

Ralph Waldo Emerson—Self-Reliance (1841)

If you're to get your highest-payoff work done today, you have to figure out just how to ignore a great deal of what's going on around you.

In your journey you must steel yourself, if that's what it takes, to ignore many things, many people, and many situations. But that's the natural part.

The hard part is that you must also come to recognize and ignore the "inner noise." The stuff you sometimes unconsciously obsess over. Things like fear, doubt, and uncertainty about the entire road you're traveling.

You might not be able to fully ignore these things, but you must recognize that how you interpret these things is what holds you back. Your reaction to these inner doubts is what binds you to conform, play it safe, and mimic the success of others.

Steven Pressfield's excellent book *The War of Art* tackles the idea of fear in this fashion:

Fear is good. Like self-doubt, fear is an indicator. Fear tells us what we have to do. Remember our rule of thumb: The more scared we are of a work or calling, the surer we can be that we have to do it.

The real art is to go boldly toward your vision—singly as Emerson put it—but ignore things like fear and pay attention to them at the same time.

This level of self-awareness alone will allow you to stay on your unique path today.

Challenge Question

What are you most fearful of right now?

_____

_____

Evolving: Congruence

September 10

Embrace Yourself

I ask not for any crown / But that which all may win; / Nor try to conquer any world / Except the one within.

Louisa May Alcott—"My Kingdom" (1876)

Truth: you cannot help others until you help yourself. The wisdom of this idea cannot be taught. You've heard it said countless times, you may even love this idea, but you must embrace it if you are to change lives, communities, industries, nations.

Embrace—accept or support (a belief, theory, or change) willingly and enthusiastically.

Challenge Question

What are you holding on to that you need to let go of? When?

_____

_____

September 11

Solving Impact

The continuity of life is never broken; the river flows onward and is lost to our sight, but under its new horizon it carries the same waters which it gathered under ours, and its unseen valleys are made glad by the offer- ings which are borne down to them from the past,—flowers, perchance, the germs of which its own waves had planted on the banks of Time.
John Greenleaf Whittier—The Prose Works of John Greenleaf Whittier, Vol II *(1866)*

What problems are you solving? That's the essential question in life, and it certainly applies to business. It's not that you should set your entrepreneurial journey in search of problems—the fun is in creating opportunities, making new stuff, building amazing relationships—but in the end, doing even these things solves someone else's problems. Intentionally or unintentionally.

"*. . . and its unseen valleys are made glad by the offerings which are borne down to them from the past . . .*"

The measure of your true impact, and hence the jolt you may need to keep at it, resides in your relationship to the problems you ultimately solve for others. This is as true in your role as a brother, friend, spouse, as it is in your role as a founder, manager, worker bee.

Problem solving seems a bit negative until you start to use it as a way to understand those you serve and interact with from their point of view. Think about it—being a good listener is solving someone's problem, showing up when needed, having a frank conversation, celebrating a win, all problem solving.

Today, try this idea out as a filter for how you think about what you do, how you interact, and maybe even the products or services you might provide.

Challenge Question

In a single sentence, what is the greatest problem you currently (plan to) solve?

_____

_____

September 12

What Is Time?

These roses under my window make no reference to former roses or to bet-
ter ones; they are for what they are; they exist with God today. There is no
time to them. There is simply the rose; it is perfect in every moment of its
existence. Before a leaf-bud has burst, its whole life acts; in the full-blown
flower there is no more; in the leafless root there is no less. Its nature is
satisfied, and it satisfies nature, in all moments alike.

Ralph Waldo Emerson—Self-Reliance *(1841)*

Almost every work cited in this book at some point turns to nature for an example or a metaphor related to living in the present.

So let's start today off talking about what it means to not live in the present, because that's where most of us spend a great deal of our life.

Not living in the present means you open yourself to becoming a victim of the ravages of time.

Here's a fun experiment for you. Google the question "Does time really exist?" and prepare yourself for some mind-altering reading.

Using your experiences from the past and dreaming about your life or your business in the future is okay. It's necessary, but it's only when our thoughts and feelings are dictated by our past or future that we need to find a way to get rooted firmly in the immediate present.

The reason nature makes such a fine example of mindfulness is that in nature, time is one giant emerging moment. There is no past, no future, really no time, so there's no way for nature to develop any bad habits related to such social constructs.

So we spend time focused on the deadline, working as a means to an end, fixated on Monday instead of Sunday, worried what others might say or not say about our best work.

We won't solve this today—this is your lifelong work. So, settle in to the practice.

Challenge Question

What are you experiencing right now, in this moment? Describe it.

_____

_____

September 13

True Potential

Every person has at times in their mind the Ideal of what they should be, but are not. This ideal may be high and complete, or it may be quite low and insufficient; yet in all that really seek to improve it is better than the actual character. Perhaps no one is satisfied with themselves, so that they never wish to be wiser, better, and more holy. No one ever falls so low, that they can see nothing higher than themselves.

Theodore Parker—*"A New Lesson for the Day"* (1856)

What is the measure of one's true potential? Potential—now there's a word charged with emotion. Oh, and it's easy to know our potential because plenty of people have opinions about ours or our lack of it.

But you already know who the biggest critic of your potential is, don't you?

It's you, or more appropriately, it's a limited "mindset" about your potential. You're limitless; we all are, if we allow it. Nobody said it was gonna be easy, but it might be worth the effort.

Consider this idea about a mindset from Carol Dweck's book *Mindset: The New Psychology of Success*: "When people change to a growth mindset, they change from a judge-and-be-judged framework to a learn-and-help-learn framework."

Are you operating from a judge-and-be-judged framework?

Don't waste the energy it takes to beat yourself up because you think you're not living up to your full potential right now. Don't wish things were different; see them for what they are and resolve to learn from them. Stop judging others and you may find you ease up on judging yourself.

Challenge Question

Can you think of a moment of joyfulness from the past week or so? What was it? Why did it happen?

_____

_____

　　　　　　　　　　　Evolving: Congruence

September 14

Entirely Happy

I was something that lay under the sun and felt it, like the pumpkins, and I did not want to be anything more. I was entirely happy. Perhaps we feel like that when we die and become a part of something entire, whether it is sun and air, or goodness and knowledge. At any rate, that is happiness; to be dissolved into something complete and great. When it comes to one, it comes as naturally as sleep.

Willa Cather—My Ántonia *(1918)*

Happiness. That's what we all want, isn't it?

But to have a goal, any goal, to achieve a goal, much less such an ambitious one like achieving happiness, you must first possess the ability to describe what a win looks like.

Or is the search for happiness such an elusive one because we have no final destination in mind? We remain hopelessly lost in our journey, but at least we're making good time.

Let's borrow Cather's description as a great starting point: "*At any rate, that is happiness; to be dissolved into something complete and great.*"

There's nothing scientific or even terribly philosophical about Cather's description—it is at once melodic, perpetual, and filled with life. (It's fitting that this is the quote inscribed on Cather's gravestone.)

Could you live with that? Would that be enough?

Challenge Question

What do you think happiness feels like? Describe it.

_____

_____

September 15

Prune and Water

Genius will live and thrive without training, but it does not the less reward the watering pot and pruning knife. Let the mind fix its own course, and it is apt to fix too exclusively on a pursuit or set of pursuits to which it will devote itself till there is not strength for others.

Margaret Fuller—Papers on Literature and Art *(1846)*

Is there more to life than feeding ourselves, binge-watching the latest Netflix exclusive, and paying the mortgage? Rhetorical? Maybe not?

We can survive—I imagine most of you reading this book know how to do that—but what if the goal is something beyond thriving?

Fuller uses the word "genius" often to describe a form of higher living and thriving, and in this passage, she injects the notion of watering and pruning as practices required for anything to both grow and perhaps thrive.

A plant will grow just about anywhere if it receives enough light and moisture. If it climbs at all, it will choose the path of least resistance—it will survive.

But to flourish, a plant needs care—it needs focus, it needs to nurture its strengths, it needs the right blend of soil, water, light. And yes, it even needs kindness, support, and encouragement, as all living things do.

This seems like a good time to share stand-up comedian Mitch Hedberg's best plant joke: "My fake plants died because I did not pretend to water them."

So, what requires watering? Gratitude, love, courage, openness?

And what requires pruning? What requires attention, with intention? Ego, commitments, possessions, negativity?

Challenge Question

Stand before a mirror—what does your smile look like? How do you want to feel when you smile?

_____

_____

September 16

Do Not Wait

No one is born into the world whose work / Is not born with them. / There is always work, / And tools to work with, for those who will; / And blessed are the horny hands of toil. / The busy world shoves angrily aside the person who stands with arms akimbo, / ntil occasion tells them what to do; / And they who wait to have their task marked out / Shall die and leave their errand unfulfilled.

James Russell Lowell—"A Glance Behind the Curtain" (1843)

Are you doing the work you were born to do? How do you know? What if it doesn't always feel like it even if it is?

How do you feel when you're not working, say, on Sunday? Calm, tense, like you're working?

Or when you're working, do you feel like time just flies, you're happy all the time, you don't even need coffee to get going in the morning? Maybe, but that's not usually how it works.

The hard truth is, the work you were born to do may not be the work you think you want to do—but your life may depend on your doing it.

No one has the answer (although others may tell you they do). There's no book that contains *your* path. You find it by looking for it, by exploring new ways and new ideas, and by paying attention.

By not waiting, by committing to finding the truth.

Challenge Question

What are you waiting for that you should not?

_____

_____

September 17

Into the Wild

Think of our life in nature,—daily to be shown matter, to come in contact with it,—rocks, trees, wind on our cheeks! the solid earth! the actual world! the common sense! Contact! Contact! Who are we? where are we?
Henry David Thoreau—The Maine Woods *(1864)*

When you think of Thoreau, you likely think of nature, wilderness, and preservation. After all, shortly after his death *Atlantic* magazine published his essay "Walking," in which he boldly states, "In Wildness is the preservation of the world."

But Thoreau lived most of his life in a city; even as he retired to Walden Pond, he still made the short walk to Concord for his mother's cookies and chances to dine with friends.

The point is that, although Thoreau advocated the preservation of wilderness, he also acknowledged that nature is as much a part of us as we are of it. In a journal, he mused, "It is in vain to dream of a wildness distant from ourselves."

So for Thoreau, wilderness was a point of view as much as a place. How we think about new adventures allows us to create our own wilderness. Our job is to explore the unknown and to *"come in contact with it,—rocks, trees, wind on our cheeks! the solid earth!"*

Fight through the fear and enter your unknown wilderness just to discover what's there.

That is how we continue to know who we are and where we are.

Challenge Question

What's something you'd like to do now but have been afraid to try?

_____

_____

Evolving: Congruence

September 18

Find Your Gifts

But the great Master said, "I see / No best in kind, but in degree; / I gave a various gift to each, / To charm, to strengthen, and to teach. / / "These are the three great chords of might, / And he whose ear is tuned aright / Will hear no discord in the three, / But the most perfect harmony.
Henry Wadsworth Longfellow—*"The Singers,"* The Complete Poetical Works of Henry Wadsworth Longfellow *(1854)*

Poetry is hard to understand for a lot of people, so here's the full context of what goes on in "The Singers." There are three musicians and people can't figure out which one is the best. So the great Master assures them they are all great for different reasons, and if you listen with that in mind, all you can hear is the most perfect harmony.

Okay, now reread the stanza and you may find it much more lyrical.

So, how do you find harmony in a world of difference? How do you find yourself and your place in the band?

Or to quote Deepak Chopra:

There are no extra pieces in the universe. Everyone is here because he or she has a place to fill, and every piece must fit itself into the big jigsaw puzzle.

Your values, the things that mean the most to you in life right now, are the keys to understanding your gifts. The musicians in Longfellow's poem employed their gifts to charm, to strengthen, and to teach.

How about you? Journal, get alone, ask your three closest friends. Don't sweat it—as long as you are actively looking, your gifts will find you.

Challenge Question

When was the last time you got lost in the present and time disappeared? What were you doing?

_____

_____

September 19

Change Oftener

I am different from other people; my mind changes oftener. People who have no mind can easily be steadfast and firm, but when a person is loaded down to the guards with it, as I am, every heavy sea of foreboding or inclination, maybe of indolence, shifts the cargo.

Mark Twain—Mark Twain's Letters *(1875)*

The transcendentalists love advocating mind-changing. But why is that we need so much encouragement to accomplish this? Why do we hold steadfast and firm to our original positions?

Think back to the last time you went to a family gathering. You entered as a strong, successful, confident, and fearless warrior. Within five minutes you transitioned into your less assured, 12-year-old self. Feel even slightly familiar?

No matter how accomplished we are, we know that people judge us by our past acts, and so we live in fear of contradicting them. Even in the face of facts, we find it hard to shift our impression—particularly concerning ourselves.

Look, the people in your past made you the person you are and that's why you love them—but you're much more than that person today. It's time to let go of their fear and contradict the world with everything that's you. And do it oftener, too.

Challenge Question

What's one thing that people in your past don't know about you anymore?

Evolving: Congruence

September 20

Real Character

I suppose no one can violate their nature. All the sallies of their will are rounded in by the law of their being as the inequalities of the Andes and Himalayas are insignificant in the curve of the sphere. Nor does it matter how you gauge and try someone. A character is like an acrostic or Alexandrian stanza; read it forward, backward, or across, it still spells the same thing.

Ralph Waldo Emerson—Self-Reliance *(1841)*

Even as we try desperately to fit into someone else's picture of our journey, our true character will shine through in the end.

Sounds like a good teen movie plot, doesn't it?

Emerson's mountain metaphor sheds some light on the reality of character. The Andes and Himalayan mountains look jagged from close up, but the *"curve of the sphere"* is insignificant if you observe them from a distance.

Sometimes crucial aspects of our true character lie dormant. The pressure to build a business will likely reveal a few jagged edges. You'll make judgment calls that turn into mistakes. You'll be gauged and tried. You may even find yourself wondering after a particularly difficult learning experience, "How did I get here? This isn't who I am!"

And that's the moment the essence of your true character will awaken and spell out who you truly are.

Challenge Question

When was the last time your true character was tested? How did you respond?

_____

_____

September 21

Release Yourself

Wherever the soul catches a glimpse, in any form, of a perfect union of Love and Truth, it rejoices in the radiant marriage-vesture, and names it Beauty. In all these forms, the soul sees the face of its Parent. It is reminded of its home, and drawn thither. Hence, next to the word "harmony," "a joyous perception of the infinite" is the most common definition of Beauty.
Lydia Maria Child—"What Is Beauty?" (1843)

The word "beauty" is not often applied to inanimate things, but a business, an entrepreneurial dream, can be a beautiful thing. What makes it so?

Perhaps Child's words can shed a global light on this question: *"Wherever the soul catches a glimpse, in any form, of a perfect union of Love and Truth . . ."*

As inspiring as those words are, how do you make them functional?

The enemy of love and truth in a business is waste. Waste in all its many forms creates dissonance and distraction.

Wasted time, wasted resources, wasted focus, wasted ideas. Waste on bloated ideas about income, possessions, and YouTube followers. Right now people are lurking outside your door, waiting to waste your time.

Being busy is the wrong thing to celebrate.

In the words of Greg McKeown, author of *Essentialism: The Disciplined Pursuit of Less*: "You cannot overestimate the unimportance of practically everything."

With simplicity comes harmony; with simplicity comes love and truth, and yes, beauty.

Challenge Question

Check your calendar right now—what are three tasks you can release yourself from?

_____

_____

Evolving: Congruence

September 22

Everyday Truth

In a clear autumnal day we may see, here and there, a massed white cloud edged with a blazing brightness against a blue sky, and now and then a dark pine swinging its top in the wind . . . ; but who can note the shifting and untiring play of the leaves of the wood, and their passing hues, when each seems a living thing full of sensations, and happy in its rich attire? A sound, too, of universal harmony is in our ears, and a wide-spread beauty before our eyes, which we cannot define; yet a joy is in our hearts. Our delight increases in these, day after day, the longer we give ourselves to them, till at last we become, as it were, a part of the existence without us.

Richard Henry Dana—"Kean's Acting" (1950)

Dana seems to explain, in somewhat flowery language, an appreciation of nature. But he was actually describing the nature of character.

We all know someone whose character, or being as it were, affects us at once. But then upon further contact, they grow on us imperceptibly . . . *"till at last we become, as it were, a part of the existence without us."*

Certainly there is something warm about them; they genuinely express interest in us, but underneath they inhabit a natural unwavering quality. They give us something new, honest, and filled with their nature.

This is the quality of self-reliance. This is everyday truth. This is a nature that is hard to name, but it is free—they do only what they intend to do because that's what they want. There's little waste, tension, or conflict.

Challenge Question

Who in your life possesses this quality? Can you observe your interactions with them?

_____

_____

September 23

Remarkable You

Every relation, every gradation of nature is incalculably precious, but only to the soul which is poised upon itself, and to whom no loss, no change, can bring dull discord, for it is in harmony with the central soul. If any individual live too much in relations, so that they become a stranger to the resources of their own nature, they fall, after a while, into a distraction, or imbecility, from which they can only be cured by a time of isolation, which gives the renovating fountains time to rise up.

Margaret Fuller—Woman in the Nineteenth Century *(1845)*

There's a song made popular by country singer Ricky Skaggs titled "Nothing Can Hurt You." The central hook in the chorus is the line "No one can hurt you like someone you love."

It's not a particularly happy lyric, but its popularity leans on the kernel of truth contained in Fuller's warning: "*If any individual live too much in relations, so that they become a stranger to the resources of their own nature, they fall, after a while, into a distraction . . .*"

Now, let's also recall that Fuller was a highly educated literary critic, editor, author, political activist, and women's rights advocate playing in a society that thoroughly marginalized women—relationships were likely hard for her.

As an entrepreneur, that relationship you have with your business is a real thing as well. Attachment to the "us" and "we" of an entrepreneurial journey can lead to issues of control and stress over how things "should be"—and the next thing you know, you've lost yourself in your business.

Your business is never going to be your soulmate. (Okay, maybe that was taking this whole relationship analogy too far.)

The point is, you're not your business; you're the one and only remarkable you. Nothing in your business—loss, riches, failure, success—changes that.

Challenge Question

What part of your identity depends on your business to feel whole?

_____

_____

Evolving: Congruence

September 24

Your Reputation

Your scruples: do they move as in a dusk? Challenge them. Make them advance and declare themselves.

Herman Melville—Billy Budd, Sailor *(1924)*

Instagram is fun. It's a great way to enhance your appearance and give people a fleeting glimpse into how awesome your life is. Or, #staruplife, the struggle is real, y'all. Just read my 47th book this month #killingit. Humbled to have a meeting with Richard Branson this week.

Okay, so it's also an amazing way to build up a wall around the truth and grace required for you and others to fully recognize who you are.

We can put a nice bow on this with words attributed to coach John Wooden:

Be more concerned with your character than your reputation, because your character is what you really are, while your reputation is merely what others think you are. The true test of one's character is what they do when no one is watching.

Your scruples advance and declare themselves through the work you do, the value you bring, the truth you live. That's all.

Self-reliance knows how great you are.

Challenge Question

When will you know that you have achieved self-reliance? What hint will you witness?

_____

_____

September 25

Immortal Impact

Honor is venerable to us because it is no ephemera. It is always ancient virtue. We worship it today because it is not of today. We love it and pay it homage because it is not a trap for our love and homage, but is self-dependent, self-derived, and therefore of an old immaculate pedigree, even if shown in a young person.

Ralph Waldo Emerson—Self-Reliance (1841)

The true accounting for your contribution to the world won't be complete until long after you are gone. That's what Emerson seems to acknowledge.

But he also appears to suggest that he realizes that in his work, and he accordingly urges us to work today with that idea of immortal impact in mind.

Do you recognize or even acknowledge that the decision you make today in your entrepreneurial journey has the potential for far-reaching positive impact in the lives of thousands, maybe millions of people? Is that exciting or scary?

Honor is not a meme; it's here to stay. Honorable work today will be honorably recognized tomorrow.

Challenge Question

How do you know when you are making a good decision? How does it feel?

_____

_____

September 26

Right to Do

From a healthy union of Affection and Thought flows Energy. When we do love to do that which we perceive it right to do, we cannot otherwise than embody it in earnest action. This is moral beauty.
Lydia Maria Child—"What Is Beauty?" (1843)

When we do love to do that which we perceive it right to do, we cannot otherwise than embody it in earnest action.

And if that wasn't enough, research conducted by Just Capital (justcapital.com) year after year demonstrates that corporations that do that which they perceive it right to do are also the most profitable.

So there's that. Check out the rankings of America's Most JUST Companies from Just Capital. Of course, don't forget; you are in charge of deciding that which you perceive is right to do, what creates energy for you, what you define as moral beauty.

Challenge Question

What's one area of your business (or life) that is out of sync with your beliefs? What's a small step you could take to realign it?

_____

_____

September 27

Seasons of Growth

Above all, we cannot afford not to live in the present. He is blessed over all mortals who loses no moment of the passing life in remembering the past. Unless our philosophy hears the cock crow in every barn-yard within our horizon, it is belated.

Henry David Thoreau—"Walking" (1861)

If you are reading this book chronologically, you are likely full on experiencing a change in the season to either fall or spring.

One of the lovely blessings of this annual exchange is that it makes it hard to ignore the natural emergence all around us—that tree that you pass every day now has bright red leaves, the park shows off yellow and orange blossoms.

There's even an official word for this—"phenology," the study of the seasonal timing of life-cycle events.

And as surely as "May flowers bring June bugs," there is a seasonal aspect to every entrepreneurial journey. The secret is to recognize your unique seasons and the time to grow with them. Emerge from planning, to discovering, to evolving, to growing. And then do it again and again until you're done (you're never done).

Recognize the signs. Note when your plans take life as you discover what works. Note when you start to understand your products, services, and customers at deeper levels—when you move from thinking to doing.

Growth is vaguely what every entrepreneur wants. The fact is that no one knows what growth looks like until they've come out the other end of it—and only then if they are paying attention during the chaos.

Note what's happening today and lose *"no moment of the passing life in remembering the past."*

Challenge Question

What can you do today that you could not do a year ago?

_____

_____

September 28

Sense of Newness

Beginning my studies the first step pleas'd me so much, / The mere fact consciousness, these forms, the power of motion, / The least insect or animal, the senses, eyesight, love, / The first step I say awed me and pleas'd me so much, / I have hardly gone and hardly wish'd to go any farther, / But stop and loiter all the time to sing it in ecstatic songs.

Walt Whitman—Leaves of Grass *(1892)*

Although the first edition of *Leaves of Grass* was published in 1855, Whitman spent most of his professional life writing, rewriting, and revising it until his death. This reading appeared in the preface of what is called "the deathbed edition." These short inscriptions gave further insight into Whitman's thinking.

In "Beginning my studies," he seems to share the joy most of us feel in starting something anew. The expectations, the limitless possibilities, the consciousness, the awakening of our senses.

As entrepreneurs pushing through fear and trying so many new things, we feel so intoxicated by the sensation of new that we are tempted to hold on and loiter—breathe it in, remember it, then turn the page and grind on.

But here's the challenge today: how can you take this sense of beginning into every step and stage along the path?

Challenge Question

When was the last time you felt fully alive starting something new? What did it feel like?

_____

_____

September 29

Original Giftedness

Human character evermore publishes itself. The most fugitive deed and word, the mere air of doing a thing, the intimated purpose, expresses character. If you act you show character; if you sit still, if you sleep, you show it.
Ralph Waldo Emerson—"Spiritual Laws" (1841)

Emerson's concept of spirituality was based largely on the idea that we must follow our own unique and original path no matter how hard society pushes back. That our character evermore publishes itself no matter, but our true character shines through only as we reclaim our original self.

But here's the problem: our self-reliance is something we have to fight for, overcome for, and regain as part of our original self. And it runs counter to what we've been told most of our life.

Parker Palmer, author of *Let Your Life Speak*, describes that fight this way:

We are disabused of original giftedness in the first half of our life. Then—if we are awake, aware, and able to admit our loss—we spend the second half of life trying to recover and reclaim the gift we once possessed.

Trying to be what we are not robs us of becoming who we might be. Today, reclaim some part of your original giftedness.

Challenge Question

What was the best non-holiday, non-special event day of your life? Why?

_____

_____

Evolving: Congruence

September 30

Failure's Message

However mean your life is, meet it and live it; do not shun it and call it hard names. It is not so bad as you are. It looks poorest when you are richest. The fault-finder will find faults even in paradise. Love your life, poor as it is. You may perhaps have some pleasant, thrilling, glorious hours, even in a poorhouse. The setting sun is reflected from the windows of the almshouse as brightly as from the rich man's abode; the snow melts before its door as early in the spring. I do not see but a quiet mind may live as contentedly there, and have as cheering thoughts, as in a palace.

Henry David Thoreau—Walden *(1854)*

Let's face it: at some point everybody gets knocked down. Things don't always go as planned, but it's how you handle adversity that will become the ultimate expression of your success.

There are only so many things you have control over, and number one on that list is how you think and feel about daily events.

We can't control the weather, what others say about us, or when someone decides to rip our ideas off as their own. We can't control failure or paradise; we can only decide what we want to learn from it—and the lessons are countless.

In some cases, what we see as a failure is a mistake or error in judgment on our part coming home to roost. Or it could just be something we weren't quite ready to pull off in precisely the manner we chose. But either way, there's a lesson if we wish to accept it.

The fantastic thing about growing as an entrepreneur is that you either flame out through resistance to things like change and failure—and oh, hard work—or you learn to accept that all is as it should be.

The key is to love the setting sun from where you are right now, or you'll always find it hard to love the setting sun no matter how high you soar by some other person's gauge of your success.

Challenge Question

Who is one entrepreneur you deeply admire? Why?

_____

_____

October

Mark Twain (1835–1910)

Don't go around saying the world owes you a living. The world owes you nothing. It was here first.

—*Mark Twain*

Source: Wikimedia

Samuel Clemens, who wrote under the name Mark Twain, was born in Missouri in 1835.

Twain lost his father at age 11, and he left school to work as a printer's apprentice at a local newspaper. These formative years at the newspaper would shape Twain's young adulthood. In 1853, he moved north to New York and Philadelphia, where he wrote for several newspapers.

However, in 1857 he moved home to fulfill his dream of becoming a riverboat captain on the Mississippi. But the American Civil War ended all river traffic in 1861 and thus Twain's burgeoning career.

He then went west to Nevada, where his brother was a prospector. After finding little success as a prospector himself, Twain returned to newspapers, writing for publications in Nevada and San Francisco.

In 1865, his story "Jim Smiley and His Jumping Frog" gained national attention. This further established his name, and Twain embarked on a trip from California to Europe, writing for various papers along the way. The stories from this trip were compiled into his first book, *The Innocents Abroad*, which became an instant hit.

Literary success was not the only positive to come out of his travels. He also met Charles Langdon in 1869, who showed Twain a picture of his sister, Olivia. Twain fell in love with her instantly, and they married two years later.

Twain and his wife moved to Hartford, Connecticut, where they lived for the next 17 years. It was here that Twain wrote some of his most famous books, including *The Adventures of Tom Sawyer* and *The Adventures of Huckleberry Finn*.

Bad investments and mounting debt forced the family to move to Europe. From 1891 to 1900, Twain undertook a lecture tour and was able to regain his financial footing. Unfortunately, he faced personal hardships during this time, including the deaths of his daughter Suzy in 1896; his wife Olivia in 1904; and his youngest daughter Jean in 1909.

Twain himself died in 1910 at his home in Redding, Connecticut.

October 1
Doing Well

Believe me, The talent of success is nothing more than doing what you can do well, and doing well whatever you do without thought of fame. If it comes at all it will come because it is deserved, not because it is sought after. And, moreover, there will be no misgivings, no disappointment, no hasty, feverish, exhausting excitement.

Henry Wadsworth Longfellow—Hyperion *(1839)*

Quite possibly the most offered business advice out there is the need to create a business plan. Not a bad idea in theory, but then "real" happens and any semblance of a plan lands in the recycling bin.

For some, the idea of going without a plan is terrifying. For others, it's the only way to stay creative and innovative. Like so many things, the answer probably lies somewhere in the awkward middle.

You can't plan for fame or even success. It happens because you do what you can do well. *"It will come because it is deserved, not because it is sought after."*

Here's the hard part: of course you want success, of course you plan for success—that's kind of the point of doing this in the first place—but you can't see the big picture of what's going on all over the universe that's working with you and against you and for your idea or counter to your plan.

Jeff Goins, author of *The Art of Work*, spells it out this way:

> But for now, if you are intentional and willing to appreciate the fact that you don't see the whole narrative, you can enjoy more of the journey.

Holding tightly to the plan is a great way to kill the joy of the ride. It isn't scary; it's an admission that you don't control anything but how you experience the journey. There is no Google Map for this. There's only you and *"no misgivings, no disappointment, no hasty, feverish, exhausting excitement."*

Challenge Question

What are you okay with being uncertain about?

_____

_____

October 2
Done Growing

Lord, when shall we be done growing? As long as we have anything more to do, we have done nothing ... Lord, when shall we be done changing? Ah! it's a long stage, and no inn in sight, and night coming, and the body cold.
Herman Melville—*Letter to Nathaniel Hawthorne, published in*
Memories of Hawthorne *by Rose Hawthorne Lathrop (1897)*

Here's another question to ponder: when shall we start growing? Melville admitted in an earlier letter to Hawthorne that "Until I was twenty-five I had no growth at all. From my twenty-fifth year I date my life."

Growth requires change, change is hard, and so growth is hard.

Stop growing and life stagnates, but as Melville seems to express, it's exhausting at times—mainly because growth doesn't happen by hoping or even setting audacious goals. It happens when you admit where you are now and accept all the chapters in your past without regret.

From this lucid place you can chart your growth.

Wouldn't it be awesome if we got a cake and celebrated each step in our personal growth, you know, instead of simply acknowledging we lived another year?

Admit we don't know it all—cake, realize we don't have to react—cake, decide to leave a toxic job—cake, hug more, forgive sooner—cake, learn how to listen to and support team members—cake, admit, without blame, that our parents' shortcomings don't define us—cake.

Maybe those are our real "birth" days?

Challenge Question

Do you tend to focus on the positive or negative traits of others? Why?

_____

_____

October 3
Growth Data

Progress, in the sense of acquisition, is something; but progress in the sense of being, is a great deal more. To grow higher, deeper, wider, as the years go on; to conquer difficulties, and acquire more and more power; to feel all one's faculties unfolding, and truth descending into the soul,—this makes life worth living.
James Freeman Clarke—Dictionary of Burning Words of Brilliant Writers *(1895)*

Few debate the positive aspects of personal growth and the progress it bodes.

But what exactly is growth? What are the metrics? In business we set growth goals and define key indicators to track our progress. In life, in the pursuit of self-reliance we have no such objective measures.

So, what's the plan?

It starts, like all tracking, with identifying what you are going to measure. But the tricky part here is now you need to come face to face with what exactly it is you're trying to grow. Just getting better won't cut it.

So is it happier, stronger, more fulfilling relationships? Or maybe richer, more successful, less stressful?

Oh, and are these even the right things? And what do we need to measure to detect growth? And can we have them all at the same time?

The only way to measure your personal growth is to pay attention to how you're thinking, feeling, doing, and being in real time day after day. Do you feel less stressed today? How did you handle that conversion? What are you assessing as right or wrong in a team member's presentation?

Mindfully witnessing your thoughts without judgment and applying a little kindness toward getting better with each interaction is the best tool you've got.

Challenge Question

What are you going to pay attention to today? How will that help you grow?

_____

_____

Growing: Change

291

October 4
Excessive Business

It is very sad for a person to make themselves servant to a single thing; their life all taken out of them by the hydraulic pressure of excessive business.—I should not like to be merely a great doctor, a great lawyer, a great minister, a great politician.—I should like to be, also, something of a person.
Theodore Parker—*as quoted in* A Dictionary of Thoughts *(1908)*

Wow. *Hydraulic pressure of excessive business.* Now that's an evocative way to describe entrepreneurship.

Truth is, in business, we're rarely as busy as we think we are; we're as busy as we tell ourselves we are.

And that leads to time-wasting tasks, blaming others for our failings, and performing at a level beneath our best work. Then, ultimately the "hydraulic pressure" overcomes us and deteriorates our ability to be something of a person.

When you're truly connected to the greater reward of your work, you'll find it easier to ignore the immediate reward of distraction.

Challenge Question

What's the first, most important task you're going to knock out today before you do anything else? Why is it important?

_____

_____

October 5
Above Time

But humans postpone or remember; they do not live in the present, but with reverted eye laments the past, or, heedless of the riches that surround them, stands on tiptoe to foresee the future. They cannot be happy and strong until they too live with nature in the present, above time.

Ralph Waldo Emerson—Self-Reliance *(1841)*

You would think there would only be so many ways to talk about mindfulness. Ah, but then you would be wrong.

An aspect of mindfulness that isn't often touched upon is that without it you can't build change.

When we spend all our time in the known past, it automatically creates our future. When we are certain just how something is going to go—because that's how it went last time—it's a sure bet that's how it will go this time around. To our mind and body, it's as automated as breathing.

But what if instead of relying on or obsessing over how something turned out in the past we used the *present* to obsess over creating a more desirable future outcome? That's how mindfulness creates the future.

If you want to get a bit quantum about this idea, you can effectively change your mind and body to live as Emerson suggests: "*above time.*"

But this requires the ability to change in the present.

As Joe Dispenza so clearly lays out in *Breaking the Habit of Being Yourself*:

[I]f we focus on an intended future event and then plan how we will prepare or behave, there will be a moment when we are so clear and focused on that possible future that the thoughts we are thinking will begin to become the experience itself.

Living in the past, we create our future; living in the present, we create our future. The only question is, which future is more desirable?

Challenge Question

If your future had no limits, what would you choose to do? Why?

_____

_____

October 6
Ready or Not

*Weep not that the world changes—did it keep / A stable, changeless state,
'twere cause indeed to weep.*
                    William Cullen Bryant—"Mutation: A Sonnet" (1862)

Not all change is good; it's just inevitable. In your entrepreneurial journey, you may encounter change that creates hardship, outdates your business, or comes at a great financial cost.

Change on your terms is one thing—but what about change over which you have no control?

Ready or not, change is going to happen. So how we grow and mature with change is the key to how we survive it. While change for the sake of change may prove risky, resistance to the seeming inevitable may cost you everything.

Change, especially hard change, creates resilience. Change can force us to get better. Change can create opportunity.

Growth and progress require change. So keep your head up, look for signs on the changing horizon, and lead through it.

It's okay to miss the good old days; just don't live in them.

Challenge Question

What area of your business do you need to be paranoid about right now?

_____

_____

October 7
Trouble Solving

Within two minutes, or even less, he had forgotten all his troubles. Not because his troubles were one whit less heavy and bitter to him, but because a new and powerful interest bore them down and drove them out of his mind for the time—just as one's misfortunes are forgotten in the excitement of new enterprises.

Mark Twain—The Adventures of Tom Sawyer *(1876)*

There's little question that the strategy for quickly moving on from our troubles is to fill the space with "the excitement of a new enterprise."

But is moving on in that fashion potentially like sticking our head in the sand? Don't like the hard work required to make this initiative profitable? No worries; just try out a new social media platform. Distraction isn't the answer; honesty is.

To leave a problem in the past, we have to first be willing to draw a line in that sand instead of digging a hole in it. We have to be able to mark the past as the past and the present as the greatest opportunity to learn.

We may need to ask for help. The solution could live in a completely new approach, testing something that's worked for a peer, or getting advice from an independent voice.

And you might have to change your mind.

Like many entrepreneurs, Tom Sawyer's troubles were often self-inflicted. Finding and knocking down the barrier we've built within that keeps us stuck in a cycle of self-sabotage may be the real problem that deserves a fix.

Is it fear of the cost of failure or fear of the cost of success at play?

Challenge Question

If nothing changes, what are the challenges in your business going to look like six months from now?

_____

_____

October 8
Some Absorbing Errand

True happiness, we are told, consists in getting out of one's self; but the point is not only to get out—you must stay out; and to stay out you must have some absorbing errand.

Henry James—Roderick Hudson *(1875)*

Entrepreneurial chaos is fertile ground for getting "in one's self." You've never done it surely, but it's likely you've heard others talk about the resistance they refer to as "head trash."

Sometimes the answer is to stop thinking so much already and just go pull some weeds. Not metaphorical weeds. Really, go out and get dirty, rake some mucked-up leaves, turn over some pots, plant some dill, change your mental and physical chemistry with intention.

Now, after the medicine of "some absorbing errand," go back to that thing that captures your ambitions, deserves your aspirations, and consumes your efforts, happy to be out of your mind.

Challenge Question

What's your go-to method to get out of overthinking things? When is the last time you did it?

_____

_____

October 9

Intentional Travel

To set about living a true life is to go on a journey to a distant country,
gradually to find ourselves surrounded by new scenes and people; and as
long as the old are around me, I know that I am not in any true sense living
a new or a better life.

Henry David Thoreau—Familiar Letters *(1865)*

Taking a vacation from time to time is so nice, isn't it? It's a chance to recharge, relax, and basically escape from real life. You've probably noticed that it takes a day or two to let go. At first, you're worrying about what you forgot, how your morning routine is going to go, and where you're going to find a good vegan restaurant (or not), but eventually you melt into the pace.

So, what if travel was more than a vacation or meeting destination? What if travel was intentional and served some everyday purpose? Perhaps you've known or admired some couple who quit their jobs, bought an RV, and took a year off. Maybe you thought it seemed noble; maybe you thought it just seemed hipsterish.

No matter; you don't have to take the giant leap, but *"gradually to find ourselves surrounded by new scenes and people"* offers an education unavailable in any other fashion.

Above all, intentional travel teaches us humility, compassion, empathy, and a whole lot about our capabilities as human beings.

If you subscribe to the notion that an eternal spirit of some sort exists that connects us all in a great big field of potential, then *"a distant country"* may be your greatest source of connection and inspiration. (Across town may be a distant land.)

Today, consider the possibility of intentional travel as a way to build your entrepreneurial dream.

And, another thing: journal every day that you travel to record new findings, but mostly to consider how you've changed.

Challenge Question

What is something beautiful you see every day? Where else could you find more beauty?

_____

_____

October 10
Abundant Trust

He who is firmly seated in authority soon learns to think of security, and not progress, the highest lesson of statecraft. From the summit of power people no longer turn their eyes upward, but begin to look about them.
James Russell Lowell—"New England Two Centuries Ago," Literary Essays *(1865)*

Funny how we scratch and claw and dig our way to the top, and then once we get there, we spend an enormous amount of time looking back and around to make sure nothing is crumbling around us.

It's the nature of how this game is often portrayed. Beat the competition, win, cash the check (or some new kind of money).

Funny thing is, few things erode progress faster than getting stuck in Paranoiaville on what feels like your slippery summit. Want to pick up some momentum again? Start down the hill, release the brakes, fly on by, and start to trust again.

Trust in abundance.

Extend trust to those who believe in you and your dreams. People, customers, partners, team members want to go on this journey with you if you'll let them. They want you to show them how to help you. They don't need you have the answers or even a plan; they just want to know you care about their climb up the hill, too. Mostly, get out of their way.

Want to win? Show up with a passionate community ready to eat marshmallows with you. (You know they're made from horse hooves, right?)

Today, turn your eyes upward, and hand out the marshmallows.

Challenge Question

If someone wrote a story about you, would you be the champion or the challenger?

_____

_____

October 11
Ever Expansive

Now, it is clear, not only that what is obvious to one mind may not be obvious to another, but that what is obvious to one mind at one epoch, may be anything but obvious, at another epoch, to the same mind . . . It is seen, then, that the axiomatic principle itself is susceptible of variation, and of course that axioms are susceptible of similar change. Being mutable, the "truths" which grow out of them are necessarily mutable too; or, in other words, are never to be positively depended upon as truths at all—since Truth and Immutability are one.

Edgar Allan Poe—"Eureka" (1848)

Poe was his era's Stephen King and as such it's not always clear if he's writing about good or evil, because he saw everything as little more than truth.

"Eureka" is oddly in line with transcendental philosophy, even though Poe was a vocal critic of many of the more noted transcendentalist writers, including Emerson. It's hard to imagine this piece is from the nineteenth century; mixed in with some pretty zany ideas are elements of prophetic science, even though it lacked any experimental proof of what he proposed. (Some claim the work is vital in later models of the big bang theory—not the TV show.)

But what's all this got to do with you?

Tucked away in the passage from today's reading is a somewhat lucid, if not complex, anatomy of the concept of intuition. Truth is connection with others. Intuition is honesty at full price. Our existence on this planet is incredibly ever expansive.

Challenge Question

In what ways is your universe expanding?

_____

_____

October 12
Do Right Now

*Greatness appeals to the future. If I can be firm enough today to do right
and scorn eyes, I must have done so much right before as to defend me now.
Be it how it will, do right now.*

Ralph Waldo Emerson—Self-Reliance *(1841)*

Today's reading is a reminder that nothing great comes from caring too much
about what others think or how they respond to your journey: to *"be firm
enough today to do right and scorn eyes."*

Can you imagine a future made better by the fact that you dreamed it
today and acted upon it today?

Building something from nothing, let alone something that is declared
great, is little more than an accumulation of what you do that is right, right
now. Maybe even the tiniest act focused on an imagined destination that only
you can picture.

It's okay to seek advice and opinions, but if that turns into trying to
morph your products or services or business to please everyone, you will
become eternally stuck in pleasing no one—including yourself.

Customers, suppliers, the guru selling the latest, greatest way to generate
leads will all suggest they know better. Only you know better. Trust that.

Challenge Question

Who do you need to stop trying to please?

_____

_____

October 13
New Wine

All want, not something to do with, but something to do, or rather something to be. Perhaps we should never procure a new suit, however ragged or dirty the old, until we have so conducted, so enterprised or sailed in some way, that we feel like new in the old, and that to retain it would be like keeping new wine in old bottles.

Henry David Thoreau—Walden *(1854)*

It's no secret that Thoreau valued ideas over possessions. He sought to minimize his material needs so that he could focus on his spiritual needs.

But maybe the wardrobe guidance contained in this passage could be seen as something more than an attempt to reduce his carbon footprint—a nineteenth-century version of Patagonia's Worn Wear initiative.

Perhaps the metaphorical act of feeling like new in the old is a reflection of authenticity.

Where do we find authentic happiness, authentic work, authentic possessions?

They can be found in being passionately employed in our work, but they can be lost as we succumb to work that leads us to busyland only to wake up one day and find that we are leading that "life of quiet desperation." And then, as though we have no choice, we reach to procure a new suit.

The suggestion here isn't simply one of buying less; it's a matter of becoming more. Thoreau urges us to consciously fuse the *doing* in life with the *being* in life—to let go of who we think we are supposed to be in order to recognize who we truly are.

Challenge Question

Do you wish you were doing something different than what you are doing now? What?

_____

_____

October 14
Creative Genius

I have come prepared to see all this, to dislike it, but not with stupid narrowness to distrust or defame. On the contrary, while I will not be so obliging as to confound ugliness with beauty, discord with harmony, and laud and be contented with all I meet, when it conflicts with my best desires and tastes, I trust by reverent faith to woo the mighty meaning of the scene, perhaps to foresee the law by which a new order, a new poetry, is to be evoked from this chaos.

Margaret Fuller—At Home and Abroad; or, Things and Thoughts in America and Europe *(1856)*

Creative genius is often seen as something that comes to the chosen few who pick up a brush or sit at a piano and craft something so original that duplication is unthinkable.

That's the storybook version anyway. The reality is likely closer to something like this.

You search high and low for something you want, but when you can't find it, you decide to make it. You wrestle with a creative way to package your offerings, and then one day, while reading a work of fiction you brought to the beach, you stumble on the perfect solution in some quirky piece of dialogue between characters. A client asks you why you've always done something a certain way, and you can't find a meaningful answer. So you build a new way.

That's creative genius; that's *"the law by which a new order, a new poetry, is to be evoked from this chaos."*

Question everything, tear apart best practices, create unusual pairings—take nothing but a notebook with you on vacation.

Creative genius is found in paying attention to what the universe is showing you in all those places you don't go looking for it.

Challenge Question

What color best defines you? Why?

_____

_____

October 15
Limiting Stories

When a resolute young person steps up to the great bully, the World, and takes it boldly by the beard, they are often surprised to find it come off in their hand, and that it was only tied on to scare away timid adventurers.
Oliver Wendell Holmes, Sr.—Elsie Venner *(1861)*

When is the last time you told yourself a story that just wasn't true? And the imagined outcome of that fable controlled not only your emotions, but your actions or inactions as well?

The stories we tell ourselves about money, or success, or failure, or even our own happiness dictate and foreshadow our eventual consequences. They color how we see the world and the abundant opportunity all around us. They force us to see people and things not as they are, but as we tell ourselves they are.

But then one day something clicks and forces us to approach a limiting story and experience it in a totally new manner, to take it *"boldly by the beard,"* and we are surprised, relieved, and maybe a little frustrated that it exercised such control over us.

But limiting assumptions are kind of like dandelions: if you don't get to the root, you'll never get control.

Think of a story you tell yourself that's holding you back. Ask yourself why you have that story. Go unearth the evidence all around you that helps you undermine your current thinking.

Write it down—you've grown so much since you first developed your old story. Just because you believe it, that doesn't make it true. Go take it boldly by the beard and yank hard.

Challenge Question

What's one thing you've done in your life that you once thought was not possible?

_____

_____

October 16

Finding Aliveness

Life consists with wildness. The most alive is the wildest. Not yet subdued to humankind, its presence refreshes. One who pressed forward incessantly and never rested from their labors, who grew fast and made infinite demands on life, would always find themselves in a new country or wilderness, and surrounded by the raw material of life. They would be climbing over the prostrate stems of primitive forest trees.

Henry David Thoreau—"Walking" (1861)

Thoreau, Emerson, and Whitman advocated the qualities of nature as a requisite aspect of spirituality. They wrote about it in romantic and poetic terms but, seated firmly as they were at the height of the Industrial Revolution, their arguments were seen at the time more as metaphor than movement.

Today, elements of their teachings (preachings) can be found in everything from politics to urban planning. Studies of happiness and even longevity include nods to living in places and environments where there is a dimension of wildness or aliveness.

What the heck; maybe we're not meant to eat food created in a lab, or perhaps sitting all day under artificial lights isn't good for our health. Maybe we need to meet more people face to face, and maybe, just maybe, we need nature to master, as Thoreau described it, "the art of life."

The life of the typical entrepreneur often suffers today from what Richard Louv, author of *The Nature Principle*, calls "Nature Deficit Disorder"—a way to describe the psychological, physical, and cognitive costs of human alienation from nature.

Thoreau asked, "What is the pill that will keep us well, serene, contented?"

His answer to this question was morning air inhaled in a place that feeds our soul.

Challenge Question

Where are you drawn to explore? Why? When?

October 17
Creating History

The student of history is like a person going into a warehouse to buy cloths or carpets. They fancy they have a new article. If they go to the factory, they shall find that their new stuff still repeats the scrolls and rosettes which are found on the interior walls of the pyramids of Thebes.
Ralph Waldo Emerson—*"Uses of Great Men,"* The Oxford Book of
American Essays, ed. Brander Matthews (1914)

Spanish-born philosopher George Santayana popularized the adage, "Those who cannot remember the past are condemned to repeat it." In a 1948 speech to the House of Commons, Winston Churchill paraphrased the quote slightly when he said, "Those who fail to learn from history are condemned to repeat it."

Both meant this as a warning to those who did not study the failings of past as a guide to the future.

What if you saw your entrepreneurial journey in a much different light? What if by recognizing that your "new stuff still repeats," you created your own history?

Starting today, could you look at content creation and journaling in the way that a documentarian might? Could you start to document every aspect of your journey as a way to learn from yourself, learn from your mistakes, your triumphs, your daily observations of the mundane as well as the thrilling?

You have much to teach yourself by stopping and taking note, and there's a very practical element from a brand standpoint. Sharing your journey and using your documenting practice is one of the strongest ways to connect with your audience and invite them to join you on your journey.

Challenge Question

What's the hardest part about being an entrepreneur? (That might make a great blog post.)

_____

_____

Author's Note: Today's reflection is provided by my daughter, Jenna Jantsch.

October 18
Unexplored Lands

All the past we leave behind; / We debouch upon a newer, mightier world, varied world, / Fresh and strong the world we seize, world of labor and the march, Pioneers! O pioneers!

Walt Whitman—Leaves of Grass *(1865)*

A pioneer is a person among the first to explore or settle a new country, area, or idea. Whether it is a physical location or part of your mental journey, think about all of the space you have covered. Where have you traveled to get to where you are today?

Many times initial change is viewed in a negative light. How has the change created by your journey been negative? How has it been positive? Think about those times of transition, when something's been hard and viewed poorly in the beginning but completely worth it in the end.

What knowledge did you gain from the trek? Sit with this knowledge and let it ground you. Find the confidence in what you've earned from that experience.

Now use that energy to take the next step. Where do you want to go from here?

Challenge Question

Where will you pioneer today? How will you pioneer today?

_____

_____

October 19

Knowledge Without Wisdom

You may disarm the hands, but not the brains, of a people, and to know
what should be defended is the first condition of successful defense. Simple
as it may seem, it was a great discovery that the key of knowledge could turn
both ways, that it could open, as well as lock, the door of power to the many.
James Russell Lowell—*"New England Two Centuries Ago,"* Literary
Essays *(1865)*

Many would claim that the key to success in business is knowledge.

Ah, but only knowledge, without wisdom, the wisdom that consistently results in appropriate action, is a trap.

Knowledge is found in a story of how one of your entrepreneurial heroes, aided by the insight of hindsight, achieved their version of success. (Spoiler alert: it didn't really happen like that. They most likely tried something and eventually pivoted into the thing that they were doing on the side that turned into the real winner—research Slack and Flickr cofounder Stewart Butterfield.)

Wisdom is found in knowing that your story is not their story, and though you may learn valuable lessons from their advice, it is foolish to think they know what's best for your journey.

Apply wisdom, your truth, to everything you take in and your *"key of knowledge"* will open the congruent door.

See, the real truth is, you can become one of your entrepreneurial heroes.

Challenge Question

What idea are you holding on to that's keeping you from thinking bigger?

_____

_____

October 20
Decide Growth

Very early, I knew that the only object in life was to grow.
Margaret Fuller—Memoirs of Margaret Fuller Ossoli *(1852)*

Do you think it's humanly possible to stay the same? Our brains and our bodies don't think so. In some capacity they are becoming less at this very moment.

That's the hand we are dealt.

But mental and spiritual growth, improvement, learning, changing, doing, and being something entirely new stops only when we choose to stop.

Sure, you can take up mountain biking or add a third language if that's your thing, but the opportunity to grow happens in every moment. Choosing to react (or not react) in a certain way that hasn't served you in the past is growth.

Are you excited about the possibility of every new day?

If not, then maybe you've let yourself stop.

Today, look for something new, teach someone, choose a way to grow, and let it help you define something bigger, more meaningful for tomorrow.

Challenge Question

What knowledge or skills do you possess that you could teach to others?

_____

_____

Growing: Change

October 21
Expert on You

Good and bad are but names very readily transferable to that or this; the only right is what is after my constitution; the only wrong what is against it.
Ralph Waldo Emerson—Self-Reliance *(1841)*

There's a good chance you're trying to change someone's status quo—even if it's your status quo—and that's going to eventually threaten people.

Humans like status quo; in fact, they go out of their way to create institutions and rules and policies and laws and doctrine in order to guarantee the status quo.

The transcendentalist movement was founded on challenging the status quo and saying "Enough! We're going to think and act for ourselves and remain true to what we believe."

Seth Godin, author of *Tribes*, likes to buck the status quo and offers this advice: "If you aren't upsetting someone, you aren't changing the status quo."

Don't let anyone tell you that your purpose or idea or dream is the wrong one. You may need to develop a thick skin, but you don't have to listen. You're the only expert on you.

Go crack something today.

Challenge Question

Who in your life is most threatened by your evolution? Why?

_____

_____

October 22

Little Corner

Travel is fatal to prejudice, bigotry and narrow-mindedness, and many of our people need it sorely on these accounts. Broad, wholesome, charitable views of people and things can not be acquired by vegetating in one little corner of the earth all one's lifetime.

Mark Twain—Innocents Abroad *(1869)*

Twain's words are as truthful today as they were in the nineteenth century. (Perhaps more so.)

Moving outside of one's little corner of the earth provides two divergent possibilities: growth or misery. Seek the one that works for you.

You don't explore to run from yourself; you do it to find yourself.

Challenge Question

What is something beautiful you see every day? Where else could you find that?

_____

_____

October 23
Your Creator

Character, reality, reminds you of nothing else; it takes place of the whole creation. A person must be so much that they must make all circumstances indifferent. Every true person is a cause, a country, and an age; requires infinite spaces and numbers and time fully to accomplish their design; and posterity seem to follow their steps as a train of clients.

Ralph Waldo Emerson—Self-Reliance (1841)

You are not a user, a vendor, a customer, a boss, a team member—you are your creator.

Emerson wrote that *"[e]very true person is a cause, a country, and an age"* because he contended that each of us is endowed with a soul and that alone makes each of us divine. (This of course freaked a lot of people out at the time as well.)

He taught in this sense that we are capable of self-reliance because we've been given the ability to trust our judgment. Conforming to the wishes of others was to sin against one's integrity.

Emerson's vivid message throughout *Self-Reliance* is that we live in integrity only when we pursue our unique destiny.

So, turns out you are already so much. Who knew?

Challenge Question

What do you feel is the essence of your destiny? Are you living it?

_____

_____

October 24
Future Design

Look not mournfully into the Past. It comes not back again. Wisely improve the Present. It is thine. Go forth to meet the shadowy Future, without fear, and with a courageous heart.
Henry Wadsworth Longfellow—Hyperion (1839)

The past is the past—except when we keep inviting it into the present where we create our future.

As we move through each day, our memories, charged with emotions from the past, unconsciously re-create these past emotions in our present reality. And the song stays stuck on repeat.

Okay, so if this is true—that we are limiting our progress by living in a predictable future predicated on the past—what if we told our brain to shut up about the past and we put everything we had into the present moment so we could live, today, in the future we design?

Simple, yes. Easy, maybe not.

Even though traditional advice on present-minded living suggests that you not consider the future, if by designing your desired future, without the baggage of the past, you are destined to create or will it into existence by your actions today, wouldn't that be a richer way to live?

"Go forth to meet the shadowy Future, without fear, and with a courageous heart."

Challenge Question

What is your biggest regret in life? Are you ready to move on?

_____

_____

October 25
Celestial Fire

All the means of action— / The shapeless masses, the materials— / Lie everywhere about us. What we need / Is the celestial fire to change the flint / Into transparent crystal, bright and clear. / That fire is genius!
Henry Wadsworth Longfellow—"The Spanish Student" (1843)

It would be pretty easy to interpret today's reading as a call to swell up that fire in your entrepreneurial belly. (The metaphor is there for the taking.)

But that would risk oversimplifying the entrepreneurial journey into the hustle-and-grind camp.

The *"celestial fire to change the flint"* comes more accurately from developing keen self-awareness.

By understanding your strengths and, more important, your weaknesses, you gain the power to make decisions "unreliant" on your ego. (To be "unreliant" on one's ego is sort of synonymous with being reliant on one's self, or self-reliant. How's that for making the ego the villain?)

Let's face it: it takes more work to admit our weaknesses than to carve out our strengths, but to trust ourselves at that level is to become more completely self-reliant.

Now, lead by filling those gaps; surround yourself with people and resources that shore up your weaknesses.

Analytics and details can make or break your business. Hate the details? Be self-aware enough to realize there are those strange humans who love the details.

Challenge Question

What is your greatest weakness? (No, this is not an interview question; you really have to figure this out.)

_____

_____

October 26
Upon Rereading

No one can learn what they have not preparation for learning, however near to their eyes the object. A chemist may tell their most precious secrets to a carpenter, and they shall be none the wiser. Our eyes are holden that we cannot see things that stare us in the face, until the hour arrives when the mind is reopened; then we behold them, and the time when we saw them not is like a dream.

Ralph Waldo Emerson—"Spiritual Laws" (1841)

Have you ever gone back and reread a book only to find yourself stumbling upon some bolt of wisdom that you inexplicably missed in the last reading? It's as if the author read your mind and through some electronic feat of magic edited the book while it sat on your reader or shelf.

Now, staring you right in the face is the exact thing you need to hear today in order to forge ahead.

For all of its miraculousness, the mind seems to obscure things from our view until we are ready to go looking for them.

But, another thing is at play here: you've traveled some distance since you last picked up that book, and your new understanding is a measure of this. Since the book never changes, its constant state persists as the measure of your growth.

And for that reason, rereading should be at the top of every entrepreneur's to-do list. Quite often we read books because they show up on someone's "must reads" list, yet they contain ideas we barely understand until we've attempted and struggled to accomplish some aspect essential to the book's core idea.

Emerson's *Self-Reliance* has endured the test of time and still offers something more upon the twentieth or thirtieth reading.

When you encounter any challenge, an intentional, purposeful rereading of a meaningful work may reveal a gem you are now prepared to receive.

Challenge Question

What book will you reread next? Why?

_____

_____

Growing: Change

October 27
Be Good for Something

Pursue, keep up with, circle round and round your life, as a dog does his master's chaise. Do what you love. Know your own bone; gnaw at it, bury it, unearth it, and gnaw it still. Do not be too moral. You may cheat yourself out of much life so. Aim above morality. Be not simply good; be good for something.

Henry David Thoreau—Familiar Letters *(1894)*

In society, morality is often defined as a set of standards that should be universal. Of course, Thoreau and most of the authors represented in this book believed that universal standards were little more than a tool to oppress self-reliance.

Thoreau removes to some extent the shades of gray by suggesting a more universal standard: be good for something.

Today, lift someone up.

Challenge Question

How have you been helped by someone in your past? Send them a note.

_____

_____

October 28

Extraordinary Dreamers

If his inmost heart could have been laid open, there would have been discovered that dream of undying fame, which, dream as it is,' is more powerful than a thousand realities.

Nathaniel Hawthorne—Fanshawe (1828)

Entrepreneurs are extraordinary dreamers.

And maybe you've heard that's a bad thing.

Turns out, everything that was ever created was imagined before it was real.

We must first dream to create things that don't exist today. We must dream to give meaning to our passion well before it becomes our reality. We must dream because reality tells us we have boundaries while our dreams are limitless.

Ultimately, we must dream to create a thousand realities.

Now, before you define your big-fat-dream-in-the-sky, answer this question: who would you have to become in order to turn this dream into a reality? Dismiss that part, and the train won't leave the station.

Challenge Question

Who would you have to become in order to turn your dreams into reality?

_____

_____

October 29

Confidence and Doubt

Your moonlight, as I have told you, though it is a reflection of the sun, allows of bats and owls and other twilight birds to flit therein. But I am very glad that you can elevate your life with a doubt, for I am sure that it is nothing but an insatiable faith after all that deepens and darkens its current. And your doubt and my confidence are only a difference of expression.

Henry David Thoreau—Familiar Letters *(1865)*

If you had no doubt, you were certain something was going to work, c'mon, how fun could that really be?

You're gonna have doubt; you want doubt, because otherwise someone else would just do it in place of you. Your doubt is a sign that the thing you are doing just might be worth doing.

Thoreau encourages his friend to elevate his life with a doubt, and that's precisely the point of view all entrepreneurs need to carry into the battle against their fears.

You possess the confidence to be wrong, patient, and brave simultaneously.

"And your doubt and my confidence are only a difference of expression."

Challenge Question

What do you want instead of doubt? What value would that add to your life?

_____

_____

October 30
First Drafts

Artistic growth is, more than it is anything else, a refining of the sense of truthfulness. The stupid believe that to be truthful is easy; only the artist, the great artist, knows how difficult it is. That afternoon nothing new came to Thea Kronborg, no enlightenment, no inspiration. She merely came into full possession of things she had been refining and perfecting for so long.
Willa Cather—Song of the Lark *(1915)*

Some days you've get to create anew; some days your job is to take "*full possession of things [you have] been refining and perfecting for so long.*" The trick is knowing one from the other. Enlightenment and inspiration trickle in around numberless days of editing, tweaking, testing, and recasting.

But it is a mistake to ignore these tasks or relegate them to the empty corners of your business, because this is where you discover the sense of truthfulness in your business.

First drafts, while important, are where most people stop. There's little truth in first drafts; no one has purchased your first draft and perhaps they never will. Ship, refine, ship, perfect, ship, evolve, ship the truth (for now).

Challenge Question

What are your expectations for this stage of your business? Are they realistic?

_____

_____

October 31
To Think Is to Act

Why should we be cowed by the name of Action? 'Tis a trick of the senses,—no more. We know that the ancestor of every action is a thought.
Ralph Waldo Emerson—"Spiritual Laws" (1841)

Emerson continues in his essay to put an even finer point on this: *"To think is to act."*

Not much of a leap here, then, to suggest that your thoughts control your eventual destiny.

So be careful what you think. (It's kind of like you're carrying around a loaded gun all day.)

Our thoughts can motivate us to do things we once thought were beyond our ability. Our thoughts can lift and change the trajectory of someone's future.

Our thoughts can also reinforce the myth of our life.

This might be the point to suggest that we can also freely change our thoughts and, in doing so, impact our words, actions, habits, personality, and destiny any time we choose.

The only thoughts we control are our own, and that's a great place to start and end. This is where we often get bumped off course—trying to change the world around us.

Wayne Dyer, author of numerous self-development books, offers the following advice: "Never underestimate your power to change yourself; never overestimate your power to change others."

At the end of each day, you might find it helpful to take stock and see how many little, seemingly insignificant things went extremely well. The first step to creating thoughts that create positive action is to appreciate how great we've got it on the whole. (Oh, and meditate.)

Challenge Question

What's one problem you're thankful you don't have?

_____

_____

November

Frederick Douglass (1818–1895)

Without a struggle, there can be no progress.

—*Frederick Douglass*

Source: Wikimedia

Born into slavery in Maryland, Frederick Douglass escaped to freedom in the North, where he became a vocal advocate for the abolitionist movement, racial equality, and women's rights.

Douglass did not know his exact date of birth, only the year: 1818. He was raised in the country but was sent to Baltimore at age eight to work for a ship carpenter. It was in the city that he was first exposed to abolitionist ideas.

In 1833, he was sent back to the country. Farm life was miserable, and Douglass was whipped regularly. In 1836 he planned to escape, but his plot was discovered and he was jailed.

In 1838, he was sent back to Baltimore. He again planned to escape and enlisted the help of Anna Murray, a free black woman. This time he was successful, and Douglass settled in New Bedford, Massachusetts. He was joined by Murray, whom he married.

In Massachusetts, Douglass educated himself further and became involved in abolitionist causes. He gained widespread attention following a speech at the Massachusetts Anti-Slavery Society's annual convention.

He began to speak all across the United States, and in 1845 he published his first autobiography, *Narrative of the Life of Frederick Douglass*. But, fearing re-enslavement, he decided to travel to Europe, where he toured for two years. While he was overseas, abolitionists gathered funds to purchase his freedom outright, which allowed Douglass to safely return to the States.

He relocated to Rochester, New York, where he started his weekly paper, the *North Star*. He also became involved in the women's rights movement at this time, speaking about the need for equality for all people in the United States.

When the American Civil War broke out, Douglass advocated tirelessly for emancipation. He recruited African American soldiers for the Union and met with Abraham Lincoln, advocating for equal pay and treatment for black soldiers.

Following the war, he moved to Washington, DC, and served in the cabinets of five presidents. He continued to speak regularly on the importance of racial and gender equality until his death in 1895.

November 1

True Calling

Each person has their own vocation. The talent is the call. There is one direction in which all space is open to them. They have faculties silently inviting them tither to endless exertion. They are like a ship in a river; they run against obstructions on every side but one; on that side all obstruction is taken away, and they sweep serenely over a deepening channel into an infinite sea.

Ralph Waldo Emerson—"Spiritual Laws" (1841)

How do you know when you've found your calling?

Here's one clue: the truest measure of our significance is not what we do, but what happens to others when we do it.

Impact like this doesn't happen overnight; it happens because you've mastered your craft. Maybe it never feels as though it fully happens. Maybe someone will have to tell you it happened.

But this is how you will know you have found your true calling.

Today, enter into every act by considering the impact it can produce for others.

Challenge Question

Do others know the real you and what you stand for? How do you know?

_____

_____

November 2
Future Forward

The continuity of life is never broken; the river flows onward and is lost to our sight, but under its new horizon it carries the same waters which it gathered under ours, and its unseen valleys are made glad by the offerings which are borne down to them from the past,—flowers, perchance, the germs of which its own waves had planted on the banks of Time.

John Greenleaf Whittier—"The Scottish Reformers" (1844)

Eventually, you'll begin to wonder about the legacy of your work. Maybe not today, or even tomorrow, but that day will arrive.

It's in many ways the natural measurement of what may be your life's body of work. "What difference did I make?" you might end up asking.

But this is like traditional accounting: "How did we do last year?"

The self-reliant entrepreneur instead may ask, "What impact do we want to have in 10 years, 20 years?"

Often people relate this type of forward thinking with the kind of innovation that disrupts and creates products that no one knew they needed until now.

But it's more likely that your impact will flow from a consistent adherence to the founding principles that guide your life and that of your entrepreneurial journey.

This isn't something that is calculated day-to-day; it's something that is felt in hindsight. But it's intentional—it has a destination in mind—and that's how your legacy will be built.

It's not what you did; it's what you stood for. It will be found in the *"unseen valleys made glad"* by what you offered today and tomorrow.

Challenge Question

What values and beliefs most influence your actions?

_____

_____

November 3
Change Stuff

New times demand new measures and new people; / The world advances, and in time outgrows / The laws which in our father's times were best; / And doubtless, after us, some purer scheme / Will be shaped out by wiser people than we, / Made wiser by the steady growth of truth.
James Russell Lowell—A Glance Behind the Curtain *(1843)*

Lowell wrote the words in today's reading mostly likely with a quill or fountain pen on vellum paper. While we've outgrown the writing mechanism, his words continue to blossom.

The world will always need the self-reliant entrepreneur because the world will always change. We change stuff; that's why we do this mostly.

Getting rich is on the list, but doing something that utterly changes us and in the process changes our world, that's where the fun is, that's where *"the steady growth of truth"* is found.

Challenge Question

How do you know you're changing? You, your team, your customer?

_____

_____

November 4

Enjoy Your Reward

People think that if a person has undergone any hardship, they should have a reward; but for my part, if I have done the hardest possible day's work, and then come to sit down in a corner and eat my supper comfortably—why, then I don't think I deserve any reward for my hard day's work—for am I not now at peace? Is not my supper good? My peace and my supper are my reward.

Herman Melville—*Letter to Nathaniel Hawthorne, published in* Memories of Hawthorne *by Rose Hawthorne Lathrop (1897)*

Every year wealthy and famous people commit suicide. While there are many reasons they may have been unhappy, it wasn't because they weren't rich and famous.

Even in much smaller ways, entrepreneurs often stumble after achieving some measure of success for fear of losing what they've gained.

Success is a worthy goal. Contentment, however, is the only objective that will deliver inner peace.

Today, discover ways to be more accepting. Things are usually never as good or as bad as we make them. Nothing will ever be perfect.

Today, find reasons to smile more. Even if you're just laughing at what a mess you've created.

Today, look around and witness the many things you have to be grateful for.

Today, work hard, eat your supper, and enjoy your peace.

Challenge Question

What can you be grateful for today?

_____

_____

November 5
Service Driven

If I can stop one heart from breaking, / I shall not live in vain; / If I can ease one life the aching, / Or cool one pain, / Or help one fainting robin / Unto his nest again, / I shall not live in vain.
Emily Dickinson—*"Life,"* The Collected Poems of Emily Dickinson
(1855)

Some entrepreneurs start their venture based purely on serving those in need. Others, like Toms Shoes, start a business to fill a need and create an aspect, giving away shoes, that also serves those in need.

For these businesses, one of the primary measures of success is service to others. This success metric helps tell the story of their business and engage those who would become a part of that story.

Here's the thing, though: while service is an overt characteristic of these businesses, it is the eventual purpose of every business. Every business consistently provides value to someone—or it doesn't stick around very long.

You may never *"help one fainting robin unto his nest again,"* but there's a mission in your work. Whose life is made even moderately better? What problem is lessened? How many businesses benefit from your work? Answer these questions, set goals around these objectives, and create your own service-driven metric.

You may be just starting out and your value to others and the market may be unclear, but start to measure the little ways your business is making a difference. Make that part of your story, and you might be surprised how empowering this new focus can become.

Challenge Question

How can you begin to measure the impact of your work on others?

_____

_____

November 6
Artistic Material

I think of few heroic actions, which cannot be traced to the artistical impulse. Those who do great deeds, do them from their innate sensitiveness to moral beauty. Such persons are not merely artists, they are also artistic material. Washington in some great crisis, Lawrence on the bloody deck of the Chesapeake, Mary Stuart at the block, Kossuth in captivity, and Mazzini in exile—all great rebels and innovators, exhibit the highest phases of the artist spirit. The painter, the sculptor, the poet, express heroic beauty better in description; but the others are heroic beauty, the best belov'd of art.

Walt Whitman—"Talk to an Art-Union" (1839)

Painters and sculptors often admit that they are uncertain about what they will create when they start; they just know that they have to find the truth and beauty in the canvas or hunk of marble. And that drives them as much as any notion of creating a work of art.

Really, I do not know whether my paintings are surrealist or not, but I do know that they are the frankest expression of myself.

Frida Kahlo

The depth of your drive to create and impact will most likely dictate how many hurdles you are willing to overcome. And there will be hurdles, as you find the truth and beauty, *"frankest expression"* of yourself, in your own canvas.

You might not know where you're headed. You don't need to know that just now; stay open to becoming "artistic material," and you'll find a way to get to the right place.

Challenge Question

What work of art best represents why you do what you do? Don't know? Then find one.

_____

_____

November 7
Chasing Fame

Enduring fame is ever posthumous. The orbs of virtue and genius seldom culminate during their terrestrial periods. Slow is the growth of great names, slow the procession of excellence into arts, institutions, life. Ages alone reflect their fullness of lustre. The great not only unseal, but create the organs by which they are to be seen. Neither Socrates nor Jesus is yet visible to the world.

Amos Bronson Alcott—"Orphic Sayings" (1842)

Even a tiny sliver of fame and recognition can be kind of intoxicating. But seeking it as anything more than the accidental by-product of doing good work is to ask for something you do not understand.

The Stoics, who influenced many of the transcendentalists, had much to say about seeking fame—in particular, the Roman emperor Marcus Aurelius:

Give yourself a gift: the present moment. People out for posthumous fame forget that the Generations To Come will be the same annoying people they know now. And just as mortal. What does it matter to you if they say x about you, or think y?

(Would have been a nice tweet back in 180 AD.)

You know the top 50 so and so's list to follow in your industry. There's a really good chance most of them have little to offer you but a lot of Twitter followers.

Fall in love with your work, add value to every conversation, master your craft, achieve success on your terms, and don't wait for the accolades.

Challenge Question

Are you looking for something outside of yourself that you already have?

_____

_____

November 8
Turning Point

If I understand the idea, the Bazar invites several of us to write upon the above text [The Turning Point of My Life]. It means the change in my life's course which introduced what must be regarded by me as the most important condition of my career. But it also implies—without intention, perhaps—that that turning-point itself was the creator of the new condition. This gives it too much distinction, too much prominence, too much credit. It is only the last link in a very long chain of turning-points commissioned to produce the cardinal result; it is not any more important than the humblest of its ten thousand predecessors. Each of the ten thousand did its appointed share, on its appointed date, in forwarding the scheme, and they were all necessary; to have left out any one of them would have defeated the scheme and brought about some other result. I know we have a fashion of saying "such and such an event was the turning-point in my life," but we shouldn't say it. We should merely grant that its place as LAST link in the chain makes it the most conspicuous link; in real importance it has no advantage over any one of its predecessors.

Mark Twain—"The Turning-Point of My Life" (1906)

Twain's reading requires very little reflection.

He is simply reinforcing the idea that every step in the journey, struggles included, are part of what we are meant to experience on our path. Accept that and you welcome everything with the balance it deserves.

If you stay at this long enough and achieve any measure of what others call success, someone may ask you, "What was the secret to your success?" And to that you may reply, "Everything."

Challenge Question

If you could start all over again, what would you do differently? Careful—this is a trick question.

_____

_____

330   Growing: Impact

November 9
New Energy

I consider this mutability of language a wise precaution of Providence for the benefit of the world at large, and of authors in particular. To reason from analogy, we daily behold the varied and beautiful tribes of vegetables springing up, flourishing, adorning the fields for a short time, and then fading into dust, to make way for their successors. Were not this the case, the fecundity of nature would be a grievance instead of a blessing. The earth would groan with rank and excessive vegetation, and its surface become a tangled wilderness. In like manner the works of genius and learning decline, and make way for subsequent productions.

Washington Irving—"The Mutability of Literature: A Colloquy in Westminster Abbey" (1885)

Every generation of entrepreneurs has something to offer the next generation.

If you are young and just starting your entrepreneurial journey, learn everything you can from those who toiled 10, 20, 30 years ahead of you. You don't have to make copies of their journey, but you can borrow the strategies and tactics that may have lost favor with your peers and still retain an element of fundamental truth.

If you are seasoned, you must know that it is wise to routinely look back and evaluate new tools, new techniques, new languages, new energy so that you can continue to grow and evolve with new opportunities and changing behavior.

This has to be more than advice noted well; it must become for you a substantial growth behavior and practice no matter the stage of your business. You're never done, you've never made it, stay in the game, always challenge yourself to grow, learn, teach, and evolve.

Your ability to impact others rests in your ability to impact yourself.

Challenge Question

Who will you study and learn from today?

_____

_____

November 10
Expanding Force

The objection to conforming to usages that have become dead to you is that it scatters your force. It loses your time and blurs the impression of your character.

Ralph Waldo Emerson—Self-Reliance *(1841)*

There's a quote that shows up in a lot of success writing attributed to author Jim Rohn that goes like this: "You are the average of the five people you spend the most time with."

Sure, there's some truth in this—until the advice concludes that you must hang around only with people who support, inspire, and validate you.

There's little doubt that our deepest relationships often form with people who believe many of the same things as we do. But to wrap yourself in a bubble of those who think, look, and act like you is to limit who you can become.

We need to interact with people who will help us broaden our views, introduce us to new things, and most of all challenge our well-held beliefs.

We don't need to change our beliefs, but we do need to constantly question why we believe the things we do.

Emerson refers to the idea of "scattering our force." Yes, fighting back, trying to convince others, becoming emotionally invested in our point of view, will scatter our force. But accepting, learning, and seeking to understand those whose opinion differs from yours is how you expand your force.

In the Japanese grappling martial art of Aikido there is said to be no winner or loser—the goal is for all to have a successful ending. Even in defending themselves from a physical attack, students are taught not to expend their force in defense but to blend with the attacker's force to diffuse the situation.

This is how entrepreneurs look to grow.

Challenge Question

How can you step outside of your bubble and experience other points of view?

_____

_____

Growing: Impact

November 11
Written Words

A written word is the choicest of relics. It is something at once more intimate with us and more universal than any other work of art. It is the work of art nearest to life itself. It may be translated into every language, and not only be read but actually breathed from all human lips;—not be represented on canvas or in marble only, but be carved out of the breath of life itself.
Henry David Thoreau—Walden *(1854)*

If you're one of the lucky ones, your parents hung on to a box of possessions from their parents. And in that box was a collection of beautifully scripted, thoughtfully crafted handwritten letters and notes.

People don't hand-write notes anymore, but we should.

Notes are a powerful way to express gratitude. These days the recipient will be pleasantly surprised, but the aspect of note writing that people underestimate is how much the formal act of sharing your kind thoughts will do for you.

Sure, emailing, texting, liking as you scroll, are all a lot easier. But stepping back and taking a moment to express your thanks, recognize an accomplishment, or simply compliment someone on the loving relationship they have with their child via an age-old mechanism requiring a stamp for delivery is good medicine for all.

Don't expect a response or action on the part of the recipient; just put two or three of these into the world each day and witness how good this simple act makes you feel.

Challenge Question

Who will you send your first handwritten note to?

_____

_____

November 12
Time Treasure

I like the independent feeling; and though not an easy life, it is a free one, and I enjoy it. I can't do much with my hands; so I will make a battering-ram of my head and make a way through this rough-and-tumble world.

Louisa May Alcott—Her Life, Letters, and Journals *(1914)*

The inspiring promise of entrepreneurship is complete independence. At least that's what the brochure says, right? What's your reality been?

What few tell you is that it's possible to be totally free and totally out of control at the same time. And then the promise starts to feel more like sacrifice than reward.

Freedom is granted only to those who take it, and that means coming to grips with the treasure of your time. (A "battering ram" for a head doesn't hurt in this conquest either.)

If freedom to you means hitting fresh powder on a Tuesday morning during ski season, it will only cause stress unless Tuesday afternoon is spent focused on making a difference in your business.

It's not about time management; it's about a commitment to working on the things that matter—and 75 percent of the things we spend (waste) our time on don't matter in the end.

What's the most important objective of your business, who are you most trying to impact, what priorities trump all today? Focus only on those few high-payoff activities, do less of everything else, and go hit the trails—that's freedom, that's control.

No, it's not an easy life; it's a free one.

Challenge Question

What is your biggest priority today? Why does working on it matter more than anything else?

_____

_____

Author's Note: Today's reflection is provided by my daughter, Sara Nay.

November 13
By Example

The same reality pervades all teaching. A person may teach by doing, and not otherwise. If they can communicate, they can teach, but not by words. They teach who give, and they learn who receive.

Ralph Waldo Emerson—"Spiritual Laws" (1841)

In his book *The Coaching Habit*, Michael Bungay Stanier shares the following thought: "Silence is often a measure of success." As an entrepreneur, you need to ask a lot of questions, but the real trick is to gain the control to sit back and fully listen for the answers with patience. If your question is met with silence, this often means a person is considering your inquiry with deep thought instead of sharing the first thing that comes to mind.

If your question is met with a question, lob it right back in their court—they probably know the answer but are waiting for you to empower them to think on their own.

This is growth. This is how you lead by example.

Today, pay close attention to how you're setting an example.

Challenge Question

What is your best opportunity to lead by example today?

_____

_____

November 14
On Immortality

Would I could die today that this aching sense of immortality might be sat-isfied or cease to ache. The difficulty remains the same when I struggle with the extension of never never never—just as I repeated the exercise in child-hood; can't form an idea, can't stretch myself to that which has no end . . . It is this impossibility of losing oneself, though ages pass over the change, that argues immortality.

Mary Moody Emerson—The Selected Letters of Mary Moody Emerson
(1774–1863)

For a little family history context, Mary Moody Emerson was Ralph Waldo Emerson's aunt and earliest teacher.

Currently, biological immortality is still just a major plot element in Indiana Jones–type movies or maybe a goal of the anti-aging research being done by Google.

There is, however, an element of immortality in the work done by many entrepreneurs—at least in the sense that their work, innovations, and contributions lend to the lives of others long after they are gone (planned or unplanned).

Books, for example, are often said to be a path to an author's immortality. (Some it might make utterly forgettable.)

In nature, a forest lives in immortality through regeneration of old growth and new growth from events such as fires.

So today's thought is this somewhat theoretical question: do you (should you) consider the long-term impact of your work as part of your plan? Would that change any element of your work? Would you ultimately have more impact if you intended to? Is that even a worthy part of the equation?

Challenge Question

What element of your work will live on long after you? Who will benefit?

_____

_____

November 15
Owning Your Legacy

A few fine essays do not float a person into immortality, but the generous character, the heart sweet in all excesses and under all chances, is a spectacle too beautiful and too rare to be easily forgotten. A person is better than many books. Even a person who is not immaculate may have more virtuous influence than the discreetest saint. Let us remember how fondly the old painters lingered round the story of Magdalen.

George William Curtis—*"Thackeray in America,"* The Oxford Book of American Essays, *ed. Brander Matthews (1914)*

Entrepreneurs rarely think about something as vague as legacy as they start their journey—and there's a good reason.

Legacy isn't a section of a business plan; it's what happens when you share your passion, take care of yourself and your family, and remain true to your values.

It's what happens because you've spent your time raising others up. It's what happens because you've shown the real you in every circumstance. It's what happens because you've spent your days working for what you believe in.

Why think about this now? Because you're writing it every day anyway?

Challenge Question

What is the one thing you want to be known for most? Are you living it?

_____

_____

November 16
Challenge Enough

The ancients summed up the whole of human wisdom in the maxim, Know Thyself, and certainly there is for an individual no more important as there is no more difficult knowledge, than knowledge of themselves, whence they come, whither they go, what they are, what they are for, what they can do, what they ought to do, and what are their means of doing it.

Orestes Brownson—The American Republic *(1865)*

Brownson's reading begs to be answered.

Today, can you ponder and answer? Can you agree there's work to be done? Can you search for deeper knowledge of yourself?

Where did you come from?

Where are you going?

Who are you?

What do you stand for?

What can you do?

What should you do?

What are your means for doing it?

No Challenge Question; I've given you enough challenges today.

November 17
Natural Wonderment

As the leaf is to the tree, so is the individual to society. Tear away a single leaf from the towering crest, and the trunk does not seem to suffer: nevertheless, one small thread withers, one channel dries up, one source of beauty and use fails; and, from that moment, a certain sidewise tendency marks the growth.

    Caroline Healey Dall—The College, the Market, and the Court *(1867)*

Trees turn up often in all forms of literature used as strong metaphors for things not fully understood.

Authors of the era, such as Thoreau, Bryant, Cooper, and Emerson, wrote frequently about the sacredness of nature. None claimed to understand the source of their spiritual experience, but Thoreau, in particular, believed that trees held the secret.

Throughout his over two million words in journals, he repeatedly noted the knowledge possessed by trees.

Author Richard Higgins used Thoreau's journals to write a book dedicated to Thoreau's fascination with trees. In *Thoreau and the Language of Trees*, he notes the following:

> The trees, he wrote, knew things that he did not and would never know. "You are so far in them as they are far before you," he wrote on January 30, 1841. "Their secret is where you are not and where your feet can never carry you."

Throughout this book we've touched on the importance of using our outer experiences to help us forge better inner experiences. Perhaps a sense of wonder about the nature of trees holds the ultimate potential for such an experience.

Challenge Question

What aspect of your business creates a sense of wonderment for you? You might consider sitting under a majestic white pine (*pinus strobus*) or maybe a rangy American sycamore (*platanus occidentalis*) when you answer today's question.

_____

_____

November 18
Self-Helping

We come to them who weep foolishly, and sit down and cry for company, instead of imparting to them truth and health in rough electric shocks, putting them once more in communication with their own reason. The secret of fortune is joy in our hands. Welcome evermore to gods and people is the self-helping individual. For them all doors are flung wide; all tongues greet, all honors crown, all eyes follow with desire.

Ralph Waldo Emerson—Self-Reliance (1841)

There are a few ways you could go with today's reading—for example, when asked your opinion, speak the truth. (The whole rough electric shock thing might be excessive, though.)

Another viable interpretation is to consider that the "*joy in our hands*" is the fact that there will never be another person exactly like you. That we all become that "self-helping individual" when we realize our only job is to trust that the universe is here to help us step into our greatness all on our own.

We may want and, at times, need help keeping on track, but we can never let someone else to formulate our path. (This includes gurus and mentors.)

Challenge Question

Where will your life be in a year from now if you continue doing what you're doing today?

_____

_____

November 19

Greatness of Our Fates

My actual life is unspeakably mean compared with what I know and see that it might be. Yet the ground from which I see and say this is some part of it. It ranges from heaven to earth, and is all things in an hour. The experience of every past moment but belies the faith of each present. We never conceive the greatness of our fates. Are not these faint flashes of light which sometimes obscure the sun their certain dawn?

Henry David Thoreau—Letter to Mrs. Emerson (1843)

Do you come to the end of a day thinking, "I'm capable of so much more than I am doing right now?"

If not, you're a lucky one. Entrepreneurs, even in the face of evidence to the contrary, rarely feel accomplished enough, far enough, done enough. We know we have more potential than is being rewarded.

Of course, we probably define potential as something unreachable in this lifetime.

In part, it's what keeps us going; in part, it's what makes us mental.

And then one day through some combination of courage, usefulness, doubt, hard work, stumbles, lurches, and discoveries, we trust ourselves and the universe enough that we get lucky. (Please note the author is being sarcastic here.)

But we keep going precisely because *"We never conceive the greatness of our fates."*

Have faith in every present moment, chill out, and pat yourself on the back every now and then.

Challenge Question

To what extent do you think you shape your own destiny, and how much comes down to fate?

_____

_____

November 20

In the Open Light

You talk as if you had always lived in that wild, unprofitable element you are so fond of, where all things glitter, and nothing is gold; all show and no substance. My people work in the secret, and their works praise them in the open light; they remain in the dark because only there such marvels could be bred.

Margaret Fuller—At Home and Abroad; or, Things and Thoughts in America and Europe *(1856)*

Relentless self-promotion probably creates more stress for entrepreneurs than making payroll.

Why? Because all too often it's a lie that gets harder and harder to uphold. Look at your typical top 20 list to follow for this and that; dig beneath the façade, you will find few who have accomplished much approaching what you want to accomplish. (Yes, this isn't the first time you've read this idea.)

The true success stories often shun the spotlight in favor of making something more useful out of their efforts—including money.

Take note of what author David Zweig calls a "quite elite" in his book titled *Invisibles*.

Entrepreneurs seeking some measure of self-reliance are more wired to give credit than take credit and derive satisfaction in the work itself and the value it produces.

Some professions require more self-promotion than others. The good that you can do won't reach as many people as possible if you do not promote, but seeking status for the sake of status has never been a steady path to self-fulfillment.

Do work that has value for others, self-promote in a way that has value for others, seek others who do their work in the dark—and your work will be praised one day in the open light.

Challenge Question

What is your first reaction when someone compliments you for your work? Does it serve you well?

_____

_____

November 21
Future Forward

And I honor the person who is willing to sink / Half their present repute for the freedom to think, / And, when they have thought, be their cause strong or weak, / Will risk t' other half for the freedom to speak, / Caring naught for what vengeance the mob has in store, / Let that mob be the upper ten thousand or lower.

James Russell Lowell—"A Fable for Critics" (1848)

What is reputation? What is your reputation? Do you have any idea? Let's allow author Seth Godin to weigh in on this:

Reputation is what people expect us to do next. It's their expectation of the quality and character of the next thing we produce or say or do.

We control our actions (even when it feels like we don't) and our actions over time (especially when we think no one is looking) earn our reputation.

seths.blog

Okay, now you got it?

But here's the hard part. You control your actions, but others control your reputation. You can tell people to trust you all you like, but your trust-worthiness will come at the hands of what others say and confirm about you.

Might be in an online forum, at a conference, or on a review site, but that's your reputation and that's the part that is slightly out of your control.

Again, from Godin: "The single best way to maintain your reputation is to do things you're proud of."

Simple, yet painfully truthful advice.

Challenge Question

What would someone who knows you say if a friend asked them for a referral? Write down the words you think they would use.

_____

_____

November 22

Insist on Yourself

Insist on yourself; never imitate. Your own gift you can present every moment with the cumulative force of a whole life's cultivation; but of the adopted talent of another, you have only an extemporaneous, half possession. That which each can do best, none but their Maker can teach them. No one yet knows what it is, nor can, till that person has exhibited it. Where is the master who could have taught Shakespeare?

Ralph Waldo Emerson—Self-Reliance *(1841)*

The first sentence of today's reading is perhaps the strongest call to action in the entire essay.

"Insist on yourself; never imitate." This mantra is all you need to take into every day as you continue to explore that which only you can do best.

You are your Maker. Your own gift is a giant bowl of stew made up of every person, every interaction, every experience, every thought, and every observation.

No one else has what you have.

Today, insist on yourself.

Challenge Question

What in your life or your business feels like an imitation?

_____

_____

November 23
Brief Moments

There is a difference between one and another hour of life in their authority and subsequent effect. Our faith comes in moments; our vice is habitual. Yet is there a depth in those brief moments which constrains us to ascribe more reality to them than to all other experiences.

Ralph Waldo Emerson—"The Over-Soul" (1841)

Today's reading plays out on many practical levels.

Our real work comes in moments; our wasted time is habitual.

Our creativity comes in moments; our imitation is habitual.

Our strong relationships come in moments; our Instagram liking is habitual.

The list could go on, but you probably get the point.

Today, witness those brief moments and "*ascribe more reality to them than to all other experiences.*" (Maybe cut some of the habitual.)

Challenge Question

How will you catalog your brief moments today and every day?

_____

_____

November 24

Reputation and Character

Influence follows close upon the heels of character; and whatever we are, that we shall in the end be acknowledged to be.
Caroline Healey Dall—Historical Pictures Retouched: A Volume of Miscellanies, in Two Parts *(1860)*

Are you most often who you are or who people think you are? That might neatly sum up the difference between reputation and character, but eventually they are one and the same.

As Emerson famously said, "What you are shouts so loudly in my ears I cannot hear what you say."

So maybe the better question is, what does it take to build or reveal true character?

Consider this aphorism attributed to many, including Emerson:

We sow a thought and reap an act;
We sow an act and reap a habit;
We sow a habit and reap a character;
We sow a character and reap a destiny.

So let's conclude that character is built from our habits. But here's the hard part: people don't fall in love with our habits. They fall in love with who we are. Creating and adhering to a strict list of "good habits" may indeed move you closer to some goals, but it may also stifle your true character.

When writers develop characters for their stories, they are advised above all to show the parts that make them real.

Revealing what makes us real means that we have to be willing to, be vulnerable, admit what we really care about, what we believe, and what we don't know.

Challenge Question

What character trait showcases the most authentic part of who you are?

_____

_____

November 25

The East Wind

What makes the value of your life at present? What dreams have you, and what realizations? You know there is a high tableland which not even the east wind reaches. Now can't we walk and chat upon its plane still, as if there were no lower latitudes? Surely our two destinies are topics interesting and grand enough for any occasion.

Henry David Thoreau—Familiar Letters *(1865)*

How would you sum up your life right now? Not your net worth, your life worth?

A lot of entrepreneurs give up on their dreams because they aren't making enough or as much money as their peers.

In hindsight, some wonder what the cost was of not following their dreams.

This is the place where it would be logical or at least trendy to suggest you quit your job, travel around the world, and while you're at it learn to surf. Only you can decide worth in this case.

Maybe that's following your dream (go for it), but when Thoreau asked, *"What makes the value of your life at present?"* he was more concerned with raising your conviction to follow your destiny, no matter what shape it took.

Every entrepreneur will hopefully at some point learn that *"there is a high tableland which not even the east wind reaches."*

It might be helpful to note here that throughout history and literature the east wind is often portrayed as mischievous, destructive, or evil. (The writers of the Old Testament really had it out for the east wind.)

So, perhaps what Thoreau is suggesting is that if we follow our heart, even when consumed with self-doubt, there is a reward in the end.

Challenge Question

What would you have to give up to follow your dreams? Is it worth it?

_____

_____

November 26
Thinking for Yourself

I admire great persons of all classes, those who stand for facts and for thoughts; I like rough and smooth, "scourges of God" and "darlings of the human race.". . . But I find a person greater when they can abolish themselves, and all heroes, by letting in this element of reason, irrespective of persons; this subtilizer, and irresistible upward force, into our thought, destroying individualism; the power so great that the potentate is nothing."
Ralph Waldo Emerson—"Uses of Great Men," The Oxford Book of
American Essays, ed. Brander Matthews (1914)

There was a lot going on in America at the time of Emerson's writing: the legal practice of human slavery, significant religious upheaval, a cultural and moral divide so vast that it led to a civil war, and the beginning of the fight for women's rights.

There's a lot going on in the world still today, and there probably always will be. The call for individualism issued by Emerson, particularly as he suggested across all classes, may never be completely answered, but it's surely less polarizing than the opposite. You could rephrase this as merely thinking for yourself.

To practice self-reliance, one must "*stand for facts and for thoughts*"— agree and disagree and agree to disagree, but above all know what is good and right in your heart alone. Okay, and take responsibility for your acts, stop comparing yourself to others, make your own decisions, and maybe change your own oil. (But that last one is optional.)

Want data? Studies have shown that people who adopt Emerson's individualistic or self-reliant view report a greater sense of well-being and live longer. (See "The Interaction Between Individualism and Wellbeing in Predicting Mortality: Survey of Health Ageing and Retirement in Europe" at www.ncbi.nlm.nih.gov/pmc/articles/PMC5765189/.)

Challenge Question

What's one thing in life you had to learn before you could form a reliable opinion of your own? What changed?

_____

_____

November 27

Crafting Your Biography

When I read the book, the biography famous, / And is this then (said I) what the author calls a person's life? / And so will someone when I am dead and gone write my life? / (As if anyone really knew aught of my life, / Why even I myself I often think know little or nothing of my real life, / Only a few hints, a few diffused faint clues and indirections / I seek for my own use to trace out here.)"

Walt Whitman—Leaves of Grass *(1855)*

For those interested, a quick Amazon search will turn up at least four Whitman biographies and a more exhaustive one will turn up many more housed in university libraries.

So, maybe you're not thinking about your biography just yet. No worries; just know that you're crafting it every day. You didn't know that?

Perhaps the most telling line in the stanza about this is *"Why even I myself I often think know little or nothing of my real life."*

His admission is arguably both an apology and a plea.

In many ways the journey to self-reliance is a journey to become aware of yourself—to witness how you discover and change. And perhaps this is the real biography of everyone's life.

So, to date, what would the chapters of your biography be titled? (Leave a bunch blank as some pretty epic stuff is probably left.)

Challenge Question

What things or events make you feel threatened or insecure? How do you know?

_____

_____

November 28
Brand Reliance

To him no vain regrets belong / Whose soul, that finer instrument, / Gave to the world no poor lament, / But wood notes ever sweet and strong. / O lonely friend! he still will be / A potent presence, though unseen,— / Steadfast, sagacious, and serene; / Seek not for him—he is with thee.
    Louisa May Alcott—*"Thoreau's Flute"*—Her Life, Letters, and Journals
    (1914)

More entrepreneurs should read poetry (maybe).

Some might find it hard to comprehend; it does bring a certain aliveness to things tangible and intangible. Perhaps there are copywriting lessons to be had.

The passage from today's reading deserves some context. Alcott wrote this shortly after Thoreau tragically succumbed to tuberculosis, thus the title, "Thoreau's Flute." (Gossip was that she was in love with him.)

In a thought more observational than instructional, entrepreneurs, or creators of any sort for that matter, have a tendency to personify aspects of their business. And, perhaps this is the real essence of a brand.

Now, in the era of the "personal brand" seeking, this tends to lead to the pop-culture YouTube persona and that's not what is meant here.

Seeking self-reliance leads to a strong brand because elements of the brand are accidentally personified through your passion to serve, your authentic point of view, your staying the course, and a whole bunch of showing up. (It doesn't hurt that you mostly zig when people say zigging is crazy.)

Maybe we can call this "brand-reliance."

Challenge Question

What aspects of your business represent what you stand for (even if you don't realize it yet)?

_____

_____

November 29
Express Authenticity

And indeed who can see the works of a great artist without feeling that not so much the private as the common wealth is by them indicated. I think the true soul—humble, rapt, conspiring with all, regards all souls as its lieutenants and proxies—itself in another place—and say of the Parthenon, of the picture, of the poem,—It is also my work.

Ralph Waldo Emerson—Letter to Nathaniel Hawthorne—published in
Memories of Hawthorne *by Rose Hawthorne Lathrop (1897)*

The passage from today's reading is an excerpt of a letter Emerson sent to his friend and writing companion Nathaniel Hawthorne, bemoaning the fact that none of his lectures were suitable to share outside of his immediate family. Of course, the group of lectures referenced would include several, such as *Self-Reliance*, which would eventually come to be immortalized.

Even wracked with doubt about his own works, he understood that they were both of him and from him and that he had little choice to create them or share them.

Ironically, even as he expressed that he found them lacking by the literary standards of those he compared them to, he felt they uniquely represented who he was (his soul).

And also ironically, we choose the path of self-reliance not as a way to create independence but as a way to express authenticity.

In terms of self-reliance, this may be the highest moral measure.

Honor those gut feelings, embrace your discomfort, keep an open mind, but stick to what you value.

Challenge Question

When was the last time your acts were not in alignment with your true values?

_____

_____

November 30
Unseen Many

What means the fact—which is so common, so universal—that some soul that has lost all hope for itself can inspire in another listening soul an infinite confidence in it, even while it is expressing its despair?
Henry David Thoreau—Letter to Mrs. Lucy Brown (1843)

So often in life we underestimate the impact we have.

We may feel that we have little to give, that our businesses has achieved next to nothing, and yet, there are those who rely on what we do. They don't need us to be something we're not; they need us to remind them that they are strong and amazing, even though we may not feel that way today.

There will be days that we don't want that kind of accountability, but let it be a positive driving force and let it push and motivate us to become even more. (If you have kids, you know they are watching even if you don't think they are.)

See, all of our frailty, success, actions, failures, breakthroughs, and stumbles as entrepreneurs are lessons for those who will learn and grow from them.

Never underestimate the motivation your journey provides to the unseen many.

Challenge Question

Is there something you've tried in your business that led to disappointing results? What could others learn from that?

_____

_____

December

Willa Cather (1873–1947)

The world is little, people are little, human life is little. There is only one big thing—desire.

—Willa Cather

Source: Wikimedia

Wilella "Willa" Cather was born in Back Creek Valley, Virginia, in 1873. Her parents were well established in the community, but the American Civil War had greatly affected life in Virginia. And so in 1883, the family moved to Nebraska.

They initially settled in the country, but after their first year relocated to the town of Red Cloud. Here, a young Cather was introduced to art, culture, and immigrants from all around the world.

Upon graduating high school, Cather attended the University of Nebraska. She originally planned to study medicine but soon became enamored with writing. She served as editor for the school newspaper and yearbook, and she wrote for two local papers: the *Lincoln Courier* and the *Nebraska State Journal.*

Her experience in journalism took her to Pittsburgh following graduation, where she became the editor of *Home Monthly* and wrote for various publications. Her writing caught the eye of S. S. McClure, one of the most famous editors of the day. He published a number of her pieces before eventually inviting her to join his magazine in 1906.

She moved to New York and became managing editor of *McClure's*, also ghostwriting pieces during her tenure there. While a formative experience, it also monopolized her time. In 1912, she decided to leave the magazine to focus on her own writing.

During the 1910s, she published four novels, including *My Ántonia* and *One of Ours*, which won the Pulitzer Prize. She was even more prolific in the 1920s and early '30s, writing six more books and garnering greater recognition. She appeared on the cover of *Time* magazine, was elected to the National Institute of Arts and Letters, and was awarded the *Prix Femina Americain* by the country of France.

In the late 1930s her writing slowed significantly, as she grew older and dealt with the loss of her mother, two brothers, and a dear friend. Her last novel, *Sapphira and the Slave Girl*, was published in 1940.

Cather died in 1947 at her home in New York.

December 1
Gratitude in All Things

Cultivate the habit of being grateful for every good thing that comes to you, and to give thanks continuously. And because all things have contributed to your advancement, you should include all things in your gratitude.
Ralph Waldo Emerson—Journals of Ralph Waldo Emerson *(1909)*

Gratitude in all things—now that's an ambitious objective.

Entrepreneurs face frustrating obstacles on a daily basis. We work hard and come to believe that we deserve certain fruits of this effort.

When you seek gratitude in all things, challenges become opportunities to experience grace in every moment. You can begin to see a sense of entitlement as nothing more than selfishness.

When we expect things to go our way, we are no longer thankful for what we have achieved or overcome.

The next time you face an unexpected outcome, stop and ask what this moment is here to teach you.

Let go of your expectations in every moment, and grace will wash over you.

Challenge Question

Of what are you most thankful for today?

_____

_____

December 2

There Is No Try

I like trees because they seem more resigned to the way they have to live than other things do. I feel as if this tree knows everything I ever think of when I sit here. When I come back to it, I never have to remind it of anything; I begin just where I left off.

Willa Cather—O Pioneers! *(1913)*

A great deal of stress in our lives is caused by some form of not being who we were meant to be. This even includes the energy expended trying to be a loving, kind, or positive person.

Like the tree in today's reading, what if you spent more time allowing rather than trying?

Simply be who you are and practice bringing your unique gifts to the world.

Hey, and the good news is that it's so much easier that way.

Go into silence or meditation today and toss out every label you've applied to yourself—forget your job, your age, your community, your family order, and for that moment resign yourself to live as you were meant to.

Challenge Question

What can you stop trying and start allowing today?

_____

_____

December 3
Ragged Edges

The symmetry of form attainable in pure fiction cannot so readily be achieved in a narration essentially having less to do with fable than with fact. Truth uncompromisingly told will always have its ragged edges.
Herman Melville—Billy Budd, Sailor (1924)

There is no symmetry of form attainable in the creation of your journey. The ragged edges are what shapes our form, our truth, uncompromisingly untold. Celebrate them. Amplify them. Own them. Life without them is imitation.

Challenge Question

What little ragged edge of yours could be an advantage if you used it?

_____

_____

December 4
Neither Good nor Bad

We should have a sense of mental as well as moral honor, which, while it makes us feel the baseness of uttering merely hasty and ignorant censure, will also forbid that hasty and extravagant praise which strict truth will not justify. A person of honor wishes to utter no word to which they cannot adhere.

Margaret Fuller—Life Without and Life Within *(1859)*

As an entrepreneur, you'll always find yourself riding a wave of mental perplexity.

You'll work to help the world understand that you've got the goods while simultaneously dealing with those in your life who want to believe you're that person you once were. If you've ever oared a canoe, it's kind of like that: a constant balance between forward momentum and tipping for no good reason.

The trick is to push aside both. Seek neither praise nor the words of those who fear your success. Do you and be proud of that. If praise comes, accept it gracefully, but then keep doing you. If criticism comes, accept it with the same grace but then keep doing you.

Think of neither as good nor bad. (Not easy, but the water is cold.)

Here's the truth: no one is capable of knowing you but you.

Today, see if you can go an hour or two without assigning any particular meaning to what you see and hear.

Challenge Question

What is one critical view, event, or statement that you can release today?

_____

_____

Growing: Grace

December 5
Something Wonderful

This curious world which we inhabit is more wonderful than it is conve-nient; more beautiful than it is useful; it is more to be admired and enjoyed than used . . . We rejoice in it as one more indication of the entire and universal freedom that characterizes the age in which we live,—as an indi-cation that the human race is making one more advance in that infinite series of progressions which awaits it.

Henry David Thoreau—Familiar Letters *(1865)*

Let's face it: this curious entrepreneur thing is sometimes more wonderful than convenient. And at other times, more beautiful than it is useful.

But it is certainly *"one more indication of the entire and universal freedom that characterizes the age in which we live."*

To think any other way is to abuse this freedom. It's not our right; it's our honor to get to do this.

It's wonderful, it's beautiful, it's a pain, it's a chore, it's like doing burpees. Well, maybe not quite like that, but you get that, once the effort is put in, only something wonderful can come of it.

Make peace with the hard and let's never take this present for granted.

Challenge Question

What is the most wonderful thing you get to experience? The most inconve-nient?

_____

_____

December 6
Precision and Balance

The fruition of beauty is no chance of miss or hit—it is as inevitable as life—it is exact and plumb as gravitation. From the eyesight proceeds another eyesight, and from the hearing proceeds another hearing, and from the voice proceeds another voice, eternally curious of the harmony of things with mankind . . . This is the reason that about the proper expression of beauty there is precision and balance.
                    Walt Whitman—Preface *to* Leaves of Grass *(1855)*

We don't balance anything by trying. Everything balances itself, and something seemingly so imprecise as that then becomes precision and balance.

That's perhaps a more elegant way of saying, "Hang on, everything's gonna be all right."

Trust that even though it just . . . may . . . not . . . feel . . . like it—*the fruition of beauty is no chance of miss or hit*. Remember, those challenges are little packages of goodness tipping the universe back your way. Growing pains, let's call them that. Chaos before the storm. (Have faith.)

Today, express your beauty, that's your only job, be an expression of your vision.

Challenge Question

What does balance feel like to you? Test it—is that balance or is it complacency?

_____

_____

December 7
Human Discovery

Nature is the best dictionary and school of eloquence; genius the pupil of sun and stars, woodlands, waters, the fields, the spectacle of things seen under all aspects, in all seasons and moods. Blot these from his vision, and the scholar's page were of small account. Letters show pale and poor from inside chambers and halls of learning alone.

Amos Bronson Alcott—Concord Days *(1872)*

Amos Bronson Alcott was an innovative educator and Louisa May Alcott's father. *Concord Days* is a memoir of sorts relating his time spent with Emerson, Hawthorne, and Thoreau.

The primary thrust of today's reading holds some sage advice for entrepreneurs: "*Letters show pale and poor from inside chambers and halls of learning alone.*"

Our best ideas on paper or in some digital form are nearly worthless from an economic standpoint until informed by human discovery. Never underestimate how far your "sure thing" can miss the mark. You will likely live, breathe, think, and feel every element of your ideas before they ever enter the scope of consideration for those you wish to influence.

It's not a bad thing; it just means you've got to get out there and test your ideas, discover what connects, what needs more explanation, what makes no sense at all. You can't do this in study hall; this task asks you to look someone in the eye and feel their response.

Today, it's possible to build a successful business without any human interaction whatsoever—something just a generation ago would have found both implausible and maybe a bit bewildering.

Just because technology allows us to cater to our introverted selves doesn't mean we can discount the value of one true human connection. (Hug it out with someone; you'll never regret it.)

Challenge Question

What's the hardest part of your business to explain? Ask a friend or customer to explain it to you in their words.

_____

_____

December 8
Employing Time

Have regular hours for work and play; make each day both useful and pleasant, and prove that you understand the worth of time by employing it well. Then youth will bring few regrets, and life will become a beautiful success.

Louisa May Alcott—Little Women *(1868)*

Here's the problem with time: it's the only thing we can't make, manage, or control.

We can't speed it up, slow it down, or put it in place for safekeeping. The big bucket of stress in our lives comes from the fact that we are convinced time is something we can direct.

Stop trying to wrestle time to the ground and admit it's not possible. However . . .

Time is indeed something we can waste, much like the first few squirts from a tube of toothpaste (or insert your own analogy).

Consider this: the biggest positive gains on any given day usually come from brief spurts of time spent.

If that's so, then what if the goal became managing focus in an attempt to work fewer hours? Wait, what?

What if we worked at getting better at focus management; do what needs to be done most and figure out what doesn't need to be done at all. Maybe this new relationship with focus versus time could allow you to drop the reflex that tells you to sit at a desk from 9 to 5, or worse.

When results achieved versus time spent becomes the main measure of output, you may eventually find you can work 20 or 30 hours a week rather than 60 or 70.

Try this for a while: make your only time-management goal to shrink your workweek, instead of seeing what else you can cram into each day.

Challenge Question

What time do you plan to quit working today? What, then, will you need to get done first?

_____

_____

December 9

On This Rotation

Rotation is the law of nature. When nature removes a great person, people explore the horizon for a successor; but none comes, and none will. Their class is extinguished with them. In some other and quite different field, the next person will appear; not Jefferson, not Franklin, but now a great salesperson; then a road-contractor; then a student of fishes; then a buffalo-hunting explorer, or a semi-savage Western general.

Ralph Waldo Emerson—Uses of Great Men *(1849)*

Emerson's message is painfully clear: no matter our eventual impact, our individual spirit will be extinguished with us.

There will be others, and they will be equally unique in their contributions.

But let's not wait for an invitation. Let's kick ass on this rotation.

Challenge Question

What's one thing you should definitely stop putting off? When are you going to do it?

_____

_____

December 10
Feminine Energy

Every new relation and every new scene should be a new page in the book of the mysteries of life, reverently and lovingly perused, but if folded down, never to be read again, it must be regarded as only the introduction to a brighter one.

Sophia Ripley—"Woman," The Dial *(1841)*

The transcendentalists were social reformers as a lot. About the only thing they agreed on universally was what might have been called their "liberalness." The period featured the emergence of strong female voices given a platform, perhaps, for the first time.

Ripley's essay, appearing in the movement's official publication, *The Dial*, attempts to describe "ideal or perfect women." Although it does contain language relating to traditional domestic roles at the time, it also explores feminine energy in ways that transcends gender. (It's worth a search to read the entire essay.)

And, you ask, how's it going to apply to your entrepreneurial journey?

A healthy business values feminine and masculine energy, to see a problem and want to fix it, even if it's not broken, and to view every new relation and every new scene as a new page in the book of the mysteries.

This topic is too colossal to tackle in this space, but today, consider it, pay attention to it, and see if you find some truth in its existence.

Challenge Question

What is your default response when challenged? Think about a recent event. Do you know others who responded differently than you?

_____

_____

December 11

Defining Beauty

Wherever the soul catches a glimpse, in any form, of a perfect union of Love and Truth, it rejoices in the radiant marriage vesture, and names it Beauty. In all these forms, the soul sees the face of its Parent. It is reminded of its home, and drawn thither. Hence, next to the word "harmony," "a joyous perception of the infinite" is the most common definition of Beauty.

Lydia Maria Child—"What Is Beauty?" (1843)

Child's essay is an attempt to describe a thing called beauty.

Not in ways you might find portrayed in make-up ads, fashion mags, billboards, and television spots.

In the essay she comes to the conclusion that it is not a physical or even tangible thing but that it is something felt. While everyone gets to define what real beauty is to them, when pressed most express it as an inner feeling.

So, what is beauty to an entrepreneur? How do you feel beauty in your life, in your work? How do you blend truth and love in your entrepreneurial journey?

Maybe it's in doing things that others won't, in finding ways to do things that require money you don't have, in doing things you were told were impossible.

Those answers might surprise some, but not you; you're unusual.

That's what is so awesome about doing your own thing. It's beautiful any way you want to frame it.

Challenge Question

What makes you feel beautiful?

_____

_____

December 12

On a Tangent

I say that conceit is just as natural a thing to human minds as a centre is to a circle. But little-minded people's thoughts move in such small circles that five minutes' conversation gives you an arc long enough to determine their whole curve.
Oliver Wendell Holmes, Sr.—The Autocrat of the Breakfast-Table *(1858)*

You've got to love a good geometry metaphor.

Circles will play a role in your growth on your journey. Think of it in terms of networking. We need circles of influence to spread our message. That's how it works today. Our expanding and overlapping circles hold more potential than any billboard in Times Square.

But there's always a but, right? They also have the potential to constrict, as Holmes suggests: *"little-minded people's thoughts move in such small circles."*

Further in the essay he adds this: *"A circle of clever fellows, who meet together to dine and have a good time, have signed a constitutional compact to glorify themselves and put down him and the fraction of the human race not belonging to their number."*

We must intentionally leap between the radical centers of intersecting circles in order to find and expand our true tribe. (Radical center is a geometry term, the power center of three circles, but dang, it fits here.)

Do this, and your entrepreneurial and life circles take a shape more like a heptagram—a seven-pointed star that also happens to appear on the flag of the Cherokee Nation.

Width and diversity in our circles brings the richness required for expansion, universal connection, and growth. In other words, we find ourselves over and over again in these changing shapes.

Challenge Question

What circles do you need to break from? What circles do you need to find, join, and intersect?

December 13
Being Noble

Be noble! and the nobleness that lies / In other men, sleeping, but never dead, / Will rise in majesty to meet thine own: / Then wilt thou see it gleam in many eyes, / Then will pure light around thy path be shed, / And thou wilt never more be sad and lone.

James Russell Lowell—"Sonnet IV" (1890)

Nothing very challenging about today's reading other than the smog of the classic portrayal of the hero having an occasional big noble moment no matter what a slacker they've been in the rest of the movie.

No, Lowell is talking about being noble, everyday noble, not doing a noble thing.

Challenge Question

What is the most noble act you have witnessed? How did it impact you at the time?

_____

_____

December 14
Indescribable Repose

There are some strange summer mornings in the country, when he who is but a sojourner from the city shall early walk forth into the fields, and be wonder smitten with the trancelike aspect of the green and golden world. Not a flower stirs; the trees forget to wave; the grass itself seems to have ceased to grow; and all Nature, as if suddenly become conscious of its own profound mystery, and feeling no refuge from it but silence, sinks into this wonderful and indescribable repose.

Herman Melville—Pierre; or, The Ambiguities *(1852)*

Do you ever have days like Melville describes here? Maybe on vacation, maybe at your desk. It's funny how sometimes, something like a river kicks in and everything just feels right.

Psychologists and hackers alike want us to believe that we can tap into this mental state they might call "flow" whenever we like by simply putting ourselves in it.

But it might not be that straightforward. It is a natural state, and like any state of nature, you don't control it—you access it by letting go and riding it.

Chances are you find it when you are doing something immersive.

Challenge Question

In what aspect of your work do you find yourself letting go and even losing awareness of time and self? Flow is probably there.

_____

_____

Growing: Grace

December 15
The Math of Movement

The invigorating air did them both good, and much exercise worked whole-some changes in minds as well as bodies. They seemed to get clearer views of life and duty up there among the everlasting hills; the fresh winds blew away desponding doubts, delusive fancies, and moody mists; the warm spring sunshine brought out all sorts of aspiring ideas, tender hopes, and happy thoughts.

Louisa May Alcott—Little Women *(1868)*

You've probably heard that sitting at a desk in front of a computer screen for some odd eight or nine hours is worse for you than, say, running with scissors, among other things.

Hey, but who has time to break that grip?.

Funny thing about *"life and duty up there among the everlasting hills"* or the gym or the sidewalk—it replaces more time than it takes.

You won't have to work very hard to find scholarly articles that relate activity to improved mood, reduced stress, and enhanced cognitive thinking—all things our busy mind craves.

No one needs to be reminded of this; we just have to figure out how to make it a priority.

Try this: want to have an extra hour or two of productive work in your day? Take two 20-minute walks during your workday. It's a pretty simple math equation. (Dance parties count too.)

Challenge Question

Where will you schedule your active breaks each day? Put them on your calendar.

_____

_____

December 16
Climb on Your Own

We should endeavor practically in our lives to correct all the defects which our imagination detects. The heavens are as deep as our aspirations are high. So high as a tree aspires to grow, so high it will find an atmosphere suited to it.

Henry David Thoreau—Familiar Letters *(1865)*

In the state of Colorado, there are at least 54 peaks that top 14,000 feet above sea level. There are those who aspire to "bag" as many fourteeners as they can in their lifetime. Nothing wrong with that healthy pursuit, particularly if you like to hike and climb with lots of other people with the same aspirations (maybe carrying the same map).

At the same time, there are 637 peaks over 13,000 feet, some just a few feet shy of the coveted fourteener status. On any given weekday during the summer or winter, there's a very good chance you could climb one of those peaks without seeing another person outside of your party. (Some are also far more technical than their more famed range mates.)

The choice to ascent one or the other is less of a choice of difficulty and more of aspiration. Some who choose to "bag" thirteeners don't aspire for less; they aspire for something that speaks to them alone perhaps.

It's easy to think that what we hope to accomplish in our work and in our lives must be chosen from the standard members of the bucket list set, when only our heart knows our true path.

It's not enough to know that you don't have the same dreams as everyone else; you've got to go imagine how high you can climb on your own.

Maybe check out a thirteener and see what it's like to go that way.

Challenge Question

What goals are you chasing because you were told very early on that it was part of the normal track?

_____

_____

December 17
District of Nature

As plants convert the minerals into food for animals, so each person converts some raw material in nature to human use. The inventors of fire, electricity, magnetism, iron, lead, glass, linen, silk, cotton; the makers of tools; the inventor of decimal notation; the geometer; the engineer; the musician, severally make an easy way for all through unknown and impossible confusions. Each person is, by secret liking, connected with some district of nature, whose agent and interpreter they are, as Linnæus, of plants; Huber, of bees; Dalton, of atomic forms; Euclid, of lines; Newton, of fluxions.
Ralph Waldo Emerson—Uses of Great Men *(1849)*

In this reading Emerson seems to describe something akin to "entrepreneurial photosynthesis."

Physiologically speaking, humans are not capable of harnessing the sun to activate the chemical reactions needed to sustain our bodies as plants do, but converting some raw material, even thought, into something useful is the burden of every business.

Emerson's belief that we are all here for our singular purpose is fortified by his thought that "*[e]ach person is, by secret liking, connected with some district of nature.*"

At the time, he was referring to human nature rather than entrepreneurial nature, but is there much difference?

A distinctive element of Emerson's self-reliance (as long as we're staying in the science theme) is symbiosis. That we are self-reliant, we have our own path, but not self-subsistent, we rely on connectedness and collaboration in order to thrive.

Challenge Question

What is your district of nature? Who do you need to rely on to access it?

_____

_____

December 18
To the Morning

It was the cool gray dawn, and there was a delicious sense of repose and peace in the deep pervading calm and silence of the woods. Not a leaf stirred; not a sound obtruded upon great Nature's meditation . . . Gradually the cool dim gray of the morning whitened, and as gradually sounds multiplied and life manifested itself. The marvel of Nature shaking off sleep and going to work unfolded itself to the musing boy . . . All Nature was wide awake and stirring, now; long lances of sunlight pierced down through the dense foliage far and near.

Mark Twain—The Adventures of Tom Sawyer *(1876)*

Good morning. (Even if it's not morning where you are now.)

Entrepreneurs famously code and write and design late into the night and often miss what Twain so mystically describes in today's reading.

Morning comes on slowly as our days should. Morning allows us to choose the tone for our day. Morning affords the weightlessness to decide our priorities. Morning allows the space to make decisions about how we want our day to unfold, including when we want to be done.

There's a Dan Fogelberg song ("To the Morning") that includes these inspiring lyrics:

> And it's going to be a day
> There is really no way to say no
> To the morning.

The morning is our chance to restart every day; it's our time, it's our family's time. You'll give plenty away today to your business and to others, but start today, even for just a moment, with "*a delicious sense of repose and peace in the deep pervading calm and silence.*"

Now, coffee.

Challenge Question

What time would you need to get up in order to have 30 minutes of "me" time every morning? How can you make that happen? What would make you look forward to it?

_____

_____

Growing: Grace

December 19
Worth Amazing

The cost of a thing is the amount of what I will call life which is required to be exchanged for it, immediately or in the long run.
Henry David Thoreau—Walden (1854)

Thoreau just doesn't make it easy, does he? Ah, but life isn't easy; it's just amazing.

When asked why she risked jail rather than move seats, Rosa Parks said in her biography, *My Story*, "I sat down because I was tired."

Some would suggest in that moment she sparked a movement, but the cost of the thing she would exchange just became too high. Perhaps right then courage seemed cheap in comparison.

If we're going to exchange life for something, it should be worth amazing. (Hard question coming.)

Challenge Question

Is the cost you're exchanging for life worth it now and in the long run? Don't answer this question too quickly. It has layers.

_____

_____

December 20

Diversity of Thought

Let us be wise, and not impede the soul. Let it work as it will. Let us have one creative energy, one incessant revelation. Let it take what form it will, and let us not bind it by the past to man or woman, black or white.
        Margaret Fuller—Woman in the Nineteenth Century *(1845)*

Fuller was an abolitionist and women's rights advocate, and she spent her life promoting equal rights for all. Not an easy task for anyone, let alone a woman, in mid-nineteenth-century America.

Today, while there is a measure of equality that is assumed and more organizations work to create environments that welcome and foster diversity, Fuller seemed to imply a deeper diversity of thought with her suggestion of one creative energy. Something more akin to empathy.

Beyond the call to recognize physical equality, she invites us to explore something greater: to recognize and appreciate everyone's unique insight and way of thinking.

One of the most potent ways to begin to develop diversity of thought is through diversity of reading. Does this mean reading books written by a person who doesn't look like you, a person of color, an LGBTIQ+ person, a person from another culture, a person with whom you disagree? Maybe, but it also means expanding your range of topics unrelated to your business.

Perhaps, more than anything else Fuller is calling for compassion through diversity of thought—intentionally pushing beyond our normal range is how entrepreneurs add empathy to the world.

Challenge Question

What is a topic that you currently don't understand or appreciate? Start there.

_____

_____

Growing: Grace

December 21

When You Grow Up

Humanity must ever reach out towards a New Eden. Succeeding genera-tions smile at the crude attempts, and forthwith make their own blunders, but each attempt, however seemingly unsuccessful, must of necessity con-tain a germ of spiritual beauty which will bear fruit.
Amos Bronson Alcott—Bronson Alcott at Alcott house, England, and
Fruitlands, New England *(1908)*

Did anyone ever tell you when you were young that you could be anything you dreamed of being?

Chances are, particularly if you grew up white and male, you believed them for quite some time. But then, one by one you started to realize you had limitations. You were never going to hit a major league curveball, you weren't particularly interested in the dynamics of rocket propulsion, and why would anyone want to be the president of an entire country?

"You can be anything you want" is horrible advice. Not because people aren't capable of remarkable things, because it sends us off chasing things oth-ers want for us rather than investing in figuring out what we are meant to do.

Perhaps something like "You can be anything your heart eventually reveals you are meant to be" is far better advice. Now go figure that out and don't forget to check out the wide path you've traveled already as you look for clues.

Accept your limitations, not those imposed by others who want to keep you in your rightful place, but those that just aren't part of your potential. Many entrepreneurs find who they are meant to be when they get fired.

It's a bummer that turns into a gift. The word "no" or one door closing to us is sometimes an invitation to "yes" and an amazing new door opening.

Keep searching for your meaning and truth, and then you'll discover you are indeed limitless.

Challenge Question

What did you think you wanted to be when you grew up? What does that reveal about you now?

_____

_____

December 22
Measure of a Life

I want to do something splendid . . . something heroic or wonderful that won't be forgotten after I'm dead. I don't know what, but I'm on the watch for it and mean to astonish you all someday.
Louisa May Alcott—Little Women *(1868)*

Entrepreneurs strike out for many different reasons. Perhaps, at first, it's to fill a gap that they've experienced while trying to solve their problems. Or maybe it's merely to take an idea and see how far and fast they can run with it. (Jo Marsh would have been an amazing entrepreneur.)

As we stick with it, pivot, scale, and evolve, we ultimately find that our entrepreneurial vision is the tool that allows us to make meaning and impact in the lives of others as equally as it enables us to make a living.

There are those who set out from the start to right an injustice, but most stumble upon greatness directly through the eventual execution of a solution that brings value to others.

Realization of this impact is how you measure a life. The point is that you get to decide what's heroic or wonderful. If you don't stop occasionally and accept just how great your impact has become already, you'll forever wonder what the point of all of this is.

Making just one person's life better today is, in itself, an astonishing feat.

Challenge Question

Whose life has been made better by what you do?

_____

_____

December 23
Redeem Some Portion

I do not know what to say of myself. I sit before my green desk, in the chamber at the head of the stairs, and attend to my thinking, sometimes more, sometimes less distinctly. I am not unwilling to think great thoughts if there are any in the wind, but what they are I am not sure. They suffice to keep me awake while the day lasts, at any rate. Perhaps they will redeem some portion of the night ere long.

Henry David Thoreau—Familiar Letters *(1865)*

Have you ever written something and upon reading it through, thought, "It's okay, I don't know, maybe it will work." Something like that anyway.

But then you put it aside because there is always more work to do. And then you read it the next day and think, "This is crap, or this is brilliant, particularly if I change this one little thing."

It's the way of genius, of creativity; we don't sit at our green desk and attend to our thinking like there's an on or off switch.

Often the best way to improve anything, particularly our thinking, is to go to bed and see it again in new light. Or take it with you on a jog and see how it works itself out in your mind.

Or, and this is the worst, do you get your best ideas in the middle of the night?

So, here's what science says: we can't be creative whenever we want because we're full of fear most of the time and our brain revolts. That could be sort of paraphrasing the research, but the fight-or-flight mechanism triggered by the slightest bit of fatigue or stress turns some things in our mind.

So, want to be smart today? Meditate before you do something, do a couple of laps, watch a Tig Notaro routine on YouTube. Let it marinate and come back to it with a fresh perspective.

Challenge Question

When is the last time you got a brilliant insight like a flash of lightning? What were you doing when it happened?

_____

_____

December 24
About Something Else

Nothing is so common-place as to wish to be remarkable. Fame usually comes to those who are thinking about something else—very rarely to those who say to themselves, "Go to, now, let us be a celebrated individual!" The struggle for fame, as such, commonly ends in notoriety—that ladder is easy to climb, but it leads to the pillory which is crowded with fools who could not hold their tongues and rogues who could not hide their tricks.
Oliver Wendell Holmes, Sr.—The Autocrat of the Breakfast-Table *(1858)*

Another pretty strong indictment for the act of chasing fame. (Ba-dum ching!)

Know anyone who might utter something like this, even if only through their acts: *"Go to, now, let us be a celebrated individual!"*

You were meant for a ladder harder to climb.

Challenge Question

Look at your last 10 social media updates; do they hint of the struggle for notoriety or of thinking of something else?

_____

_____

December 25
Small Achievements

We need only look on the miracle of every day, to sate ourselves with thought and admiration every day. But how are our faculties sharpened to do it? Precisely by apprehending the infinite results of every day.
Margaret Fuller—Woman in the Nineteenth Century *(1845)*

In the climb to meet our goals, months fade into years, and sometimes into decades and the little, everyday accomplishments go unmarked.

But here's a funny thing about many goals: they are like the horizon on a long, flat, stretch of prairie highway. As you drive toward the horizon, it moves heartlessly away from you at an equal speed.

So, it can feel as though you've made no progress at all even though you've worked tirelessly. Or worse, you can sense that others around you are making far more progress—and their social media posts can only serve to remind you of this disturbing fact.

What if you began to take stock of every gain, no matter how minor, and celebrated every win no matter how trifling? It's the accumulation of actions you take every day to get just a little better that eventually delivers you to your destination.

Consistently working on daily habits, acknowledging the big results in celebrating small things, is how you win. Turn around; look how far you've come.

There's certainly a place for one-, three-, and even five-year goals, but this is not a zero-sum game we are playing, and the ultimate goal is to find the miracle in every single day.

Make today magnificent.

Challenge Question

What's one small step you can take today to get a little better? Who can you celebrate with?

_____

_____

December 26
How to Wait

The wisest person could ask no more of Fate / Than to be simple, modest, brave, true, / Safe from the Many, honored by the Few; / To count as naught in World, or Church, or State, / But, inwardly in secret to be great; / To feel mysterious Nature ever new; / To touch, if not to grasp, its endless clue, / And learn by each discovery how to wait.

James Russell Lowell—"Jeffries Wyman" (1891)

Concepts like scrum, lean, agile, iterate, and minimally viable product (MVP) crept into the business vocabulary as ways to suggest faster ways to do things, including fail.

There's nothing inherently wrong with that idea, but stick with this a while and you'll discover the magic of waiting for the gears to align. Not to be perfect, but to be orchestrated.

From a practical perspective, patience is sort of sexy. The less desperate you seem to want a sale, the more the buyer wants you. That's a hard one but a valuable one.

Ask a question, and then be silent and wait. Bite your lip if you must, but wait.

Patience permits you to set timelines that allow for everyone's point of view and working style.

Go stomping through the subalpine woods and you'll never see a wild animal. Go quietly, sit quietly, and wait. And (as long as you're not wearing some hideous fragrance), mule deer, moose, alpine chickadees, and maybe even a pika or two scrambling in the rocks may wander within feet of you. (A black bear may as well, but that's the risk of all of this.)

Today, as you have a conversation, consciously consider how the other person is feeling about the conversation.

And learn by each discovery how to wait.

Challenge Question

Can you recall a time when impatience in a situation might have cost you? What did you learn?

_____

_____

Growing: Grace

December 27
Experimental Truth

I somehow cling to the strange fancy, that, in all persons, hiddenly reside certain wondrous, occult properties—as in some plants and minerals—which by some happy but very rare accident (as bronze was discovered by the melting of the iron and brass at the burning of Corinth) may chance to be called forth here on earth; not entirely waiting for their better discovery in the more congenial, blessed atmosphere of heaven.
Herman Melville—Hawthorne and His Mosses *(1850)*

Do you ever sense that you have one true calling, that we all have one true calling, even if we never quite settle into it?

That instead of telling life what we are meant to do, maybe we should be asking and listening for what life hopes to do with us?

Some do this without knowing and one day wake up to realize, through the gift of hindsight, they are doing something they couldn't not do. Others, still under the spell of what they were taught by someone else, struggle to live up to what's expected of them.

What if we were able to view our lives as one giant experiment in finding our calling? So that everything wasn't necessarily good or bad but a chance to ask, "What truth is life telling me here?"

Mahatma Gandhi's autobiography, titled *The Story of My Experiments with Truth*, promoted the idea that life is a series of experiments. An experiment is defined as a success if something is learned as a result of an experiment. So, Gandhi was able to reframe past and future events not as a success or failure but as something to be learned or not learned. Imagine what could happen to the past if you relived it through that filter.

What, not ready to compare yourself to Gandhi?

Think how much more fun it could be to follow your passion knowing you couldn't fail; you could only learn.

Challenge Question

What past event or belief could you revisit to uncover a lesson learned? How would you apply this new learning?

_____

_____

December 28
The Most Harmless Thing

All profound things, and emotions of things are preceded and attended by Silence . . . Silence is the general consecration of the universe. Silence is the invisible laying on of the Divine Pontiff's hands upon the world. Silence is at once the most harmless and the most awful thing in all nature. It speaks of the Reserved Forces of Fate. Silence is the only Voice of our God . . . Like the air, Silence permeates all things, and produces its magical power, as well during that peculiar mood which prevails at a solitary traveler's first setting forth on a journey, as at the unimaginable time when before the world was, Silence brooded on the face of the waters.

Herman Melville—Pierre; or, The Ambiguities *(1852)*

Noise may be the fastest-growing threat to human health and creativity. And not just audible noise, but data noise as well.

It's nonstop—and it's kicking our creative butts whether we know it or not.

And yet Melville's description of silence accurately portrays an element of today's relationship with the absence of noise: "*Silence is at once the most harmless and the most awful thing in all nature.*"

When we go into silence, such as during mediation, there's an element of dread that often shows up first. Our brains are so addicted to noise that they immediately revolt. (That's why meditation is so hard for some.)

We need more silence in our lives if we are to accomplish our best work.

Today, try this: take a couple silence breaks. Turn off everything, sit and take some deep breaths, and lower your stress immediately. Then ask yourself a question you've been wrestling with and see if your thinking is a little calmer.

Challenge Question

What questions would you like silence breaks to answer?

_____

_____

Growing: Grace

December 29
Path Awareness

May I be active as a spirit of love, / Since thou hast taken me from that path which Nature / Seemed to appoint, O, deign to open another, / Where I may walk with thought and hope assured; / . . . Had I but faith like that which fired Novalis, / I too could bear that the heart "fall in ashes," / While the freed spirit rises from beneath them, / With heavenward-look, and Phœnix-plumes upsoaring!

Margaret Fuller—Life Without and Life Within (1859)

How do you know if you are on or have been taken from the path that "*nature seemed to appoint*," as Fuller poses? Have you ever stopped to consider that seemingly big concept?

Are you on the path you were meant to be on?

What sign would you need to know? What role does faith play in your belief? Does it even matter?

If, as many of the writers in this work suggest, we all have our fate to chase, isn't this kind of a big, stressful deal?

Maybe, but maybe not.

We can get far too hung up on thinking of our path as some specific physical calling. What if it is a path that leads to our ability to find happiness in whatever we decide to do? Sure, there may be things each of us are more suited to do with our skills and interests, but how we handle the obstacles no matter is the key to "*walk with thought and hope assured*."

Consider this thought from Ryan Holiday, author of *The Obstacle Is the Way*:

The obstacle in the path becomes the path. Never forget, within every obstacle is an opportunity to improve our condition.

Does that change things? If only by reframing how you think about your path then, well, yes, possibly.

Challenge Question

What is the biggest obstacle in the way of you achieving your dreams? Is it real? Have you given juice to it? Could it become your new path? (4 for 1 today)

_____

_____

Growing: Grace

December 30
Grace to Your Art

For his heart was in his work, and the heart / Giveth grace unto every Art.
Henry Wadsworth Longfellow—"The Building of the Ship" (1870)

Longfellow's poem "The Building of the Ship" describes in some detail the building and launching of a sailing ship. While for him the ship symbolized the formation of the Union of States, the metaphor rings true for the building of a business.

The shipbuilder in the poem is an old master who is teaching a young apprentice to build using "only what is sound and strong."

He vows that the ship "should laugh at all disaster, and with wave and whirlwind wrestle!"

Are you starting to see the metaphor? What if we went into every step of our business with this approach? Would we take more care, use better materials, insist on our best work, apprentice those who would take on our craft?

It's harder this way—maybe it's even scary this way—but it matters to your heart. It's how you do your best work no matter what it is or how much prestige others attach to it.

Today, give grace to your art.

Challenge Question

Do you feel as though the work you are doing is making a difference? For whom?

_____

_____

December 31
Temple Mind

I never lived, that I remember, what you call a common natural day. All my days are touched by the supernatural, for I feel the pressure of hidden causes, and the presence, sometimes the communion, of unseen powers. It needs not that I should ask the clairvoyant whether "a spirit-world projects into ours." As to the specific evidence, I would not tarnish my mind by hasty reception. The mind is not, I know, a highway, but a temple, and its doors should not be carelessly left open. Yet it were sin, if indolence or coldness excluded what had a claim to enter; and I doubt whether, in the eyes of pure intelligence, an ill-grounded hasty rejection be not a greater sign of weakness than an ill-grounded and hasty faith.

Margaret Fuller—Summer on the Lakes *(1844)*

You've likely heard the phrase "your body is a temple" more often than "your mind is a temple."

The temple mind is the doorway to the temple body.

So, if the mind is the gateway to physical well-being and the doors are carelessly left wide open, we can't really expect to get what we want.

Carelessly left wide open is not the same as not being guarded about what information you consume—but filling your head up with cuddly affirmations will only go so far.

You've got to become the master and gatekeeper of your thoughts before you can change them.

You can hear something very negative about yourself and choose to believe it's the reason you never get what you want. Or you can withhold self-judgment and go to work on understanding the underlying events and emotions that give this thought its power.

Today (and all of next year), resolve to pay attention to more of the thoughts that turn up at your temple door. Ask more questions of them—why are they here, where did they come from, what have they come to teach you?

Challenge Question

What is the first thought that comes to mind when you hear the word grace?

_____

_____

See you next year!

About the Author

John Jantsch has owned a business for almost three decades. And while it may appear he knows what he is talking about, he is simply observing and documenting the entrepreneurial condition through his own unique journey. He is the best-selling author of *Duct Tape Marketing* and *The Referral Engine*, among others. His works have been translated into 10 languages and his writing has appeared in publications such as *Inc., Entrepreneur*, and *Southwest: The Magazine*. He lives with his wife in Kansas City, Missouri, and at 8,689 feet above sea level in Coal Creek Canyon in Colorado.